FUNDAMENTALS

OF

MANAGERIAL

ACCOUNTING

AND FINANCE

Third Edition

Roger W. Mills

Professor of Accounting and Finance

Henley Management College

John Robertson

Senior Lecturer in Accounting and Finance

Cranfield University, Shrivenham Campus

Printed and bound in Great Britain by Butler and Tanner Ltd

3rd Edition: December 1993
6th Reprint: January 1999

LIBRARY OF CONGRESS CATALOGING IN PUBLICATION DATA

Mills, Roger W.
Fundamentals of Managerial Accounting and Finance - 3rd Edition

Roger W. Mills   John Robertson

Included bibliographies and index

ISBN   1 873186 05 3

1. Financial Accounting, Cost Accounting, Management Accounting
I. Title   II.   Robertson J.

Published by:

Mars Business Associates Ltd

62 Kingsmead

Lechlade

Glos. GL7 3BW

Tel: 01367 252506

A B O U T   T H E   A U T H O R S

Roger W. Mills, B.Tech (Hons, Brunel), MSc (Brunel), (Phd. (Brunel), is a Professor of Accounting and Finance at Henley Management College where he is Head of the Accounting and Finance Faculty.

Roger trained as an accountant in industry and is a Fellow of the Chartered Institute of Management Accountants (FCMA), Chartered Institute of Secretaries and Administrators (FCIS) and a the Association of Corporate Treasurers (FCT). He is the co-author of a number of books on accounting and finance and is the author of numerous articles.

Professor Mills is also the PricewaterhouseCoopers Consultant Professor on Shareholder Value and Managing Director of Global Alliance International Ltd. His particular areas of specialisation are strategic financial and value analysis, corporate finance, business valuation, merger and acquisition analysis and corporate restructuring.

John Robertson, Dip ML (Lancaster), Phd. (Brunel), is Senior Lecturer in Accounting and Finance at Cranfield University, Shrivenham Campus. Teaching to 2nd and 3rd year undergraduates following degrees in Engineering, Computing and Logistics, also full and part time Masters programmes in Defence Administration (MDA). He gives regular guest lectures in a number of Universities.

John is a Fellow of the Chartered Institute of Management Accountants (FCMA) and the Chartered Association of Certified Accountants (FCCA). Author and co-author of a number of articles on financial ratios, ratio models and shareholder value. Author of a research monograph, <u>Measuring Changes in Financial Health through Ratio Analysis</u>.

Preface

This book has been written specifically with the MBA student in mind. Such students we know from our experience need to be financially aware and also to understand the language of accounting for both the MBA course and their career in management, but they do not need to know everything about managerial accounting and finance unless they intend to specialise. We have therefore assumed that the reader of this book will have his or her sights upon general management in the true sense of the word and will seek other sources for purposes of specialisation.

The book is organised in the ten chapters shown in the following illustration:

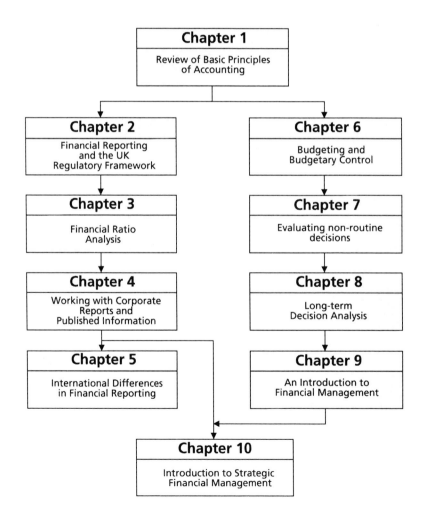

Chapter 1
Review of Basic Principles of Accounting

Chapter 2
Financial Reporting and the UK Regulatory Framework

Chapter 6
Budgeting and Budgetary Control

Chapter 3
Financial Ratio Analysis

Chapter 7
Evaluating non-routine decisions

Chapter 4
Working with Corporate Reports and Published Information

Chapter 8
Long-term Decision Analysis

Chapter 5
International Differences in Financial Reporting

Chapter 9
An Introduction to Financial Management

Chapter 10
Introduction to Strategic Financial Management

The relationship between the chapters is as follows: Chapter 1, basic principles of accounting, assumes that you have had little formal exposure to the main financial statements used within an organisation and the rules and conventions used in drafting them. It will take you through these quite gently and, in common with all chapters, has examples and questions for you to attempt.

On completion of this Chapter there are two alternative routes. First, you can pursue Chapters 2, 3, 4 and 5 which are concerned with how to read, interpret and analyse financial reports in the form of published accounts and published information. The UK regulatory framework for financial reporting is discussed in Chapter 2, followed by the principles of financial ratio analysis in Chapter 3, and its practical application and ratio models in Chapter 4. Chapter 5 takes the discussion of financial reporting a stage further by reviewing international developments within the context of the European community and the United States, as well as international regulatory influences and endeavours.

Alternatively, from Chapter 1 you can pursue the route through Chapters 6, 7, 8 and 9. These chapters focus upon internal, as opposed to external and published, managerial accounting and financial issues. The important area of budgeting and budgetary control is discussed in Chapter 6 followed by issues associated with non-routine, but often very important, decisions of a short and long term nature in Chapters 7 and 8. Chapter 9 provides an introduction to financial management and draws together many issues in earlier chapters.

The last Chapter provides an introduction to Strategic Financial Management. Within strategy the financial dimension can be vital in terms of providing an indication about the value of the business and its parts. This chapter discusses the approaches available for undertaking such valuation and you will find it draws upon many areas covered within the book. It is important and in our opinion an appropriate final chapter because it firmly places the value of managerial accounting and finance within a general management context.

Preface to the third edition

In response to popular demand we have included answers to the numeric exercises at the end of the book.

Roger W. Mills   John Robertson

November 1993

Contents

CHAPTER 9 AN INTRODUCTION TO FINANCIAL MANAGEMENT

CHAPTER 10 INTRODUCTION TO STRATEGIC FINANCIAL MANAGEMENT

REVIEW OF BASIC PRINCIPLES OF ACCOUNTING

LEARNING OBJECTIVES

When you have finished studying this chapter and completed the exercises you should be able to:

❑ Prepare a balance sheet in different formats and be able to show the effect of transactions.

❑ Prepare profit and loss accounts and comment on the difference(s) between profit and cash.

❑ Prepare cash flow forecasts and interpret the results.

❑ Understand the relationship between the three main financial statements; balance sheet, profit and loss account and cash flow forecast.

❑ Describe the generally accepted accounting principles of separate identity, money measurement, timing, realisation, consistency, prudence, matching and materiality.

❑ Understand the distinction between assets and expenses and their treatment in the financial statements of a business.

❑ Explain the alternative treatments for depreciation and goodwill and show the effect of each on the main financial statements.

1.1   Introduction

The successful study of accounting and finance is dependent upon the assimilation of a number of basic principles. Rather than deal with all of these by way of a comprehensive introduction, in this chapter, we have selected only those needed for the earlier chapters of the book. In these earlier chapters, the particular focus of attention is upon the principles, content and layout of the main financial statements.

This chapter provides an overview of accounting for both those with little or no background in the subject and for those with some background who wish to review some fundamental principles. Specific reference will be made to important terminology and to what financial statements do and do not portray. To know what financial statements do not communicate is just as important as knowing what they do communicate.

Fundamental principles are discussed in the chapter without employing some of the specific accounting techniques (like double-entry bookkeeping) and jargon (like debit and credit). It is directed at answering two important questions often asked by managers and other parties with an interest in an organisation: How well did it or will it perform over a given time period? How does it or will it stand at a given point in time? The accountant answers these questions with two main financial statements which we shall consider at length in this chapter - the profit and loss account and the balance sheet.

Our focus of attention in the chapter is directed at 'for-profit' organisations and, in particular, limited liability companies. Such organisations typically revolve around a similar, usually regular, cycle of economic activity. For example, retailers and most businesses buy goods and services and modify them by changing their form or by placing them in a convenient location, such that they can be sold at higher prices with the aim of producing a profit. The total amount of profit earned during a particular period heavily depends on the excess of the selling prices over the costs of the goods and services (the mark-up) and the speed of the operating cycle (the turnover). However, as we shall demonstrate, profit is not the only important focus of attention. Cash is equally important and must be carefully monitored as well. Quite how profit, cash and financial position can be monitored and the relationship between them will be demonstrated in this chapter.

1.2   Main financial statements

F inancial statements are used by organisations to summarise aspects of past, present and future performance. These financial statements are the result of applying certain principles, like double-entry book keeping and some are reliant upon accounting conventions, a basic knowledge and understanding of which is essential in most of what follows.

Our discussions in this chapter focus upon the following three main financial statements and the difference in the information conveyed by each of them:

1. The Balance Sheet

2. The Profit and Loss Account

3. The Cash Flow Forecast

1.2.1   The balance sheet

The balance sheet is the financial statement used to illustrate an organisation's financial position. It can be likened to a snapshot because it is a static representation of an organisation's financial position in the form of its total liabilities and total assets at a particular point in time.

The balance sheet is reliant upon the following simple principle:

TOTAL LIABILITIES = TOTAL ASSETS

In developing this principle in this chapter our focus of attention will be upon those liabilities and assets to be found in the balance sheet of a limited liability company. However, the principle, though not the terminology used is also applicable to most types of organisation. What are liabilities and assets? We provide a short review of each of them.

Total liabilities:

These are monetary obligations arising from past events and can be thought of as being the sources of finance used by the business. They include 'liabilities' to the owners, known as shareholders' (owners') funds (equity), which are usually categorised as share capital and reserves (such as retained profit), and liabilities to external sources of finance in the form of long-term loans and short-term sources like trade credit (creditors) and bank overdrafts. The sources of finance and how they may be generally categorised is illustrated in *Figure 1.1*

Figure 1.1   Total liabilities

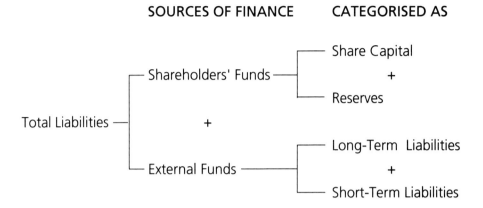

Total assets:

These are those resources obtained from the sources of finance which are expressed in monetary terms. Assets to be found in a company balance sheet are those in its possession, whether owned or controlled, and which are expected to yield future economic benefits. As shown in *Figure 1.2*, assets are usually referred to as being 'fixed' or 'current'. Fixed assets are those like land and buildings, machinery, vehicles, which are intended for use in the business and are not intended for sale as part of normal trading activity. Current assets form part of the working capital of a business and are instrumental in the generation of profit within the business. They include stock, debtors and cash held for use within the business.

Figure 1.2   Total assets

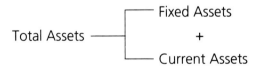

The balance sheet is therefore comprised of a number of liabilities and assets, the totals of which equal one another. This is illustrated in *Table 1.1* where we have attached some values to the individual categories of total liabilities and total assets to be found in the balance sheet of a typical manufacturing company.

Table 1.1   Balance sheet as at (a given date)

	£'000		£'000
Shareholders' Funds:		**Fixed Assets:**	
Share Capital	30,000	Land and Buildings`	20,000
Reserves	20,000	Machinery	10,000
		Vehicles	15,000
External Funds:			
Long-Term Loans	10,000	**Current Assets:**	
Creditors	20,000	Stock	15,000
		Debtors	15,000
		Cash	5,000
TOTAL LIABILITIES	**£80,000**	**TOTAL ASSETS**	**£80,000**

We will use TOTAL LIABILITIES, TOTAL ASSETS and selected individual items to illustrate the operation of the principle of double-entry bookkeeping which is instrumental in ensuring the equality of the two totals. We commence with a simple example to show what happens if £5 million of stock is purchased on credit:

	£'000		£'000
INCREASE Creditors	5,000	INCREASE Stock	5,000
TOTAL LIABILITIES	**85,000**	**TOTAL ASSETS**	**85,000**

An equal amount of £5 million is added to creditors and stock on each side of the balance sheet, thereby increasing each side by the same amount but maintaining the balance between total liabilities and total assets.

The result of such a purchase would be the following revised balance sheet:

Table 1.2   Balance sheet as at (a given date)

	£'000		£'000
Shareholders' Funds:		**Fixed Assets:**	
Share Capital	30,000	Land and Buildings	20,000
Reserves	20,000	Machinery	10,000
		Vehicles	15,000
External Funds:			
Long-Term Loans	10,000	**Current Assets:**	
Creditors	25,000	Stock	20,000
		Debtors	15,000
		Cash	5,000
TOTAL LIABILITIES	**£85,000**	**TOTAL ASSETS**	**£85,000**

In reality any purchase of stock would normally be undertaken with a view to making a subsequent sale for a profit. Let us consider with reference to the balance sheet in *Table 1.2* what happens in such circumstances. We will assume that this stock purchase which had cost £5 million is sold to a customer on credit for £10 million. The effect of the credit sale is that both total liabilities and total assets increase by £5 million. In terms of individual items and total liabilities and total assets the effect is:

	£'000		£'000
INCREASE in Reserves	5,000	DECREASE in Stock	5,000
		INCREASE in Debtors	10,000
TOTAL LIABILITIES	**90,000**	**TOTAL ASSETS**	**90,000**

The reason for this increase is that £5 million profit on the sale has been made which is reflected as both an increase in assets and liabilities. The increase in assets is obvious but the reason for the increase in the liabilities side in the form of reserves is more elusive and warrants particular consideration.

Companies usually require profit to meet tax obligations and other matters of company policy such as dividend payments. Any profit remaining after such deductions and kept within the business is a source of future growth and is referred to as retained profit, or revenue reserves. Such reserves are not usually to be found in the form of cash assets. That this may be so can be seen with reference to the credit sale example where there has been no increase in cash as a result of the transaction. The debtors balance rather than the cash balance increased as a result of the sale. The increase in the debtors balance will lead to an increase in cash, but not in the time period covered by this balance sheet.

We have revised the balance sheet in *Table 1.3* to show the result of the credit sale for profit:

Table 1.3   *Balance sheet as at (a given date)*

	£'000		£'000
Shareholders' Funds:		**Fixed Assets:**	
Share Capital	30,000	Land and Buildings	20,000
Reserves	25,000	Machinery	10,000
		Vehicles	15,000
External Funds:			
Long-Term Loans	10,000	**Current Assets:**	
Creditors	25,000	Stock	15,000
		Debtors	25,000
		Cash	5,000
TOTAL LIABILITIES	**£90,000**	**TOTAL ASSETS**	**£90,000**

Our discussion of the balance sheet and its portrayal of financial position has also touched upon profit and cash. Whilst profitability and cash flow effects can be illustrated with reference to the balance sheet alone, it is normal to use a profit and loss account and cash flow statement for such purposes. This is because the balance sheet is used typically to show the financial position at an instant in time, but the profit and loss account measures performance for a span of time and the cash flow statement the effect of economic activity upon cash flow.

There is an important relationship between the profit and loss account and balance sheet. As indicated in *Figure 1.3*, the balance sheet shows the financial position at an instant of time, but the profit and loss account measures performance for a span of time, whether it be a month, a quarter, or longer. The profit and loss account is the major link between balance sheets:

Figure 1.3   Relationship between Balance sheet and Profit & Loss Account

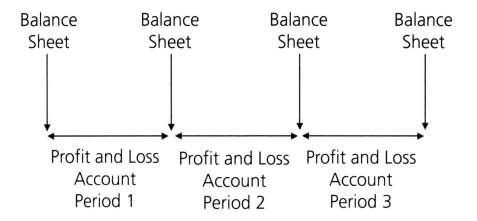

1.3   Profit, cash flow and financial position

We will now consider each of these financial statements but our focus of attention will be upon matters of principle rather than of detail. In particular, presentation requirements to be found in most company accounts will be ignored until the next chapter.

One vital feature of the profit and loss account and cash flow statement for you to be aware of is that different principles are applied in drafting each of them. The application of these different principles means that for the same period cash and profit results will rarely be the same, hence the importance of having the two statements to convey the necessary information required for managing a business.

In contrast with the balance sheet format shown and discussed earlier, you will often encounter that where total assets are placed above (known as vertical) rather than alongside total liabilities (known as horizontal). This type of format illustrated in *Table 1.4* is common in U.K. annual reports, although you should be aware that no single layout is used exclusively world-wide. As you will see when we consider international differences in financial reporting practices, different balance sheet layouts are used in different countries. Even within the European Community (EC), where significant moves have taken place to standardise profit and loss accounts and balance sheets via legal instruments known as directives, alternative layouts are permitted and those which have been adopted differ between EC member states.

Table 1.4   Balance sheet as at (a given date)

	Column 1 £'000	Column 2 £'000
Fixed Assets:		
Land and Buildings	20,000	
Machinery	10,000	
Vehicles	15,000	45,000
Current Assets:		
Stock	15,000	
Debtors	25,000	
Cash	5,000	45,000
TOTAL ASSETS		90,000
Shareholders' Funds:		
Share Capital	30,000	
Reserves	25,000	55,000
External Funds:		
Long-Term Loans	10,000	
Creditors	25,000	35,000
TOTAL LIABILITIES		**£90,000**

You will note that the balance sheet in *Table 1.4* contains exactly the same information as that in *Table 1.3*. One key point to note is the use of two columns rather than one. Such a columnar layout is often a source of confusion for newcomers to accounting, but it need not be. Column 1 shows the value of individual assets and liabilities which are added together to represent sub-totals for the various categories of asset and liability in column 2. Thus, the £45 million in column 2 represents the sum total of the individual fixed assets in column 1.

To facilitate our discussion of the differences between the three financial statements we will assume that a number of other business transactions have taken place in the next accounting period. The transactions for this period have been summarised as follows:

1.   £10 million of stock has been purchased and sold for £20 million cash.

2.   Wages and expenses of £5 million have been paid in full prior to drafting the profit and loss account.

Let us consider whether these transactions generate any profit and their effect upon cash flow. As indicated earlier, we could measure any profit (or growth) using just a balance sheet, but in common with general practice we will use a profit and loss account.

What does the profit and loss account show that the balance sheet does not? As illustrated earlier, the profit and loss account summarises the revenue generated and the costs incurred in the trading period between two balance sheet dates. Where the revenue exceeds the cost there is a profit and where the cost exceeds the revenue a loss is incurred. For our example the profit and loss account is illustrated in *Table 1.5.*

Table 1.5   Profit and Loss Account (for a given period)

	£'000
Sales	20,000
less Cost of Sales [1]	15,000
Profit	5,000

[1] *Purchases £10,000 + wages £5,000*

The profit and loss account illustrates that the effect of trading as summarised by our example transactions, is the generation of £5 million of profit, which in this case has been retained in the business. Profit that is retained forms an important link between successive balance sheets. This is illustrated in *Table 1.6*, where the balance sheet prior to the transactions, the 'opening' balance sheet, and that after the transactions, the 'closing' balance sheet, are found side by side in two columns. The use of such comparative balance sheets is common practice. You only have to refer to the published accounts of any UK public company for an example of such practice.

Observation of the opening and closing balance sheets illustrated in *Table 1.6* shows that reserves (which have been boxed) have increased by £5 million and that there is an additional £5 million cash in current assets.

Table 1.6   Balance sheets as at (a given date)

	Opening		Closing	
	£'000	£'000	£'000	£'000
Fixed Assets:				
Land and Buildings	20,000		20,000	
Machinery	10,000		10,000	
Vehicles	15,000	45,000	15,000	45,000
Current Assets:				
Stock	15,000		15,000	
Debtors	25,000		25,000	
Cash	5,000	45,000	10,000	50,000
TOTAL ASSETS		£90,000		£95,000
Shareholders' Funds:				
Share Capital	30,000			
Reserves	25,000	55,000	30,000	60,000
External Funds:				
Long-Term Loans	10,000		10,000	
Creditors	25,000	35,000	25,000	35,000
TOTAL LIABILITIES		£90,000		£95,000

In a profitable environment the result of recording accounting transactions will be that the assets of the business will increase rapidly. On a regular basis, at least annually for publication purposes, companies prepare profit and loss accounts to determine the amount generated by and retained in the business. The amount retained is added to the revenue reserves forming part of shareholders' funds, thereby increasing the total liabilities section. In this way the benefit to shareholders from profitable activity is recognised in the form of growth in the assets.

The additional £5 million cash included in the closing balance sheet of *Table 1.6* would also usually be expressed in detail in a cash flow statement. A simple cash flow statement is illustrated in *Table 1.7* which, because all transactions were cash based and no credit was involved, looks identical to the earlier profit and loss account *Table 1.5*.

Table 1.7   Cash flow statement (for a given period)

	£'000
Cash Sales	20,000
less Cash Costs	15,000
Cash Increase	**£ 5,000**

While in this case the profit and cash generated from this group of transactions is identical, they can be different and this is usually the case. The reason for this is that the production of a profit and loss account is reliant upon a number of generally accepted principles, which are not required or used in producing cash flow statements. In addition to their application in measuring profit (or loss) in the profit and loss account, these principles listed in *Table 1.8* are applied in determining the financial position in the balance sheet.

Table 1.8   Generally Accepted Accounting Principles

❑ **Separate identity**. An organisation is deemed to have a separate existence from its owners. This means that personal transactions are excluded from business accounts.

❑ **Going concern**. An organisation is assumed to continue in operational existence for the foreseeable future.

❑ **Money measurement**. Accounting only records those events which may be described and measured in money terms.

❑ **Timing of reports**. A time period is fixed as a basis for measurement of profit or loss.

❑ **Realisation**. Accounting recognises only those profits which have been realised in the accounting period. Other than in certain specific situations profit is only accounted for when the earning process is virtually complete.

❑ **Consistency**. The accounting treatment of particular items should be the same from period to period; if changed, the difference should be revealed.

❑ **Prudence or conservatism**. Provision should be made for all potential costs whereas, as indicated, profits should not be accounted for until realised. This means that a far more conservative approach is adopted towards accounting for profit than is the case for costs.

❑ **Accruals/Matching**. Accounts have to ensure that costs are matched with their associated revenues.

❑ **Materiality**. Non standard usage in accounting practice is permissible if the effects are not material.

The implication of such principles for profit and financial position in comparison with cash can be illustrated. First, the fact that the legal effect of a transaction is used in measuring profit for a period means that the sales and purchases for inclusion in a profit and loss account relate to both cash and credit transactions. This is in contrast to the cash flow statement in which all cash receipts and payments made during the time period in question are recorded, irrespective of the time period to which they relate. Second, within the profit and loss account and balance sheet a measure of the annual fall in value of fixed assets, known as depreciation, is charged against income in the profit and loss account. This contrasts with the cash flow statement where, if we assume a fixed asset is purchased for cash, the full amount will be shown even though only a proportion of the cash sum will form depreciation in the profit and loss account.

In our experience, many individuals find the effect of depreciation upon profit in comparison with the implications of an asset purchase upon the cash flow statement difficult to understand. The difference in the effect upon profit and cash is most readily understood with reference to the following simple example concerning an item of capital expenditure costing £15 million and paid for by cash which has an estimated useful economic life of five years at the end of which time it will be worth nothing. In the year of purchase there would be a cash outflow in the cash statement of £15 million, in contrast with a depreciation charge against profit in the profit and loss account for a proportion of this sum. The proportion charged as depreciation can be calculated in many different ways, but one common method of calculating it is to make an equal charge against profit in each of the five years of the assets life, giving an annual charge in this case of £3 million (£15million ÷ 5 years). Clearly the £15 million cash outflow will eat further into cash in year 1 than the £3 million annual charge will eat into profit hence there will be a difference in the results portrayed in the profit and loss account and cash flow statement simply because of the different principles applied in accounting for fixed assets. This is illustrated in *Figure 1.4*.

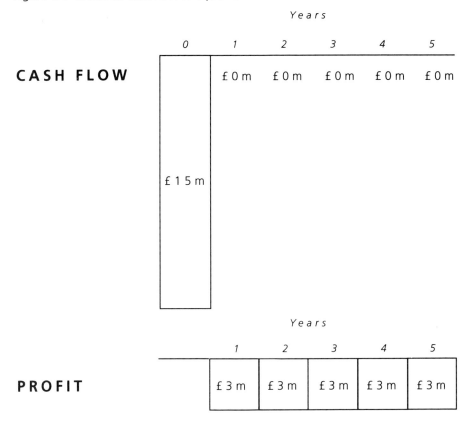

Figure 1.4 *Effect on cash flow and profit*

How these principles operate in practice to produce differences between cash flow and profit is best understood will be explained in section 1.5 using a simple example.

1.4 Fixed assets, depreciation and expenses

The distinction between assets for inclusion in the balance sheet and expenses for inclusion in the profit and loss account often causes many difficulties. One useful way of making a distinction is to consider expenses as being used-up assets, whereas assets are those not appropriate to the current expense stream, but which are carried in the balance sheet until their subsequent expiration. This can be readily understood with reference to fixed assets where from the time of purchase that part assumed to have expired will be represented by the period depreciation charge. That which has not expired will appear in the balance sheet as the asset value carried forward.

Quite how accurately the value of such expenses can be gauged is a moot point. This is evident if we consider our earlier depreciation example. There we assumed that an asset costing £15 million was written off over 5 years by equal depreciation charges in the profit and loss account of £3 million. However, this is not the only basis for determining a depreciation charge. If you pick up any basic text on accounting you will find reference made to the reducing or diminishing balance method, whereby a larger depreciation charge is made in earlier than in later years, the amount of which can be readily determined if the asset has an estimated residual or scrap value. Our example which assumes no scrap value does not permit the calculation of such a charge in quite the same way, but we will demonstrate the key point of our discussion with reference to an easy to understand approximation for the reduced balance. This method is called the 'sum of the digits', or the 'sum of the years digits'. Given the data in this case the annual depreciation charge is calculated in the manner illustrated in *Table 1.9*.

Table 1.9 Sum of year's digits method of depreciation

Year 1	5	5/15	£5 million
Year 2	4	4/15	£4 million
Year 3	3	3/15	£3 million
Year 4	2	2/15	£2 million
Year 5	1	1/15	£1 million
	15	**15/15**	**£15 million**

The basis for determining the annual depreciation charge is found simply by reversing the order of the years, such that for year 1 the depreciation charge is determined from the last year (5 in this case) which is expressed as a fraction of the sum of the digits of the years (5+4+3+2+1 in this case). Thus, 5 ÷ 15 of the £15 million value of the asset is charged against year 1 and so on for subsequent years.

There is nothing which requires UK companies to adopt one particular method rather than another, although all indications are that the majority adopt the straight line approach whereby an equal charge is made for each year of the asset's estimated useful economic life. Clearly the adoption of different methods will have an impact upon reported profits and it is important to be aware that UK companies can exercise judgement in selecting the basis for charging depreciation. This judgement means that two companies in a similar line of business can quite legitimately adopt different methods of depreciation for the same assets and each may often adopt different methods for different categories of assets.

Please do be aware that not all assets are depreciated. The most common example of a non-depreciating asset is land which may often increase in value. As a consequence, you will find that in addition to depreciation, many U.K. companies periodically revalue land which is typically shown in the balance sheet at the most recently revalued figure. What are the mechanics of such a revaluation and what is the effect upon the profit and loss account, cash flow statement and balance sheet? Let us consider this with reference to the following example, where it is assumed that the company has had a professional revaluation of all of its fixed assets, not just land, such that they now have a value of £25 million, £10 million higher than their existing value in the accounts.

Such a revaluation of fixed assets increases the fixed assets in the balance sheet by £10 million and also the reserves in the balance sheet by £10 million. However, such an increase in reserves is usually kept totally distinct from those generated through trading and is typically referred to as a revaluation reserve. Thus, unlike depreciation, the revaluation of a non-depreciating asset has no effect on the profit and loss account. However, in common with depreciation, a revaluation also has no effect on the cash flow statement because, although a new higher value has been placed upon the fixed assets, no cash movement has occurred.

In the balance sheet the effect of a revaluation of fixed assets upon affected items is:

Table 1.10   Balance sheets as at 31st December 199X

	Opening £'000	Change £'000	Closing £'000
Fixed Assets	15,000	+10,000	25,000
Total Assets	**£120,000**	**£+10,000**	**£130,000**
Reserves: Revaluation	-	+10,000	10,000
Total Liabilities	**£120,000**	**£+10,000**	**£130,000**

Many UK companies now revalue their fixed assets on a regular basis, such as once every five years. The outcome is typically a stronger balance sheet that reflects the current value of the assets and at the same time provides an increase in the equity of the business.

One potential advantage to the company of including current values of assets through revaluations on a regular basis is that it should make the cost of acquiring the company greater. The assumption for listed companies as you will doubtless have realised is that the revaluation will be incorporated by the market in the company's share price. Revaluations may also improve the ability of the company to borrow funds because the ability to borrow without recourse to the shareholders is usually limited to a percentage of assets. Anything that increases the assets will, as a matter of course, increase borrowing power.

Our discussion so far has focused upon accounting for tangible fixed assets. As indicated, intangible fixed assets such as brands and goodwill have attracted a good deal of attention in the UK. We propose to deal briefly with the accounting issues associated with just these two categories of intangible asset.

The first important point is to recognise the differences between categories of intangible asset, such as goodwill and brands. Goodwill is only accounted for when the price paid for an acquired business is greater than the value of the assets acquired, this excess being the goodwill element of the purchase price. Therefore, goodwill will be represented by a corresponding purchase transaction in the books of the company, sometimes in the form of cash. By contrast, the decision to include an intangible asset like a 'home grown' as distinct from an acquired brand in the balance sheet is can be likened to an asset revaluation where there is no specific cost consideration associated with the inclusion of the brand, merely an entry in the books to show an increase in reserves.

There are alternative views as to the treatment of goodwill in financial statements. One viewpoint is that goodwill should be eliminated from the balance sheet by being deducted from the owners' equity. This is achieved by adjusting reserves in some manner as soon as the goodwill arises following the acquisition of a business. Thus, the goodwill is assumed to be associated directly with the interests of the shareholders in the company.

By contrast, the other viewpoint is that goodwill should be shown as an asset and treated in the same manner as tangible fixed assets. Thus, goodwill would be capitalised (included in the balance sheet as an asset) and written-off over a number of years, the reason being that the benefit associated with it should be matched with the costs which give rise to it. If costs are not matched in this way, the result is overstated profits. Therefore, just as depreciation is applied to tangible fixed assets so too may it be applied to goodwill, though often any depreciation associated with an intangible asset is referred to as amortisation.

Currently, preferred UK practice is for goodwill to be written off immediately against reserves, or for a new reserve to be created such that depreciation is not required, though this may change in the future. Only if the company elects to write-off the goodwill will future profits be affected in the way illustrated earlier for the depreciation of tangible fixed assets.

Whilst, in principle, brands may be amortised, the current practice in the UK is that they are not. Changes in the value of brands are typically dealt with via the balance sheet and not through the profit and loss account, thereby appearing to have much in common with the bookkeeping entries associated with an asset revaluation.

To help you understand the alternative treatments of goodwill and their impact upon the balance sheet we will use the following basic data which refers to an acquisition. Where the purchase price paid is £200 million of which £150 million represents goodwill. We have assumed this acquisition to be made by our example company which had the balance sheet represented by the closing column in *Table 1.6.*

Example to show alternative treatments of goodwill:

Basic Data:	**£'000**
Purchase Price [1]	200,000
less Net Assets [2]	50,000
Goodwill	150,000
Projected annual profit for next 5 years	50,000

[1] Purchase financed by:

Share Capital	10,000
Share Premium	140,000
Long-Term Loan	50,000
	200,000

[2] Net assets comprise:

Fixed Assets	40,000
+ Current Assets	100,000
- Current Liabilities	90,000
	50,000

We show the effect upon the profit and loss account:

	\1 £'000	\2 £'000	Year \3 £'000	\4 £'000	\5 £'000	TOTAL £'000
[3] Projected profit	50,000	50,000	50,000	50,000	50,000	250,000
Goodwill amortised	30,000	30,000	30,000	30,000	30,000	150,000
[4] Adjusted profit	20,000	20,000	20,000	20,000	20,000	100,000

[3] Writing goodwill off immediately against reserves in the balance sheet

[4] Amortising goodwill against projected annual profit

We now show the effect upon the balance sheet of:

---

1. Writing goodwill off immediately against reserves

	Opening balance sheet £'000	£'000	Adjusted balance sheet £'000
Fixed Assets	45,000	+40,000	85,000
Goodwill	0		0
Current Assets	50,000	+100,000	150,000
Total Assets	**95,000**		**235,000**
Share Capital	30,000	+10,000	40,000
Reserves	30,000	+140,000	20,000
		-150,000	
Long-Term Loans	10,000	+50,000	60,000
Creditors	25,000	+90,000	115,000
Total Liabilities	**95,000**		**235,000**

2. Capitalising goodwill as an intangible asset

	Opening balance sheet £'000	£'000	Adjusted balance sheet £'000
Fixed Assets	45,000	+40,000	85,000
Goodwill	0	+150,000	150,000
Current Assets	50,000	+100,000	150,000
Total Assets	**95,000**		**385,000**
Share Capital	30,000	+10,000	40,000
Reserves	30,000	+140,000	170,000
Long-Term Loans	10,000	+50,000	60,000
Creditors	25,000	+90,000	115,000
Total Liabilities	**95,000**		**385,000**

Writing goodwill off immediately against reserves yields a weaker balance sheet relative to the alternative, but there is a benefit insofar as future profits will be not eroded by amortisation charges.   By contrast, there is the appearance of a healthier balance sheet as a result of capitalising goodwill as an intangible asset. Against the benefit must be weighed the disadvantage of the intangible asset being amortised against future profits. As you will discover later in the book both methods are to be found in practice (albeit in different countries).

1.5   Worked example of financial statements

Information

MEC Ltd to be formed on 1st July will immediately purchase £250,000 of fixed assets, including land valued at £50,000, using a 5 year loan. The loan is to be repaid in full at the end of the 5 year period, but interest on the loan will be paid monthly. In addition, £150,000 of capital will be provided by the injection of shareholders' funds. Its plans for the first six months to 31st December are as follows:

❑ Sales for 6 months   £6,000,000

❑ Materials used   £2,400,000

❑ Materials required to be purchased to
    allow for closing stock of £200,000   £2,600,000

❑ Labour in sales   £2,100,000

❑ Overheads (including estimated
    interest charges and £20,000 depreciation
    for the 6 month period)   £1,400,000

Expected cash receipts and payments for the first 6 months have been estimated. After making due allowance for credit periods to be allowed to customers and expected to be available from suppliers, the estimates are:

	Cash receipts from sales	Cash payments for materials
	£'000	£'000
July	430	600
August	600	600
September	600	200
October	800	200
November	1,300	200
December	1,600	200
TOTAL	**5,330**	**2,000**

All expenses other than materials are to be paid evenly each month.

1.5.1   Cash flow forecast

The first statement we will consider is the cash flow forecast, which requires a brief introduction.

Basically, this financial statement is reliant upon principles we apply in everyday life. The cash we have at any point in time is the difference between what we have received and what we have paid out. We can also apply this principle to forecast cash available or required as you will find illustrated for our example in *Table 1.11*. In this table receipts and payments over the six month period are shown for each month. The difference between receipts (part A) and payments (part B) gives cash available or required (part C). The cash available or required for each month can also be viewed in conjunction with previous months in the form of a cumulated cash balance (part D).

Table 1.11 Cash flow forecast

Part A

Receipts £'000	July	Aug	Sept	Oct	Nov	Dec	Total
Sales	430	600	600	800	1,300	1,600	5,330
5 year Loan	250						250
Share Capital	150						150
Subtotal A	830	600	600	800	1,300	1,600	5,730

Part B

Payments £'000	July	Aug	Sept	Oct	Nov	Dec	Total
Materials	600	600	200	200	200	200	2,000
Wages	350	350	350	350	350	350	2,100
Overheads	230	230	230	230	230	230	1,380
Fixed Assets	250						250
Subtotal B	1,430	1,180	780	780	780	780	5,730

Part C

	July	Aug	Sept	Oct	Nov	Dec
Balance (AB)	600	580	180	20	520	820

Part D

	July	Aug	Sept	Oct	Nov	Dec
Balance c/f, Cumulative Cash Position	-600	-1,180	-1,360	-1,340	-820	0

The cash flow forecast shows that over the course of the 6 months there will be an unsatisfactory cash position at the end of each month with the exception of December. The cash flow will be at its worst in September when the shortfall in cumulative cash will reach £1.36 million. That the cash flow position for each month will be unfavourable is indicated by the negative numbers in Part D. (*In accounting and finance, brackets are often used to convey an unfavourable or adverse position*).

The important point to note is that only cash receipts and cash payments are included in the cash flow forecast, irrespective of the time period to which they relate. How could the cash position be improved? Anything which could be done to improve the speed and size of cash inflows and delay the speed and size of cash outflows would doubtless help. The relevant actions would include improving debtor collections, delaying creditor payments and delaying payments for fixed assets. These are all 'levers' which could be pulled to improve the cash position, but cash is only one perspective. Attempts to improve cash flow by pulling such levers will usually also have an impact upon profit and financial position. We consider each of these in what follows.

1.5.2   The profit and loss account

Table 1.12   Profit and loss account for the 6 month period

		£'000
Sales		6,000
less Cost of Sales:		
Materials	2,400	
Labour	2,100	4,500
Gross Profit		1,500
less Expenses:		
Overheads	1,380	
Depreciation	20	1,400
Net (and Retained) Profit		£100

The profit and loss account in *Table 1.12* requires cost of sales to be calculated and deducted from sales to yield a gross profit for the period. The cost of sales normally has to be calculated from materials purchased during the period and a stock adjustment. In this case the necessary information has been provided so that a stock adjustment is not required.

Why is a stock adjustment normally required? This adjustment ensures that the sales revenue for a given period is compared with its associated physical cost of sales. The reason for it is best understood if we consider the case of a trader in computers who starts with no stock, buys 2,200 but sells 2,000 in a trading period. In the profit and loss account the profit or loss for the period would be measured by comparing the revenues from 2,000 computers with the costs associated with 2,000, not 2,200. The remaining 200 represent closing stock, the profit or loss on which would be measured in a subsequent profit and loss account. Because the 200 items of closing stock are irrelevant to the measurement of profit for this period, it is valued and deducted from the purchase cost of 2,200 items.

The £2.4 million for materials, together with labour costs incurred during the 6 month period of £2.1 million is deducted from sales. As indicated, the difference between sales and the cost of sales is known as the gross profit from which salaries and expenses are deducted to determine the net and (in this case retained) profit of £100,000 for the 6 months.

One important point about profit illustrated in our example profit and loss account is that there are different 'layers' of profit. These layers we have illustrated in *Figure 1.5*:

Figure 1.5   Profit and Loss account items

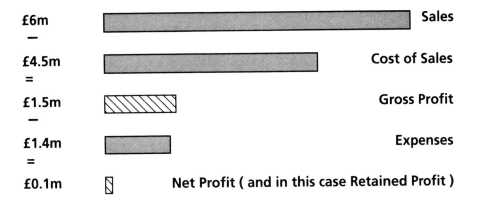

£6m		**Sales**
—		
£4.5m		**Cost of Sales**
=		
£1.5m		**Gross Profit**
—		
£1.4m		**Expenses**
=		
£0.1m		**Net Profit (and in this case Retained Profit)**

The different layers of profit illustrate the need to be cautious in discussions concerning profit. It is quite possible for communication to be confused by different parties referring to different layers without this being evident.

Whilst the cash flow forecast has been produced on a monthly basis because of limited data, the profit and loss account has been produced for the full 6 month period. This means that the only cash and profit comparisons for this example can be made for the whole 6 month period.

If we compare the 6 monthly totals relating to cash flow and profit, there are some notable differences as illustrated in *Table 1.13.*

Table 1.13 Differences between cash flow and profit

		Column 1 Cash flow forecast £'000	Column 2 Profit and loss account £'000	Difference (Column 2 Column 1) £'000
Loan		250	0	250
Share Capital		150	0	150
Sales		5,330	6,000	+670
	(A)	5,730	6,000	+270
Materials		2,000	2,400	400
Wages		2,100	2,100	0
Expenses		1,380	1,380	0
Fixed Assets		250	20	+230
	(B)	5,730	5,900	170
DIFFERENCE (A) + (B)		0	100	100

The differences between the cash flow forecast and the profit and loss account illustrate well how accounting principles affect financial statements differently. Firstly, in calculating profit the legal effect of a transaction is recognised which means that debtors of £670,000 and creditors of £600,000 are included. Secondly, there is a difference in the treatment of fixed assets. In the profit and loss account the operation of the matching principle means £230,000 less is charged against profit than is the case in the cash flow forecast. In other words the costs of fixed assets are 'packaged' in the profit and loss account over their useful economic lives as a series of annual depreciation charges which is quite different to accounting for cash flows.

This means that there is a depreciation charge for the 6 months in this example of £20,000, i.e. the useful economic life used in the depreciation calculation was clearly estimated as being 5 years.

The charging of an annual sum for depreciation against profit and the inclusion of the legal effect of transactions serves to illustrate why there may often be significant differences between the profitability and cash flows of an operation over the same time period.

1.5.3   The balance sheet

The balance sheet in *Table 1.14* is the snapshot of what the financial position is expected to be on 31st December, the last day of the 6 month financial plan.

Table 1.14   Balance sheet as at 31st December

	£'000	£'000
Fixed Assets:		
Land		50
Other	200	
less: Depreciation	20	180
		230
Current Assets:		
Stock	200	
Debtors	670	870
TOTAL ASSETS		**£1,100**
Shareholders' Funds:		
Share Capital		150
Reserves		100
		250
External Funds:		
Long-Term Loan (5 years)	250	
Creditors	600	850
TOTAL LIABILITIES		**£1,100**

The balance sheet in *Table 1.14* illustrates that on December 31st, 6 months hence, the value of fixed assets will have diminished such that they will have a net book value of £230,000. In addition to such fixed assets and stocks, both of which have an obvious physical presence, the company will also have debtors of £670,000. This £670,000 represents moneys owing to the company which, because of the legal obligation associated with them, are relevant in the calculation of profit, but not cash flow.

The sum of all assets amounts to £1,100,000 which corresponds with the total of all liabilities in the lower part of the balance sheet. Such liabilities comprise the initial injection of share capital of £150,000, the £100,000 of profit to be generated and retained over the 6 months, the longterm liability in the form of the 5 year loan, and the current liability in the form of £600,000 of creditors. In common with debtors, the £600,000 owing to creditors is relevant in the calculation of profit because of the legal obligation associated with them. However, they are also irrelevant in calculating cash flow for this 6 month period because they will involve no movement in cash, as yet.

The outcome of this 6 month plan can be summarised as being:

❐   a stable cash position as at 31st December, but with potential cash flow difficulties throughout the period;

❐   a profit of £100,000 for the six month period; and,

❐   total assets and total liabilities of £1.1 million as at 31st December.

Any attempt to change the plan will impact upon each of these. Consider, for example, the effect of allowing no credit sales and the collection of £1 million cash per month from sales for each of the 6 months. This, given the existing position would result in potential cash flow difficulties for July and August.

Table 1.15 Revised cash flow forecast

Part A

Receipts £'000	July	Aug	Sept	Oct	Nov	Dec	Total
Sales	1,000	1,000	1,000	1,000	1,000	1,000	6,000
5 year Loan	250						250
Share Capital	150						150
Sub-total A	1,400	1,000	1,000	1,000	1,000	1,000	6,400

Part B (unchanged)

	July	Aug	Sept	Oct	Nov	Dec	Total
Sub-total B	1,430	1,180	780	780	780	780	5,730

Part C

	July	Aug	Sept	Oct	Nov	Dec	Total
Balance A - B	-30	-180	220	220	220	220	670

Part D

Balance c/f, Cumulative Cash Position	July	Aug	Sept	Oct	Nov	Dec
	-30	-210	10	230	450	670

At the end of the 6 month period the cash flow forecast would show a positive balance of £670,000, reflected in the balance sheet by an entry for cash of the same amount in place of the £670,000 entry for debtors. Would profit be affected? It appears not, but this is not the case. There is one important area that always poses difficulties which we will deal with now. It concerns interest.

If you refer to the basic data used in the example you will see that the £1.4 million for expenses included estimated interest charges. Any action to reduce the potential cash deficit to be financed by borrowing will also reduce the interest charge for the period. Let us see the effect of interest by assuming that the company based its interest charge estimate upon borrowing to cover its worst position of £1.36 million (*Table 1.11*: September) and that the interest rate allowed for the six month period was 10%.

Now with the revised forecast involving no credit sales, the worst position is £210,000. In terms of the interest charge for the period there will be a reduction to be made of £115,000 ((£1,360,000 – £210,000) × 10%). In other words, the interest charge will be £115,000 lower.

If we assume that this interest is all paid by the end of the 6 month period then the cash balance on December 31st will be:

		£
	Closing Cash Balance [(1)]	0
+	Extra Income from Sales being forecast	670,000
+	Reduction in Interest Payable	115,000
=	Revised Closing Cash Balance	785,000

[(1)] *extracted from Table 1.11*

You may think this will lead to an imbalance in the balance sheet where total assets will be higher than total liabilities by £115,000. This will not be the case, because of the effect of the reduced interest charge upon profit. As well as a deduction from cash flow, interest payments are a charge against profit. This means that the £1.4 million of expenses charged against profit will be £115,000 lower and hence profit will be:

		£
	Profit Forecast [(1)]	100,000
+	Reduction in Interest Payable	115,000
=	Revised Profit Forecast	215,000

[(1)] *extracted from Table 1.12*

What happened to this profit? You will recall that it is retained in the business and shown in the balance sheet in total liabilities under shareholders' funds. Thus, the two parts of the balance sheet, total assets and total liabilities, are kept in balance as illustrated in *Table 1.16*.

Table 1.16   Balance sheet as at 31st December

	AFTER		BEFORE	
	£,000	£,000	£000	£'000
Fixed Assets:				
Land		50		50
Other	200		200	
less:Depreciation	20	180	20	180
		230		230
Current Assets:				
Stock	200		200	
Debtors			670	
Cash	785	985		870
TOTAL ASSETS		**£1,215**		**£1,100**
Shareholders' Funds:				
Share Capital		150		150
Reserves		215		100
		365		250
External Funds:				
Long-Term Loan (5 years)	250		250	
Creditors	600	850	600	850
TOTAL LIABILITIES		**£1,215**		**£1,100**

1.6   The balance sheet equation and the UK format

One stumbling block often encountered arises because of the variety of layouts encountered in both internal and published balance sheets. If you come into contact with USA and other European balance sheets you will often find assets and liabilities illustrated in a different order and sometimes grouped together in different ways. Such grouping differences can be readily dealt with if you recall the reference we made earlier to the balance sheet equation. Whether presented in horizontal or vertical format, the basic balance sheet equation is:

TOTAL LIABILITIES   **=**   **TOTAL ASSETS**

We have seen that each of these two can be sub-divided into
component assets and liabilities such as:

SHAREHOLDERS' FUNDS   **FIXED ASSETS**
+   **=**   +
EXTERNAL FUNDS   **CURRENT ASSETS**

In UK published accounts external funds are typically grouped with total assets as negative items thereby reducing the balance sheet totals. Furthermore in the UK and most EC published accounts a distinction is made those external funds which fall due within one year and those which fall due after one year. This distinction means that you may often encounter an item referred to as 'net current assets'. Net current assets are the difference between current assets and external funds falling due within one year. Another term used for such assets is 'working capital' because they represent the liquid resources available for use in generating future profit after short term obligations have been met.

The result of grouping external funding with total assets is that you will encounter items of accounting jargon which are summarised in the following illustration, and explained in the next chapter.

 FIXED ASSETS

plus **CURRENT ASSETS**

minus **CREDITORS:** amounts falling due within one year

= **TOTAL ASSETS LESS CURRENT LIABILITIES**

minus **CREDITORS:** amounts falling due after more than one year

= **NET ASSETS**

Table 1.17 Balance sheet as at 31 December (UK format)

	£'000	£'000
Fixed Assets:		
Land		50
Other	200	
less: Depreciation	20	180
		230
Current Assets:		
Stock	200	
Cash	785	
	985	
less Creditors: amounts falling due within one year	600	385
Total Assets less Current Liabilities		615
less Creditors: amounts falling due after more than one year		250
Net Assets		**365**
Capital and Reserves		
Share Capital		150
Profit and Loss Account		215
		365

Appendix A

Miscellaneous accounting calculations

Disposal of a fixed asset

A company purchased a fixed asset on 1st January 1992 for £47,000. It had an estimated economic life of seven years and an expected disposal value of £5,000. The assetwas sold on the 31st December 1995 for £15,000. The company uses the straight line method for depreciation.

What was the profit or loss on disposal?

$$\text{Straight Line Depreciation} = \frac{(£47,000 - £5,000)}{7 \text{ years}}$$

$$= £6,000 \text{ per annum}$$

	£	£
Sale Price at 31st December 1995		15,000
Cost of Asset at 1 st January 1992	47,000	
less Accumulated Depreciation	24,000	
Net Book Value at 31st December 1995		23,000
Loss on Disposal of Asset		-8,000

The loss on the disposal of the asset would be included in the profit and loss account and would result in a reduction of the profit for the period.

Goodwill arising on acquisition

On the 2nd January 1996, P Wedge Plc, acquired the systems division of A Bunker Plc for £150 million. The assets and liabilities acquired were as follows:

Fixed Assets	£20 million
Stock	£30 million
Debtors	£34 million
Creditors	£65 million

How much is the goodwill arising on acquisition?

	£m	£m
Purchase price		150
Fixed Assets	20	
Stock	30	
Debtors	<u>34</u>	
	84	
less Creditors	<u>65</u>	
Net Assets Acquired		<u>19</u>
Goodwill Arising on Acquisition		**<u>131</u>**

Share premium account

Share premium is the difference between the price paid for shares and their nominal value. A share premium account is necessary because of the requirement to record issued share capital at its nominal value. The difference between the price paid for the shares issued and their nominal value is held in a share premium account.

On the 7th March 1991, P Wedge Plc., issued 60 million new shares, with a nominal value of £0.50, at £2.50 per share.

How much is the cash consideration, the increase in issued share capital, and the amount which should be transferred to the share premium account?

	£m
Cash consideration on share issue	
(60 million x £2.50)	150
Increase in issued share capital	
(60 million x £0.50)	30
Transfer to share premium account	
(60 million x £2.50 - £0.50)	120

Exercises

1.1 The following figures have been extracted from the books of L. Driver.

	£
Sales	2,000,000
Interest Payable	20,000
Wages and Salaries	100,000
Administration Expenses	80,000
Selling and Distribution Expenses	100,000
Opening Stock at 1st January 1990	300,000
Closing Stock at 31st December 1990	400,000
Rent Received	5,000
Purchases	1,500,000
Depreciation of Vehicles	55,000

REQUIRED
1. Prepare a Profit and Loss Account for the year ended 31st December 1990.
2. For what reason(s) would you expect the net profit calculated in 1. above to differ from the cash balance at 31st December 1990?

1.2 The following figures relate to I. Ping Plc

	£m
Closing Stock at 31st March 1991	150
Discount Allowed	18
Purchases	300
Depreciation of Fixtures and Fittings	30
Sales	450
Interest Received	10
Salaries	60
Rent	14
Sales Commission	18
Opening Stock at 1st April 1990	100

REQUIRED
1. Prepare a Profit and Loss Account for the year ended 31st March 1991.
2. What do you understand by 'depreciation of fixtures and fittings'?

1.3   The following balances have been extracted from the books of Plentiturf Ltd. as at 31st January 1991

	£
Finished Stock at 31st January 1991	150,000
Profit and Loss Account	530,000
Fixed Assets	1,000,000
Issued Share Capital	500,000
Bank Overdraft	100,000
Cash	20,000
Share Premium	50,000
Debtors	170,000
Creditors	160,000

REQUIRED

1.   Prepare a Balance Sheet as at 31st January 1991 to show the value of the following:

   i.   Fixed Assets   ii.   Current Assets

   iii. Current Liabilities   iv.   Equity, or Shareholders' Funds

2.   How does a balance sheet differ from a profit and loss account?

1.4   The following balances have been extracted from the books of Nu-Grass Ltd. as at 30th April 1991

	£
Bank Overdraft	2,000,000
Cash	100,000
Vehicles at cost	700,000
Debtors	1,800,000
Long Term Loan	1,000,000
Depreciation of Vehicles	200,000
Creditors	2,500,000
Finished Stock at 30th April 1991	3,500,000
Profit and Loss Account	2,500,000
Land and Buildings	2,600,000
Issued Share Capital	500,000

REQUIRED

1.   Prepare a Balance Sheet as at 30th April 1991 to show the value of the following:

   i.   Total Assets   ii.   Current Assets

   iii. Current Liabilities   iv.   Equity, or Shareholders' Funds.

2.   What is the value of working capital in Nu-Grass Ltd as at 30th April 1991? How would you interpret the working capital position as at this date?

1.5 The following transactions have taken place since the start-up of business on 1st January 1991.

Jan	1	Started the business and paid £1,000 into the bank
	2	Purchased goods £250 on credit from G. Ashley & Co
	3	Bought equipment and paid by cheque £200
	5	Sold goods for cash £250
	8	Bought goods on credit £150 from U. Sanderson & Co
	10	Paid rent by cash £150
	19	Sold goods for cash £650
	23	Bought motor van paying by cheque £300
	30	Paid the month's wages by cash £200

REQUIRED
Prepare a Profit and Loss Account for the month and a Balance Sheet as at 31st January 1991.

1.6 1 Describe two different methods of depreciation.

2 Write a response to a manager who has sent you a note the substance of which is that his old vehicles are fully depreciated and therefore funds should automatically be available for their replacement. Explain why this is not the case.

1.7 A company which is extremely profitable has experienced a decrease in cash and a substantial increase in its bank overdraft. Explain how such a situation may arise using specific examples.

1.8 In discussion with a colleague there appears to be some confusion about the difference between cash flow and profit. Clarify the position in a brief note to your colleague including a numerical example.

1.9 What are Generally Accepted Accounting Principles and why are they important?

1.10 In what way(s) would you expext the balance sheet of a service company to differ from one involved in heavy manufacture?

FINANCIAL REPORTING AND THE UK REGULATORY FRAMEWORK

LEARNING OBJECTIVES

When you have finished studying this chapter and completed the exercises you should be able to:

❏   Understand the regulatory framework which impacts upon financial reporting in the UK.

❏   Outline the main contents of company annual reports including an understanding of the main terms used.

❏   Prepare a published profit and loss account and balance sheet from information provided.

❏   Recognise the importance and in some cases the limitations of the auditors' report.

❏   Identify the need for a statement of source and application of funds.

2.1   Introduction

In addition to being able to work with internal financial statements as discussed in the preceding chapter , you will need to have a good understanding of published financial statements. Published financial statements are to be found in the annual reports produced by UK limited liability companies publicly listed (quoted) on the Stock Exchange and, in addition to being the primary medium for companies to convey information about performance to the outside world, they are a vital source of information to competitors, suppliers and other stakeholders.   Such reports have been produced by many UK listed companies for some 30 years and ICI has been speculated as being the first to produce such a report in 1955. However, there is an even longer tradition in the USA where the earliest US annual report appears to have been that produced by US Steel in 1902.

The principles discussed so far in Chapter 1 are relevant to published financial statements, however, there are some important areas of difference between internal and published statements such as the amount, detail and timeliness of information provided.   Obviously, companies have no desire to publish potentially sensitive information and might, therefore, restrict their disclosure, but they are limited in their ability to restrict disclosure for example by the publication requirements of the UK Companies Acts.   These requirements address the minimum amount of information that should be included in accounts, the format in which it should be presented and, more recently, with how the figures are arrived at.

What form do such publication requirements take?   The Companies Acts require the following documents which are typically contained within the Company's annual report, to be presented to the annual general meeting of shareholders.

❏ A profit and loss account.
❏ A balance sheet.
❏ A directors' report of the business for the year.
❏ An auditors' report.

In this chapter we will discuss these and other features of UK financial reporting, like the statement of source and application of funds. Prior to discussing them, however, we will provide an overview of the important influences upon financial reporting, which include company law, the Stock Exchange, accounting standards and accounting policies.

Be warned, you will find some differences from our earlier discussions in terms of both the terminology used and some aspects of the layout of statements. We will highlight important differences and draw your attention to some specific areas where more than a passing familiarity will be required.

2.2   Company law

Companies Acts have been a long-standing contributor to the UK regulatory framework. Their aim has been to protect shareholders and creditors, but there has been a growing view that companies also owe duties to other groups in society. In 1975 a significant document called 'The Corporate Report' gave the basic aim of company accounts as being to measure and report on the entity's economic resources and performance. To this end, corporate reports should be 'relevant, understandable, reliable, complete, objective, timely, and comparable.'

Whilst 'The Corporate Report' exerted an important influence upon attitudes towards financial reporting, moves towards harmonisation within the European Community (EC) have been more significant in terms of legal implementation via Companies Acts which are the principal source of legal requirements for the contents of UK companies' annual reports. These Acts have had considerable impact upon the contents of published accounts. First, the 1948 Companies Act required companies with subsidiaries to consolidate their results for accounting periods in the form of group accounts. Second, the 1967 Companies Act required companies to disclose total turnover, to split it geographically, and to analyse sales and profits between different business segments. However, the Companies Acts from 1980 are particularly noteworthy and in many respects they have exerted a more significant influence than earlier ones. The first of these, the 1980 Act, introduced new rules for classifying companies into two categories, plc and ltd. Plc's tend to be, though do not have to be, listed on the stock exchange and offer shares or loan stock to the public for purchase and sale. It is worthwhile noting that the Companies Acts do not differentiate between plc companies which offer their shares or loan stock to the public and those which do not. Many companies seek plc status for purposes of conveying a better image with no specific intention of seeking a listing. In addition, the 1980 Act introduced new rules restricting the distribution of profit and assets.

The content and format of published accounts produced by companies has been affected significantly by the Companies Act 1981. This Act was influenced by the European Community (EC) 4th Directive on company law which will be discussed in more detail in Chapter 6. It specified in more detail than earlier Acts the items to be shown in published accounts and also the lay-out of these accounts in terms of the required 'statutory formats'.

Whilst the Companies Act of 1981 significantly increased the quantity, and to some extent the comparability, of information to be included in the accounts for shareholders, it enabled directors of small and medium sized companies to file with the Registrar of Companies accounts containing significantly less information than they had been required to beforehand. Before the 1981 Act the Registrar of Companies received the same accounts as were sent to shareholders. Under the 1981 Act providing a company met certain criteria, it could omit specific information from its published accounts, although a second set of accounts was required to be prepared for shareholders containing all of the statutory information. In essence the Act made a distinction between small, medium, and large companies and a company qualified for a given status if it satisfied, but did not exceed, at least two from three criteria relating to turnover, balance sheet total and average employees per week, for both the current and the previous year. One important consequence of such classification was that small companies were not required to submit a profit and loss account and medium-sized companies could begin their profit and loss account with the figure for gross profit as the starting point.

The effect of the 1981 Act was that the position of the shareholder analyst improved, but the non-shareholder analyst was relatively disadvantaged. In addition, as we will illustrate in a later chapter, the apparent benefits of comparability provided by the Act were restricted by the number of options allowed to companies (as permitted by the 4th Directive) on valuation and presentation. The Act was superseded by the 1985 Act which consolidated requirements of earlier acts and specified additional ones. For example, companies had to prepare a profit and loss account and balance sheet each year in one of the alternative permitted formats illustrating figures for the latest and preceding year. Furthermore, and of vital importance, such published accounts had to show a 'true and fair view' of the profit or loss for the year, and of the company's financial position at the year-end. As indicated in the first chapter, a 'true and fair view' does not mean that a balance sheet necessarily discloses the 'true worth' of a company. It is worth stressing that the balance sheet represents no attempt to value the business, but is merely a statement of those assets and liabilities of a business recognised by accounting rules. Many significant assets are excluded, especially intangible assets such as business 'know-how' and the value of people. For such reasons the market value of a business often differs widely from the net book value of its assets illustrated in the published accounts.

More recently, the 1989 Companies Act was passed which is effective for accounting periods beginning on or after 1 January 1990. It is the UK legal instrument to implement the 7th Directive, the concern with which is the principles to be adopted in preparing consolidated accounts. Its implementation within the UK represents an emphasis away from legal ownership towards the concept of effective control and it is partly intended to curb the use of controlled non-subsidiaries, whereby control could be effected even though the legal requirements constituting a subsidiary were not met. Now, as will be discussed in a later section in this chapter, all undertakings actually controlled by a parent must be consolidated, including partnerships and unincorporated associations carrying on a trade or business (with or without a view to profit).

2.3 Stock exchange

Companies with shares or loan stock quoted on the Stock Exchange, which we have indicated are known as 'listed companies', are subject to a listing agreement, details of which are set out in the so-called 'Yellow Book'. This specifies, among other things, certain information to be disclosed not required by the Companies Acts. The listing agreement is effected when a company's board of directors passes a resolution binding the company to observe the regulations laid down for listed companies. The effect of the listing agreement is evident in its requirements upon the Directors' Report in the annual report. The information required of listed companies includes:

1 The reasons why the trading results shown by the accounts for the period under review differ materially from any published forecast made by the company.

2 A statement by the directors of their reasons for any significant failure to comply with Statements of Standard Accounting Practice (SSAPs).

3 A geographical analysis of turnover and of contribution to trading results of trading operations carried on outside the UK (this disclosure is also required by law).

4 The name of the country in which each subsidiary operates.

5 Particulars regarding each company in which the group equity interest is 20% or more of:

   a. the principal country of operation;

   b. detail of its issued share and loan capital and, unless dealt with in the consolidated balance sheet as an associated company, the total of its reserves.

6 Statements of directors' share interests and of other persons' substantial shareholdings.

7 Detailed information regarding company borrowings.

8 Waivers of emoluments by directors and waivers of dividends by shareholders.

9 'Close' company (controlled by a small number of individuals) and 'investment trust' status.

2.4   Statements of standard accounting practice (SSAP's)

The Accounting Standards Committee was set up in 1970 by the accounting profession in response to criticisms of it raised by such events as the GEC take-over of AEI in which £9.5 million of the £14.5 million differences in reported profits was the result of different accounting practices used before and after the take-over. This and other cases served to fuel criticism about the degree of latitude legally permissible in preparing published accounts.

Statements of Standard Accounting Practice (SSAPs) up to 1st August 1990 were issued by the Accounting Standards Committee (ASC) and are now the responsibility of the Accounting Standards Board (ASB) to be discussed later. Their purpose is to offer both some regulation of disclosure, and to establish the principles by which certain of the figures are calculated. SSAPs in conjunction with requirements of company law mean that there is a specified minimum amount of information which must be provided.

SSAPs have been a major source of authority for accountants about important areas of accounting controversy and the following reasons have often been used in their support:

❑   Comparability. Those who use financial statements in the course of making investment decisions want to compare the performance of a company with the performance of all other companies. This comparison has serious limitations unless all companies draw up their financial statements on the same basis.

❑   Trend. In evaluating a company's performance it is necessary to review the results of a number of years. This review is of dubious value unless a company has drawn up its financial statements on the same basis in each year for which the results are given.

❑   Public understanding. Many readers of statements are not experts in the interpretation of accounting information. Standardised information assists the public in gaining an understanding of financial statements.

❑   Deception. If any directors wish to mislead investors it is more difficult if companies are required to comply with accounting standards.

❑   Professional integrity. The integrity of the accounting profession would suffer if two companies in similar situations could produce quite different results for the same period simply because they were able to use different accounting methods.

However accounting standards have not gone uncriticised and considerable concern has been expressed about the dominance of the views of the accounting profession in standard setting and the ingenuity shown in the non-compliance of standards by a growing minority of companies in their creative accounting practices. As indicated, standard setting had its origins in accounting controversy and one of its most notable achievements was to deflect major criticism away from the profession. However, in recent time concern has arisen and criticism levied at the accounting profession because of the non-compliance of the spirit, if not the letter, of standards. The source of such concern has been the contentious treatment of extraordinary items, goodwill and brands without exceeding the letter of the law.

A good illustration of what a UK company could achieve without actually breaching the regulatory framework in the UK was revealed by a review of the suitability of the accounting policies of *Cray Electronics*, which had once been a much-fancied, high-flying, hi-tech 'wonderstock'. The review considered the effect upon Cray's results for the year ended April 29 1989 if brought in line with best accounting practice within the electronics sector. It revealed a pre-tax profit for the year of £5.4 million instead of the £17.03 million that was actually reported. Earnings per share also dwindled to 3.3p per share, approximately 25% of the figure reported by the company. This review resulted in the publication of a revised annual report incorporating revised published accounts. However, that was not the end of the story. In August 1990 the Cray Board comprising a new management team announced that the profit for 1989 would be revised downwards yet again to £1.3 million. In essence then £17.03 million, £5.4 million and £1.3 million all represented a 'true and fair view'!

Situations like the *Cray Electronics* incident should now be a feature of the past as a consequence of the implementation of a new system of standard setting. This new system is the direct result of concerns expressed regarding standard setting in the UK culminating in a major review of the process headed by Sir Ronald Dearing. An outline of the new structure is illustrated on the next page.

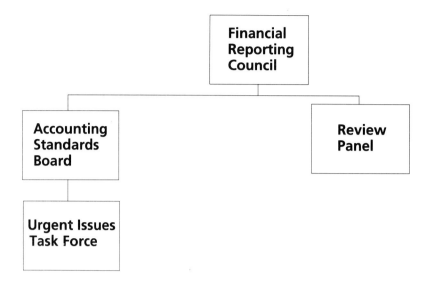

A new body, the Financial Reporting Council (FRC), with 25 members plus some observers will give a voice to all of those concerned with accounting standards, including representation from users, preparers and auditors. One key characteristic of the FRC is that it represents and involves a wide range of interested parties in the standard setting process. Formerly, the Accounting Standards Committee (ASC), which had responsibility for the setting of accounting standards, was answerable to only one constituency, the six main UK professional accountancy bodies.

One noteworthy feature of the FRC is that it is funded by the government, the accounting institutes and the city, which together ensure necessary funding to support the standard setting activities of its two subsidiaries, the Accounting Standards Board (ASB) and the Review Panel.

The ASB, has the responsibility for detailed standard setting. It took over responsibility for accounting standard setting from the ASC on 1st August 1990. It is smaller than the FRC having both a full-time chairman and technical director, together with part-time members including a committed presence from the non-practicing side of the accountancy profession. It will issue standards on its own authority, unlike the ASC, with there now being no requirement for the six main UK professional accounting bodies to approve any standards produced, and whilst the FRC will be in a position to give the ASB guidance, it will have no say over the detail of any standard. However, it is intended that the ASB will secure support and a consensus in favour of any standards produced.

As illustrated, the ASB will be supported by an Urgent Issues Task Force (UITF) whose function will be to tackle urgent matters not covered by existing standards, and for which, given the urgency, the normal standard setting process would not be practicable. This body, which will be an adjunct of the ASB and not a distinct entity in its own right, represents a new departure for UK practice but is based in principle upon the Emerging Issues Task Force which has existed for some time in the United States.

The second subsidiary of the FRC is the Review Panel, the concern of which is with the examination and questioning of departures from accounting standards. Any such departures for the Review Panel's attention are expected to be identifiable as a result of recent changes in legislation which requires companies to state whether their accounts have been prepared in accordance with applicable accounting standards and to give particulars of any material departure from those standards and reasons for them.

This new system is radically different to that which formerly existed where responsibility lay only with the ASC . In particular the existence and powers of the Review Panel with legislative backing is a totally new element in the accounting standards scene. No longer should a company be able to get away with published accounts which include a material departure from an accounting standard because the Review Panel will be able to apply to the courts and, in the event that the accounts are found not to present a true and fair view, the company may be ordered to prepare revised accounts and be obliged to circulate them to all persons likely to rely on the previous accounts. Furthermore, the courts may in such circumstances order that all or part of the costs of the application (by the Review Panel or by the Secretary of State ultimately responsible), and any reasonable expenses incurred by the company in consequence of the preparation of revised accounts shall be borne by such of the directors as were party to the approval of the defective accounts which the courts have found to be defective against the test of a 'true and fair view'.

2.5 Consolidated/group accounts

One important feature of the published financial statements contained in annual reports is that they will often be consolidated to show the results for a group of companies.

What is a group of companies? If two separate companies operate independently of each other, they will maintain separate accounting records and prepare separate financial statements. However, if one company controls the other, the result is a group comprising the controlling, holding, or parent company and the controlled or subsidiary company. Both parent and subsidiary companies retain their separate legal identity and operations and separate accounting records. Sometimes subsidiaries themselves have sub-subsidiaries, each of which is required to produce its own accounts and, if a

UK company, to file them with the Registrar of Companies. The parent company usually produces two sets of accounts contained within the one annual report:

❏ its own accounts in which the subsidiaries will be shown in the balance sheet as an investment and the dividends from them will be shown in the profit and loss account, and;

❏ its group or consolidated accounts. These show the income and expenditure, assets and liabilities of all the companies as a single economic whole and therefore usually give a much clearer and fuller picture.

A company publishing group accounts need not publish its own profit and loss account but must show how much of the group's profit is dealt with in the parent's profit and loss account.

Thus, the position with group accounts is that whereas individual legal identities are retained, the financial statements are consolidated with the purpose of providing the holders of the parent company with information about the full range of its activities including interests in subsidiaries. The result is a consolidated profit and loss account and a consolidated balance sheet obtained from aggregating the separate profit and loss accounts and balance sheets of the parent and subsidiary companies.

The notional principle of parent and subsidiary companies is straightforward, but their definition is not without its problems. As a general rule of thumb, a subsidiary arises for a company in any one of the following circumstances:

❏ when it holds a majority of the rights to vote at general meetings in any undertaking, including partnerships and unincorporated associations carrying on a trade or business (with or without a view to profit) and any rights held by any nominees;

❏ when it has the right to appoint or remove directors holding a majority of the voting rights;

❏ when it has the right to exercise a dominant influence (including at least a right to direct the undertaking's operating and financial policies) by virtue of either provisions in the memorandum or articles, or a written contract;

❏ actually exercises a dominant influence over the undertaking or is managed on a unified basis with it.

These criteria which determine the existence of a subsidiary were the result of the 1989 Companies Act, the effect of which has been to extend the meaning of a subsidiary undertaking. Judgement is now required to determine whether a parent actually controls a subsidiary, one test of which might be whether the parent company is in a position to ensure that dividends would always be paid in accordance with its instructions.

2.6   Annual reports

Most annual reports for public limited companies (plcs) contain the following:

- ❏ The Chairman's Statement.
- ❏ The Directors' Report.
- ❏ A Profit and Loss Account.
- ❏ A Balance Sheet.
- ❏ Notes to the Accounts.
- ❏ Accounting Policies.
- ❏ Historical Summaries.
- ❏ The Auditors' Report.
- ❏ A Statement of Source and Application of Funds.

The Directors' Report, the Profit and Loss Account and Balance Sheet plus the Notes to the Accounts and the Auditors' Report are all required by law. The Chairman's Statement is not a legal requirement and is not always provided. The Statement of Source and Application of Funds is a requirement by a Statement of Standard Accounting Practice (SSAP 10). Historical Summaries are not legally required of companies but have become established practice by most large companies.

2.6.1   The chairman's statement

This is generally a review of progress of the company and its business environment over the past year together with some indications of the proposed direction for the company in the forthcoming year. It is not usually the case that remarks by the chairman will be convertible into a forecast of the results for the company for the next year, although usually much of value can be gleaned from the statement in terms not only of what is included (and excluded) but the tone in which information is conveyed.

2.6.2   The directors' report

In contrast to the Chairman's Statement, the content of the Directors' Report is laid down by statute and, to a lesser extent, by the requirements of the Stock Exchange for listed companies. Furthermore, the auditors are required to comment in their report if any information given in the Directors' Report is not, in their opinion, consistent with the company's accounts. Examples of the information required to be provided in the annual report and to be found in the Directors' Report is illustrated *Table 2.1.*

Table 2.1   Examples of information required

- ❏ Names of the directors and details of their shareholdings.
- ❏ Main classes of business and any major changes.
- ❏ Important changes in fixed assets.
- ❏ Research and development activities.
- ❏ A fair review of the year's business, and the end-of-year position.
- ❏ Likely future developments.
- ❏ Any important events since the year-end.
- ❏ Details of any of its own shares a company has acquired during the year.
- ❏ Details of political and charitable contributions.

As indicated, the Report describes the principal activities of the business and must include a fair review of the development of the business during the year and its position at the end of the year, together with an indication of likely future developments. Details are required of any important events affecting the group since the year end and it should also contain a statement of the directors' interest in the shares of the company, the identity of anyone owning more than 5 per cent of the company in the case of a listed company, and if the company has acquired any of its own shares. Finally information is required about a number of other matters such as charitable and political donations, research and development, and disabled employees. A point to note, company practices vary such that items may be disclosed in the Directors' Report but alternitively, may be disclosed separately by way of a note to the accounts.

2.6.3   Published profit and loss account

We indicated earlier that the format of published profit and loss accounts and balance sheets is prescribed by the UK Companies Acts. In the case of the published profit and loss account, companies do have an element of choice insofar as the Acts provide two horizontal and two vertical alternatives. The main difference between the alternatives you will encounter concerns the way in which costs are analysed. The form you will frequently encounter and that we have adopted is illustrated in the consolidated profit and loss account in *Table 2.2*.

Table 2.2 Published consolidated profit and loss account

CONSOLIDATED PROFIT AND LOSS ACCOUNT
for the year ended 31st December 1990

	1990 £'000	1989 £'000
Sales	29,000	26,000
Cost of Sales	-21,000	-20,000
GROSS PROFIT	8,000	6,000
Distribution and Selling Cost	-2,700	-2,000
Administration Expenses	-3,000	-3,000
OPERATING PROFIT	2,300	1,000
Interest Payable	-300	-600
PROFIT/(LOSS) ON ORDINARY ACTIVITIES BEFORE TAX	2,000	400
Taxation	-700	-140
PROFIT/(LOSS) ON ORDINARY ACTIVITIES AFTER TAX	1,300	260
Extraordinary Charges	-500	0
PROFIT/(LOSS) AFTER EXTRAORDINARY ITEMS	800	260
Dividends	-300	-100
TRANSFER TO/(FROM) RESERVES	500	160
Earnings per Ordinary Share:		
Undiluted	1.5p	-1.00p
Diluted	1.25p	

The profit and loss account, in this case consolidated to show the effect on profit for the companies comprising the group, is characterised by 'layers' of profit, similar to those discussed in Chapter 1. The last item, the transfer to/(from) reserves is found by using the following 9 steps

Step

1   Add together all of the companies' revenue to obtain sales (turnover) for the group.
2   Add any other income to sales to obtain total revenue.
3   Add together the companies' costs of sales.
4   Add together the companies' distribution and selling and administrative costs.
5   Subtract the cost of sales and costs in 4. from total revenue to obtain operating profit for the group.
6   Subtract any interest payable by the group (from loans and overdrafts) from operating profit to obtain profit before taxation for the group.
7   Subtract the tax the group has to pay from profit before taxation to obtain group profit after taxation.
8   Subtract any extraordinary item to obtain the profit attributable to shareholders.
9   Subtract dividends to determine the retained profits to transfer to/(from)reserves.

What exactly is meant by the items included in the profit and loss account? We have provided a brief description in the following checklist:

❏   SALES (TURNOVER): This is the total sales or operating revenue of the group and can be goods and or services. Sales exclude VAT which companies have to collect on behalf of governments.

❏   COST OF SALES: The cost of sales includes wages and the depreciation of equipment, as well as the value of the materials and services the companies in the group have bought during the year in order to make the good or provide the services that they sell. These materials and services will include such items as raw materials, components, power for machinery and heating, maintenance bills and fuel for vehicles.

❏   GROSS PROFIT: The difference between turnover and cost of sales.

❏   OTHER COSTS: Expenses such as distribution and administration expenses are disclosed and deducted from gross profit.

❏   OTHER INCOME: Although a company or a group of companies usually has a main trading activity, it may also derive income from other different activities. For example, a company may own property which it lets. The rent it receives will be classed as 'other income'. Share of profits of related companies and income from other investments are also included here.

❑ **OPERATING PROFIT:** This is the profit made when all expenses other than interest payable have been deducted. It is sometimes called 'trading profit'.

❑ **INTEREST PAYABLE:** Interest is payable on loans and is an expense that can be charged against profit, unlike dividends.

❑ **PROFIT/(LOSS) ON ORDINARY ACTIVITIES BEFORE TAXATION:** This represents operating profit less interest payable.

❑ **TAXATION:** This includes UK corporation tax, and overseas taxes for companies operating abroad.

❑ **PROFIT/(LOSS) ON ORDINARY ACTIVITIES AFTER TAXATION:** This represents profit/(loss) on ordinary activities before taxation, less taxation.

❑ **EXTRAORDINARY ITEMS:** These include charges such as the cost of closing a factory which do not form part of normal trading. As such, they are omitted from the calculation of profit on ordinary activities and are referred to commonly as being 'below the line'.

❑ **PROFIT/(LOSS) ATTRIBUTABLE TO SHAREHOLDERS:** This is the amount that can be distributed to shareholders. Subject to any legal constraints, it is up to a company or group of companies how much is distributed and how much is retained for re-investment and expansion.

❑ **DIVIDENDS:** These are that part of after tax profit to be distributed to shareholders.

❑ **TRANSFER TO/(FROM) RESERVES:** This is the profit remaining after the deduction of all the above items. It is commonly known as 'Retained' profit.

❑ **EARNINGS PER ORDINARY SHARE (EPS):** You will have observed that at the end of the published profit and loss account illustrated in *Table 2.2* there is an entry for 'Earnings per ordinary share'. In simple terms, this shows how much each of the group's ordinary shares has earned during the year. It is calculated by dividing the profit after tax (less any preference dividends but before extraordinary items), by the average number of issued ordinary shares for the year ranking for a dividend. Where there is another equity share ranking for a dividend in the future, and/or other securities convertible into equity shares in issue, and/or options or warrants exist to subscribe for equity shares what is known as a fully diluted EPS should be disclosed. Such a fully diluted EPS shows how much each of the group's ordinary shares have earned when the effect of potential changes in the financial structure are taken into account. You should be aware that EPS is considered to be an important financial ratio which is frequently related to the market price at which a share is trading, known as the Price Earnings (PE) ratio. Both of these we consider later in Chapter 3.

Notes to the accounts

In its published form the profit and loss account is very much a summarised statement which can only provide a limited indication of how well a business has performed. In working with such a statement you will often want more information to form a more complete view, some of which you will find in supporting notes to the accounts. Do remember, however, that you will rarely find all of the information you wish because for competitive reasons companies are often reluctant to provide more than the minimum required of them.

Greater detail on all items contained within a profit and loss account are available from the notes to published accounts, the relevant note usually being cross referenced in a separate column in the profit and loss account. What form do such notes take? The following is an illustration of a note that might be found for earnings per share:

The Earnings per Ordinary Share are based on the profits after taxation and preference dividend of £1,800,000 (1988, loss £500,000) and 120,000,000 Ordinary Shares (1988, 100,000,000) being the weighted average number of shares in issue during the year.

Other notes to accounts would include:

❏ Turnover and profit or loss for each different type of business. Turnover for different geographical markets.
❏ Details of net operating costs, including raw materials and consumables, depreciation, staff costs and auditors fees.
❏ Interest payable and receivable.
❏ Details of directors' remuneration, and employees with emoluments over £30,000.
❏ The average number of employees, total wages, social security and pension costs.
❏ Details of tax.
❏ Details of extraordinary items after taxation.
❏ Details of preference and ordinary dividends.

2.6.4   Published balance sheet

Having considered the published profit and loss account, let us now consider the published balance sheet. We have provided an example which is shown in *Table 2.3.*

Table 2.3   Published Balance Sheet

CONSOLIDATED BALANCE SHEETS
as at December 31st 1989

	1989 £'000	1988 £'000
FIXED ASSETS		
Tangible Assets	7,000	5,000
	7,000	5,000
CURRENT ASSETS		
Stocks	8,000	6,000
Debtors	7,000	6,000
Cash	7,000	3,000
	22,000	15,000
CREDITORS: amounts falling due within one year	10,000	6,000
NET CURRENT ASSETS/ (LIABILITIES)	12,000	9,000
TOTAL ASSETS LESS CURRENT LIABILITIES	19,000	14,000
CREDITORS: amounts falling due after one year	7,000	3,000
NET ASSETS	£12,000	£11,000
CAPITAL and RESERVES		
Called up Share Capital	6,000	5,900
Share Premium Account	4,500	3,900
Profit and Loss Account	1,500	1,200
SHAREHOLDERS' FUNDS	£12,000	£11,000

The balance sheet in *Table 2.3* consists of the following:

1   The sum of all fixed assets within the group.

2   The sum of all current assets within the group.

3   The sum of all group liabilities falling due within one year.

4   Net current assets, which represent the difference between liabilities in 3 and current assets.

5   Total assets less current liabilities, calculated from the sum of fixed assets and net current assets.

6   Net assets, which represent the difference between total assets and all liabilities.

7   Owners equity/shareholders' funds, which is the sum of the share capital and reserves of the group.

Please do note that the contents illustrated in the consolidated balance sheets *Table 2.3*, may differ from some you will encounter in practice. Apart from differences in the nature of the business which will affect mix and even types of assets and/or liabilities, there are other reasons for example, where subsidiaries are not wholly owned, thereby giving rise to what are known as 'minority interests' (external shareholdings outside the group).

You will observe areas of similarity between published and internal balance sheets discussed earlier. However, one key point to note is that whilst the liabilities in published balance sheets are also separated with reference to the length of time of the obligation incurred, the following labels are normally used:

❑ Creditors : amounts falling due within one year

❑ Creditors : amounts falling due after one year

As indicated in the illustration in *Table 2.3*, the total in the top part of the balance sheet is calculated as follows:

FIXED ASSETS + CURRENT ASSETS - ALL CREDITORS = NET ASSETS

and that

NET ASSETS = OWNERS' EQUITY (SHAREHOLDERS' FUNDS)

The owners' equity (shareholders' funds) comprises the sum of capital and reserves and is sometimes also referred to as net worth. This section includes all of the called up share capital of a company. In some company accounts, and indeed in our example company, you will find an item in the reserves called the 'share premium account'. This arises where for example new shares are offered to existing shareholders, in proportion to the number of shares each already holds. The issue price that these shares will be sold for will usually be more than their nominal or face value but less than the market value quoted on the Stock Exchange. This discount on the market value is intended to encourage the purchase of new share issues.

As with the profit and loss account, much detail about items included in the balance sheet can be found in the notes to the accounts. Notes to the balance sheet would include:

❑ Tangible assets: showing additions, acquisitions, disposals and depreciation by main type of asset.
❑ Shares in subsidiary companies.

- ❏ Investments, short-term and long-term.
- ❏ Stocks: showing a breakdown into raw materials, work-in-progress, and finished goods if appropriate.
- ❏ Debtors, including prepayments.
- ❏ Creditors due within one year: showing a breakdown into short term borrowings, trade creditors, other creditors, accruals and deferred income, corporation taxation, other taxation including social security benefits and proposed dividends.
- ❏ Creditors due after more than one year: consists mainly of borrowing repayable between one and five years.
- ❏ Called up share capital.
- ❏ Reserves: including share premium, revaluation reserve, and other reserves.
- ❏ Profit and loss account: showing the accumulated profits as at the date of the balance sheet.

2.6.6   Historical summaries

Historical summaries are not a legal requirement, but have been provided by the vast majority large companies since their request by the Chairman of the Stock Exchange over 25 years ago. They usually cover at least five years and the more usual items included are:

- ❏ Turnover.

- ❏ Profit.

- ❏ Dividends.

- ❏ Capital employed.

- ❏ Various ratios such as earnings per share, return on capital, profit on turnover and assets per share. These have to be interpreted guardedly because, with the exception of earnings per share, there is no commonly accepted standard for any ratio.

Historical summaries are a valuable preliminary source of information about a company, a point to which we will return in a later chapter.

2.6.7   Auditors' report

By law, every limited liability company is required to appoint at each annual general meeting an auditor or auditors to hold office from the conclusion of that meeting until the conclusion of the next AGM. The auditors are required to report to the shareholders on the accounts they have examined which are laid before the company in a general meeting. It is important to understand that there is no responsibility as an auditor for the efficiency or otherwise of the business. Specifically the auditor, generally appointed by the shareholders, reports to them whether in his/her opinion:

❑   the balance sheet gives a true and fair view of the company's affairs;

❑   the profit and loss account gives a true and fair view of the profit or loss for the year; and,

❑   the accounts give the information required by the Companies Acts in the manner required.

In addition, the auditors report to the shareholders when they are not satisfied that:

❑   proper accounting records have been kept;

❑   proper returns, adequate for their purposes, have been received from all parts of the business whether visited or not;

❑   the accounts are in agreement with the accounting records and returns received from all parts of the business, and,

❑   they have received all the information and explanations required.

A 'clean' audit report would typically take the following form:

Auditors' Report

To the members of [name of the company]

We have audited the accounts, set out on pages .... to ... in accordance with approved Auditing Standards. In our opinion, the accounts, which have been prepared under the historical cost convention [as modified by the revaluation of land and buildings] give a true and fair view of the state of affairs of the company and of the group at ....19.. and of the group profit and source and application of funds for the year then ended, and comply with the Companies Act 1989.

[Name and address of auditors, and date]

It should be noted that the auditors' report uses the phrase a 'true and fair view' which indicates that the accounting policies and presentation used by the directors are acceptable, although another company in the same financial position could, by adopting different but equally acceptable policies, show a different profit.

The approved Auditing Standards referred to in the auditors' report are produced by the Auditing Practices Committee of the bodies of accountants entitled to audit the accounts of limited liability companies. They prescribe basic principles and practices members are expected to follow in conducting an audit.

On occasions you may encounter qualified auditors reports. These occasions arise in the following circumstances:

Nature of circumstances	Material but not fundamental	Fundamental
Uncertainty	'Subject to' opinion	'Disclaim' opinion
Disagreement	'Except' opinion	'Adverse' opinion

As indicated, there are four general categories of audit qualification. First, the accounts may be accepted 'subject to' a material matter about which there is uncertainty. Second, if it is a case of disagreement rather than uncertainty, the wording will be 'except' rather than 'subject to'. Far more important are the third and fourth categories of qualification where there is fundamental disagreement. Where it is a fundamental matter of uncertainty, then the disclaimer will state an inability to form an opinion as to whether the financial statements give a true and fair view. If it is a matter of disagreement then there will be an expression that the financial statements do not give a true and fair view.

For what specific reasons do audit qualifications arise? They can be best understood in terms of the two broad categories illustrated above - uncertainty and disagreement. Circumstances leading to uncertainty may include:

❏ inability to carry out necessary audit procedures, or lack of proper accounting records;

❏ inherent uncertainties, for example in relation to major litigation or long-term contracts, or doubts about the company's ability to continue as a going concern.

Circumstances giving rise to disagreement may include:

❏ failure to follow one or more Statements of Standard Accounting Practice (SSAPs) and the auditors do not concur;

❏ disagreement as to facts or amounts in the accounts;

❏ disagreement as to the manner or extent of disclosure in the accounts.

Only something important will cause auditors to qualify their report. Since most company directors are very anxious to avoid this if at all possible, a qualified audit report should always be a matter of serious concern to readers of accounts.

Thus, an audit qualifications are the exception rather than the rule, but do not believe that an unqualified audit report is necessarily a clean bill of health which guarantees that a company will not go out of business for at least another year. Such a view would be a misconception of the role of the audit report which is no more than the accounts present 'a' true and fair view. It is up to the reader to decide whether the view encourages him to believe in the company's continuing existence or to have doubts about its viability.

Extracts from selected auditors' reports with qualifications include the following:

"The accounts have been prepared on a going concern basis which assumes that adequate finance will continue to be made available to the group. Subject to the Group's principal bankers continue to provide finance, in our opinion they give a true and fair view. . .".

"The method of accounting for the group's interest in associated companies set out in note 2 on page 15 is not in accordance with Statement of Standard Accounting Practice No.1".

2.6.8   Published statement of source and application of funds

So far our discussions have omitted any reference to the statement of source and application of funds, usually referred to as the 'funds statement', which in simple terms can be thought of as being the equivalent to the cash flow statement for published accounts. Discussions about the funds statement can often become unnecessarily complex, a temptation we have chosen to avoid.

The purpose of the funds statement is to explain how far the business has managed to generate additional funds during the year, where they have come from, and how they have been used. Information contained in the funds statement is usually no more than an alternative presentation of that already contained in the profit and loss account and balance sheets. This should not be taken to infer that the funds statement cannot provide a further valuable insight into the operation of a business. Indeed, if well presented it can provide a good explanation of the changes in financial strength and standing of the business that have arisen as the result not only of trading, but also of any other major business transactions which have taken place during the year.

The funds statement is currently a requirement of a UK accounting standard (SSAP 10). There are three identifiable parts of a funds statement as can be seen in *Table 2.4*.

Table 2.4 *Source and application of funds statement*

CONSOLIDATED SOURCE AND APPLICATION OF FUNDS
for the year ended 31st December 1990

	1990[1]
(1) SOURCE OF FUNDS	**£'000**
Profit/(Loss) on Ordinary Activities BeforeTaxation	2,000
Adjustment for items not involving the movement of funds:	
Depreciation	1,000
Funds Generated From/(applied to) Operations	3,000
Net Proceeds of Share Issues	5,300
Issue of Loan Notes	8,000
Disposal of Tangible Assets	1,500
(A)	17,800
(2) APPLICATION OF FUNDS	
Purchase of Tangible Assets	6,500
Dividend Payments	100
Loans Received under Lease Contracts	1,000
(B)	7,600
(3) (INCREASE)/DECREASE IN WORKING CAPITAL (A)-(B)	10,200
Stocks	4,000
Debtors	3,000
Cash	7,000
Creditors	-3,800
	10,200

[1] *Normally two years will be found in UK published accounts.*

The three sections in the funds statement may be summarised as:

❑ A statement of sources showing where new funds have come from.

❑ A statement of applications, showing what the funds have been used for.

❑ An analysis of the increase or decrease in funds, which corresponds with the difference between the statement of sources and the statement of applications. Funds comprise of changes in the net liquid position (cash and short-term investments) and the other elements of working capital, like stock, debtors and creditors.

While the accounting standard provides a suggested format, other formats are to be found in practice. Three others that are popular can be categorised as:

❑ 'balanced' – sources and applications shown separately but with equal totals

❑ 'remainder' – applications deducted from sources leaving a residual amount

❑ 'reconciling' – analyses increases/decreases in funds for the period in terms of sources and applications, then reconciles difference with opening and closing fund balances

Within the source of funds section will be found the cash profit generated during the trading period in question, together with other sources of finance not comprising part of working capital. Similarly the application of funds will also exclude items comprising part of working capital.

An alternative to the funds statement is to produce a statement of cash-flows, a practice that has been adopted by the Federal Accounting Standards Board in the USA and seems likely to be followed in the UK. The US approach analyses cash flows under three types of activity.

❑ Financing activities: These would include proceeds from share issues and loans, the repayment of loans and finance leases and the payment of dividends.

❑ Investing activities: These include activities such as purchases and sales of fixed assets and investments and the making of loans.

❑ Operating activities: These are defined as 'all transactions and other events that are not investing and finance activities.' The cash flows are, generally, those arising from those transactions recorded in the profit and loss account.

A statement of cash flows using data from *Table 2.4* is illustrated in *Table 2.5*.

Table 2.5   Statement of cash flows

		£'000
Finance:		
Increase in Share Capital		5,300
Increase in Borrowing		8,000
Loans Repaid		-1,000
	(A)	12,300
Investment:		
Sales of Fixed Assets		1,500
Purchase of Fixed Assets		-6,500
	(B)	-5,000
Operations:		
Operating Cash Flow Before Interest		3,000
Interest Paid		0
Taxation Paid		0
Dividends Paid		-100
Increase in Stock		-4,000
Increase in Debtors		-3,000
Decrease in Creditors		3,800
	(C)	- 300
Increase/ Decrease in Cash	(A)+(B)+(C)	7,000

Although cash flow reporting is gaining popularity in the UK and has been adopted in the USA, it is important to note that funds statements continue to be a requirement elsewhere. Consequently, a sound basic understanding of the funds statement may be invaluable in working with annual reports produced outside the UK.

2.7   Interim reporting

Whilst the information provided in an annual report may be valuable, such value becomes limited with the passage of time. How can more up-to-date information be obtained? One important source is from interim reports.

In addition to a requirement to produce annual reports, the Stock Exchange's Yellow Book, Admission of Securities to Listing, requires as a minimum the following to be provided on an interim basis:

- ❏ Net turnover.
- ❏ Profit before tax and extraordinary items.
- ❏ The taxation charge.
- ❏ Minority interests.
- ❏ Ordinary profit attributable to shareholders .
- ❏ Extraordinary items.
- ❏ Dividends.
- ❏ Earnings per share.
- ❏ Comparative figures.
- ❏ An explanatory statement to include information on any events and trends during the period as well as details about future prospects.

The whole interim report must be sent not later than four months after the period to all shareholders or alternatively it must appear in two national newspapers. Such reports are not usually audited and therefore lack the authority and accuracy which annual reports appear to possess. It is also the case that there are no guidelines on the preparation of interim reports in company law or accounting standards.

Interim reporting has received relatively little attention in the UK. This can be readily understood by comparing UK practice with that in the USA. The New York Stock Exchange has required published information since 1910, the Securities and Exchange Commission (SEC) since 1946 and the American Stock Exchange since 1962. By contrast, the London Stock Exchange did not introduce requirements until 1964.

Appendix A

Formats for UK published accounts

PROFIT AND LOSS ACCOUNT (Format 1)
Turnover
Cost of Sales
Gross Profit
Distribution Costs
Administration Expenses
Other Operating Income
Interest Receivable
Interest Payable and Similar Charges
Profit on Ordinary Activities Before Taxation
Tax on Profit on Ordinary Activities
Profit on Ordinary Activities After Taxation
Extraordinary Items
Profit for the Financial Year
Dividends
Profit Retained for the Year

Earnings per Ordinary Share

PROFIT AND LOSS ACCOUNT (Format 2)
Turnover
Change in Stocks of Finished Goods and Work in Progress
Raw Materials and Consumables
Own Work Capitalised
Other External Charges
Staff Costs
Depreciation
Other Operating Charges
Interest Receivable
Interest Payable and Similar Charges
Profit on Ordinary Activities Before Taxation
Tax on Profit on Ordinary Activities
Profit on Ordinary Activities After Taxation
Extraordinary Items
Profit for the Financial Year
Dividends
Profit Retained for the Year

Earnings per Ordinary Share

CONSOLIDATED BALANCE SHEET (FORMAT 1)

Fixed Assets
Intangible Assets
Tangible Assets
Investments
Current Assets
Stocks
Debtors
Investments
Cash at Bank and in Hand
Creditors: amounts falling due within one year
Net Current Assets
Total Assets Less Current Liabilities
Creditors: amounts falling due after more than one year
Provisions for Liabilities and Charges
Net Assets
Capital and Reserves
Called up Share Capital
Share Premium Account
Revaluation Reserve
Profit and Loss Account

UK Statements of standard accounting practice

1	Accounting for the results of associated companies
2	Disclosure of accounting policies
3	Earnings per share
4	The accounting treatment of government grants
5	Accounting for value added tax
6	Extraordinary items and prior year adjustments
8	The treatment of taxation under the imputation system
9	Stocks and long term contracts
12	Accounting for depreciation
13	Accounting for research and development
15	Accounting for deferred taxation
17	Accounting for post balance sheet events
18	Accounting for contingencies
19	Accounting for investment properties
20	Foreign currency translation
21	Accounting for leases and hire purchase contracts
22	Accounting for goodwill
23	Accounting for acquisitions and mergers
24	Accounting for pension costs

Exercises

2.1   The Trial Balance of OAK Ltd as at the 31st March 1991 was as follows:-

	£	£
Vehicles (at cost)	130,000	
Purchases	720,000	
Sales		1,000,000
Depreciation of Vehicles		26,000
Stock at 1st April 1990	140,000	
Debtors	85,000	
Trade Creditors		44,000
Loan Stock 10%		60,000
Share Premium Account		25,000
Profit & Loss Account		25,000
Wages	35,000	
Rates	2,500	
Heating & Lighting	5,000	
Salaries	20,000	
Administration Expenses	65,000	
Furniture & Fittings (at cost)	18,000	
Depreciation of Furniture & Fittings		9,000
Bank Balance	50,000	
Provision for Bad Debts		3,000
Loan Interest Paid to 30th Sept. 1990	3,000	
Freehold Property	200,000	
Issued Share Capital		300,000
Bad Debts Written Off	3,500	
Directors Fees	15,000	
	1,492,000	1,492,000

REQUIRED

Prepare a published Profit and Loss Account for the year ended 31st March 1991, and a Balance Sheet as at that date.

The following notes are to be taken into account
a.   Stock at 31st March 1991; £150,000
b.   Wages outstanding at 31st March 1991; £1,500
c.   Rates paid in advance amounting to £500
d.   Depreciation of vehicles over 5 years (straight line)
e.   Depreciation of furniture and fittings, 5% of cost
f.   Provision for bad and doubtful debts, adjust to £3,500
g.   Dividend proposed, 50% of profit on ordinary activities after taxation.

2.2   The Trial Balance of BEECH Ltd as at the 31st January 1991 was as follows:-

	£000's	£000's
Issued share Capital		6,806
Profit and Loss Account		15,453
Share Premium Account		4,754
Purchases	48,200	
Sales		69,900
Bad Debts Provision		976
Rent	1,058	
Stock at 1st February1990	18,600	
Land and Buildings	11,242	
Debtors	16,937	
Creditors		12,861
Cash in Hand	1,042	
Bank Overdraft		2,479
Plant and Equipment	19,124	
Depreciation of Plant and Equipment		9,169
Marketing Expenses	1,400	
Lighting	250	
Long Term Loan at 8%		4,375
Investments	1,486	
Rates	350	
General Expenses	2,500	
Selling and Commission	1,100	
Salaries	2,800	
Bad Debts Written Off	684	
	126,773	126,773

REQUIRED

Prepare a published Profit and Loss Account for the year ended 31st January 1991, and a Balance Sheet as at that date.

The following notes are to be taken into account

		£000's
a.	Closing stocks at 31st January 1991	17,900
b.	General expenses, due not yet paid	100
c.	Bad debts, a further write off	293
d.	Bad and doubtful debts provision, adjust to	1,169
e.	Depreciation of plant and equipment	2,349
f.	Proposed dividend	437
g.	Salaries due not yet paid	300

2.3   Summarised Balance sheets for Horace and Doris Morris Ltd. for the years ending 30th April 1990 and 1991.

	April 1990 £	April 1991 £
Issued Share Capital	200,000	240,000
Share Premium Account	31,200	58,100
Profit and Loss Account	48,500	68,800
Long Term Loans	50,000	
Trade Creditors	129,700	121,900
Taxation	18,600	24,000
Land and Buildings	105,000	140,000
Vehicles	147,200	173,000
Fixtures and Fittings	6,000	3,000
Stocks	130,100	105,300
Debtors	75,200	84,700
Cash	14,500	6,800

Depreciation charged to the profit and loss account for the year ended 30th April 1991 was as follows:

	£
Vehicles	10,000
Fixtures and fittings	500

REQUIRED

Prepare a source and application of funds statement

2.4   Summarised Balance sheets for A. Retailer PLC. for the years ending 30th May 1990 and 1991.

	May 1990 £	May 1991 £
Issued Share Capital	96,900	98,900
Share Premium Account	9,800	18,100
Profit and Loss Account	77,200	116,200
Revaluation Reserve	91,500	91,500
Long Term Loans	136,200	127,200
Trade Credtiors	228,700	272,100
Bank Overdraft	8,800	6,900
Taxation	28,300	47,100
Dividend	11,800	13,400
Fixed Assets	346,700	379,000
Investments	7,300	8,200
Stocks	228,400	250,700
Debtors	90,200	128,500
Cash	16,600	25,000

CONSOLIDATED PROFIT AND LOSS ACCOUNT
for the year ended 30th May 1991

	£
Turnover	1,940,500
Profit Before Taxation	99,500
Taxation	47,100
	52,400
Dividend	13,400
Retained Profit	39,000

Note: Profit before taxation is stated after charging £36,500 for depreciation of fixed assets.

REQUIRED

Prepare a source and application of funds statement

2.5   Using the Profit and Loss Account and the Balance Sheet prepared for OAK Ltd, identify the following:-

1   Profit before taxation

2   Total assets

3   Net assets

4   Current assets

5   Liquid assets

6   Creditors: amounts falling due within one year

7   Shareholders' funds

2.6   Describe the main sections you would expect to find in the annual report of a public limited company.

2.7   Growth in earnings per share is one of the most common financial measures used by companies to report success. Illustrate how to calculate earnings per share and comment on the problems associatedwith its use.

2.8   The auditor's report may sometimes be qualified. For what reasons might audit qualifications be given? Discuss the importance to an investor of their inclusion.

2.9   What is the value of accounting standards and the framework that supports their development and enforcement in the U.K.

2.10   What is the value of the Source and Application of Funds Statement or the Statement of Cash flows in addition to the Profit and Loss Account and Balance Sheet.

FINANCIAL RATIO ANALYSIS

3.1   Introduction

One major challenge you will have to face in studying for an MBA/DMS or any other post-graduate management qualification, and as your career progresses, is to understand and make sense of internally generated and externally published financial information. In this chapter we will show how sense of financial information can be achieved using ratio analysis, whereby one piece of financial data (for example profit) is expressed in terms of another (for example total assets), then the result of which is compared with the same ratio for another time period or another company.

It is possible to calculate any number of ratios and great care has to be exercised to ensure that an approach is adopted whereby only those which are relevant and essential are selected. This can be achieved in assessing profitability by adopting a hierarchical approach involving the calculation of a 'key' ratio and further related ratios. As we will show, the 'key' ratio relates profit information from the profit and loss account to the capital employed in the business in terms of assets to be found in the balance sheet. The rationale for its calculation is much the same as that for undertaking personal investment – you need not only to know how much return or profit will be generated in absolute terms but also how it relates the amount of money to be tied up.

It is important to apply agreed rules regarding the specification of the various components of any ratio, including corporate ratios, in a consistent manner and to interpret changes in the resulting ratios against previous levels, industry averages or simple benchmarks.

Our discussion of ratio analysis is not restricted to analysing profitability. We consider other important areas of ratio analysis concerned with determining the appropriateness of a company's financial structure, liquidity and corporate performance.

We will reinforce the ratios to be discussed by using examples based upon figures taken from the balance sheet and profit and loss account illustrated in *Table 3.1.*, together with some additional information.

Table 3.1   Balance sheet, profit and loss account and share data

BALANCE SHEET AS AT 31 MARCH 1990

	£'000	£'000
Fixed Assets		
Land & Buildings	40,000	
Plant & Machinery	27,000	
Other Fixed Assets	2,000	69,000
Current Assets		
Stock	44,000	
Debtors	18,000	
Cash	6,000	68,000
TOTAL ASSETS		**137,000**
Shareholders' Funds:		
Share Capital		30,000
Profit & Loss account		57,000
External Funds:		
Long-Term Loans		10,000
Creditors -amounts owing within one year:		
Creditors		40,000
TOTAL LIABILITIES		**137,000**

PROFIT AND LOSS ACCOUNT FOR THE YEAR ENDED 31st MARCH 1990

	£'000	£'000
Sales		150,000
Materials	60,000	
Administration Costs	25,000	
Employee Costs	33,000	
Interest Payable	2,000	120,000
Net Profit Before Tax		**30,000**
less Taxation		10,800
PROFIT ATTRIBUTABLE TO SHAREHOLDERS		**19,200**
Share details:		
Nominal Value (pence)		100
Market Value (pence)		512
Earnings Per Share (pence)		64

3.2   A framework for evaluating business level performance

In this section we will illustrate how the key financial ratio, Return on Total Assets (ROTA) % may be used as an analytical tool for gauging profitability performance at the business-level. Providing the necessary financial data is available it can be further sub-divided so that more detailed analysis of a number of interrelated ratios can be calculated.

3.2.1   Return on total assets (ROTA)%

Let us commence by calculating ROTA %. The profit element in the ROTA% calculation is operating profit, and total assets within the calculation are simply the sum of fixed assets and current assets, which you should note are the same as total liabilities. The data required for its calculation is shown in *Table 3.2*, which has been extracted from *Table 3.1*.

Table 3.2   Basic data for calculation of profitability ratios

	Latest Year	Extracted From
	£,000	
Fixed Assets	69,000	Balance Sheet
Current Assets	68,000	
Profit Before Taxation	30,000	Profit and Loss Account
Interest Payable	2,000	

Using this information we can calculate ROTA% to give an indication of the return which a company achieves on its total assets:

$$\text{ROTA\%} = \frac{\textbf{Profit Before Taxation Plus Interest Payable}}{\textbf{Total Assets}} \times 100$$

$$= \frac{£32 \text{ m}}{£137 \text{ m}} \times 100$$

$$= 23.4\%$$

The resulting ROTA% of 23.4 shows that 23.4%, or 23.4 pence of profit is being generated before tax plus interest payable per £ of total assets employed.

ROTA% can be used to show whether or not a company is producing higher or lower level profit per £ of total assets than it did in the previous year and/or relative to competitors' performance.

But, what happens if the ROTA% calculated is lower than that generated in the previous year or by competitors? Is there any way of identifying possible reasons? The answer is yes. ROTA% is the 'key ratio' at the top of a business level ratio hierarchy which can be analysed in more detail by the introduction of information about sales from the profit and loss account. Introducing sales for the period of £150 million enables another level of interrelated ratios within the hierarchy to be calculated:

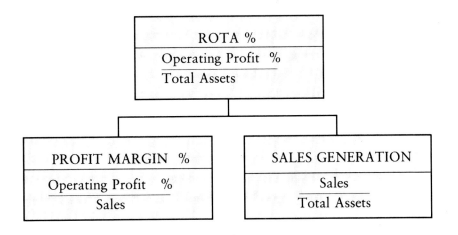

By expanding the key ratio we can see how the level of profitability is being achieved, which could be from a higher or lower operating profit as a percentage of sales, known as the 'profit margin' ratio, from a higher or lower level of sales to total assets, known as the sales generation ratio, or from a combination of the two.

3.2.2   Profit margin

$$\frac{\text{Operating Profit}}{\text{Sales}} \times 100$$

The profit margin is calculated from profit before taxation plus interest payable divided by sales, and is expressed as a %. It shows what percentage or how many pence of profit is on average generated for each £ of sales.

The expected value of this ratio will differ quite considerably for different types of businesses. A high volume business, such as a retailer, will tend to operate on low margins that make the assets involved work very hard. By contrast a low volume business, such as a contractor will tend to require much greater margins.

Using the data in *Table 3.1* and the information about sales, the profit margin is:

$$\text{Profit Margin\%} = \frac{\text{Profit Before Taxation Plus Interest Payable}}{\text{Sales}} \times 100$$

$$= \frac{\text{£32 m}}{\text{£150 m}} \times 100$$

$$= 21.3\%$$

The ratio of 21.3% shows that the average profit margin across all products is 21.3% or 21.3 pence of profit before taxation plus interest payable is generated per £ of sales. However, it is not without potential interpretive problems in that it can hide both high and low margin, and even loss making products.

You will of course be able to recognise that an increase in the ratio can be achieved by increasing the profit figure, decreasing the sales figure, or from a combination of the two. The important point to consider at this stage is that given the relationship between ROTA% and the profit margin %, any action that would improve the profit margin % should, other things equal, improve the ROTA%. If in comparing results with previous years or another company the profit margin % is found to be considerably lower it can be further analysed with a view to identifying likely problem areas. What might these be? The following headings indicate appropriate areas for further analysis.

❏ Percentage growth in sales.

❏ Product mix from various activities.

❏ Market mix for profit and sales by division and geographical area.

❏ Expansion of activities by merger or acquisition.

❏ Changes in selling prices (usually only available from management accounts and not from published accounts).

❏ Changes in costs.

We saw in Chapter 2 that companies are required to provide an analysis of turnover and contribution to operating profit between principal activities. This information is typically found in the notes to the accounts as illustrated in *Table 3.3*.

Table 3.3 Analysis of Turnover and Operating Profit

Division or principal activity	Turnover		Operating profit	
	£'000	%	£'000	%
A	60	40	9	30.0
B	36	24	10	33.3
C	24	16	4	13.3
D	24	16	5	16.7
E	6	4	2	6.7
	150	100	30	100

In *Table 3.3* we can see that Division B contributes 24% of the total turnover and 33.3% of the total operating profit. In practice you will find that companies either provide the information in absolute values or as a percentage. For a complete analysis you should obtain figures for previous years, in this way you will be able to determine trends in turnover and/or operating profit by division (and/or geographic area).

Changes in cost can also be readily analysed from published accounts as we will illustrate shortly with reference to our example company. Main categories of cost from the profit and loss account can be expressed as a percentage of sales, with a view to identifying those costs which require further investigation. The logic behind such investigation is that any cost reduction should, other things being equal, feed through to the profit margin % and therefore improve ROTA%. Do bear in mind that profit margin % and associated ratios will vary from industry to industry. Low volume businesses are often reliant upon higher margins than high volume businesses such as retailing (e.g. a petrol station), which often operate on low margins such that cost control can be absolutely critical to success.

Businesses often have very little ability to influence their profit margin which is usually constrained by market forces. For example, retailers would have to be very brave (or stupid) to increase prices much beyond that which the market will allow. Significantly higher prices are unlikely to have any positive effect upon the profit margin unless the products concerned are viewed as necessities for which no substitutes are readily available.

Profit margin: analysis by cost

We have indicated that the analysis of ratios by cost permits the identification of important movements that take place within the overall cost structure of the business. Let us now consider this with reference to our example but do bear in mind that companies in different industry sectors might use other ratios which relate to the particular cost structure of that industry.

The following ratios have been calculated from the information provided in *Table 3.1*.

Material Costs as a Percentage of Sales:

$$= \frac{\text{Material Costs}}{\text{Sales}} \times 100$$

$$= \frac{£60 \text{ m}}{£150 \text{ m}} \times 100$$

$$= 40\%$$

Administration Costs as a Percentage of Sales:

$$= \frac{\text{Administration Costs}}{\text{Sales}} \times 100$$

$$= \frac{£25\text{ m}}{£150\text{ m}} \times 100$$

$$= 16.7\%$$

Employee Costs as a Percentage of Sales:

$$= \frac{\text{Employee Costs}}{\text{Sales}} \times 100$$

$$= \frac{£33\text{ m}}{£150\text{ m}} \times 100$$

$$= 22\%$$

Before we leave the profit margin cost ratios let us consider the effect on the profit margin % if material costs are reduced by £4 million. The revised profit margin % would be calculated as follows:

$$= \frac{\left(£32\text{ m} + £4\text{ m}\right)}{£150\text{ m}} \times 100$$

$$= 24\%$$

The result is an increase in the profit margin from 21.3% to 24.0%, a clear benefit.

3.2.3 Sales Generation

The sales generation ratio, the second component of ROTA % is calculated by dividing sales for the year by total assets.

$$\frac{\textbf{Sales}}{\textbf{Total Assets}}$$

The ratio shows the value of sales generated for each £1 of total assets. The higher the value obtained the better. Using the information from *Table 3.1* and that about sales, the ratio is:

$$\textbf{Sales Generation} \quad = \quad \frac{\textbf{Sales}}{\textbf{Total Assets}}$$

$$= \quad \frac{\textbf{£150 m}}{\textbf{£137 m}}$$

$$= \quad \textbf{£1.09 to £1}$$

The above ratio indicates that the company has generated £1.09 of sales for each £1.00 of total assets.

If a company wishes to increase this ratio, it can either increase sales and/or decrease the level of total assets. In common with the profit margin % changes in the sales generation ratio will have direct impact upon ROTA% Any improvement in sales generation should, other things equal, cause an improvement in the ROTA%.

The sales generation ratio can also be further analysed so as to identify how well various assets are being utilised. For example, it could be sub-divided into:

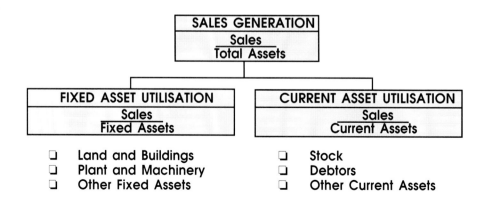

Sales divided by fixed assets and sales divided by current assets show the value of sales generated by each type of asset. Action taken to reduce the level of fixed assets and/or current assets will, other things equal, increase the sales generation ratio and ROTA%.

Analysis of fixed asset utilisation

A more detailed analysis of sales divided by fixed assets (fixed asset utilisation) can also be achieved. In this case the aim is to measure the amount of sales generated from each major category of fixed asset. The following ratios have been calculated from information provided in *Table 3.1*.

Land and Buildings

$$= \frac{\text{Sales}}{\text{Land and Buildings}}$$

$$= \frac{£150 \text{ m}}{£40 \text{ m}}$$

$$= £3.75 \text{ to } £1$$

Plant and Machinery

$$= \frac{\text{Sales}}{\text{Plant and Machinery}}$$

$$= \frac{£150 \text{ m}}{£27 \text{ m}}$$

$$= £5.56 \text{ to } £1$$

Other Fixed Assets

$$= \frac{\text{Sales}}{\text{Other Fixed Assets}}$$

$$= \frac{\text{£150 m}}{\text{£2 m}}$$

$$= \text{£75 to £1}$$

Analysis of current asset utilisation

The aim of the current asset utilisation ratios is to measure the amount of sales generated from each major category of current asset. Using the data provided in *Table 3.1* the main current asset utilisation ratios are:

Stock

$$= \frac{\text{Sales}}{\text{Stock}}$$

$$= \frac{\text{£150 m}}{\text{£44 m}}$$

$$= \text{£3.41 to £1}$$

You will notice that we have used sales as the denominator for this ratio which includes an element of profit. While it would have been preferable to use cost of sales, we have not done so because it is not consistent with the hierarchical framework which uses sales and it may be difficult to identify a true cost of sales from published accounts.

Debtors

$$= \frac{\text{Sales}}{\text{Debtors}}$$

$$= \frac{£150\text{ m}}{£18\text{ m}}$$

$$= £8.33 \text{ to } £1$$

Other Current Assets

$$= \frac{\text{Sales}}{\text{Other Current Assets}}$$

$$= \frac{£150\text{ m}}{£6\text{ m}}$$

$$= £25 \text{ to } £1$$

Just as with the profit margin %, sales generation ratios vary from industry to industry. Heavily capital intensive industries, like telecommunications, may operate on very low ratios whilst others in the service sector with few fixed assets and no stock may have high ratios. A comparison of profitability ratios is shown below:

	ROTA	PROFIT MARGIN	SALES GENERATION
	%	%	
Retailer (books/stationery)	14.0	3.8	3.68
Retailer (department store)	15.5	13.7	1.13
Manufacturer (confectionery)	12.6	8.7	1.45
Telecommunications	13.1	21.9	0.60

You will appreciate that the most desirable position would be to have high profit margin % and high sales generation ratios. This usually is not easy to achieve because there will often be a trade-off between the two. The relationship between the two ratios must also not be overlooked.

You should note that any breakdown of the sales generation ratio by business unit or division from the published accounts of UK companies has historically been impossible in the majority of cases because details of divisional net assets have not been required. A UK accounting standard now requires such disclosures which will permit divisional sales generation ratios to be calculated.

3.3   Liquidity ratios

An analysis of profitability ratios alone is totally inadequate for obtaining a well balanced view of performance. Whilst profitability is undeniably important, the need to achieve a satisfactory liquidity position is vital for survival. It is a fact that many companies which have failed were profitable but unable to maintain a satisfactory level of liquidity. Just how liquidity can be gauged we consider in this section with reference to the current and liquid ratios.

3.3.1   The current ratio

The current ratio is calculated by dividing current assets by current liabilities. It attempts to measure the ability of a company to meet its financial obligations within one year.

$$= \frac{\text{Current Assets}}{\text{Current Liabilities}}$$

$$= \frac{\text{£68 m}}{\text{£40 m}}$$

$$= \text{£1.70 to £1}$$

For decades, the interpretation of the current ratio has suffered against an unrealistic rule of thumb which states that current assets should be double that of current liabilities for all companies. This implies that the proportions of current assets and current liabilities should be the same for a fast food company with small stocks and virtually no debtors, through to the company undertaking a long term contract with high stocks, high debtors, creditors and bank overdraft.

It should be noted that a high current ratio is not necessarily a good sign; it could mean that a company has idle facilities. For example, all other things being equal, the current ratio would increase if a company were to increase its stocks or increase its debtors. Similarly, the current ratio would decrease if a company took actions to decrease its stocks or decrease its debtors. We cannot say without further information, whether these actions are necessarily good or bad, therefore care should be taken when attempting to interpret both the size of the current ratio, and the movements year on year.

3.3.2 The liquid (or acid test) ratio

The liquid ratio or acid-test ratio is calculated from current assets minus stock divided by current liabilities. It attempts to measure a company's ability to pay its way in the short-term without having to liquidate stock. Simply it is 'the acid test', can we pay our way?

$$= \frac{\text{Liquid Assets}}{\text{Current Liabilities}}$$

$$= \frac{\pounds 24 \text{ m}}{\pounds 40 \text{ m}}$$

$$= \pounds 0.60 \text{ to } \pounds 1$$

What do we mean by paying our way in the short-term? In this context, the short-term is often considered to be up to 13 weeks, and paying our way to mean that we can pay our debts as and when they fall due. It does not mean that every business needs to maintain a level of liquid assets to cover all current liabilities. Anyone looking at the liquid ratio for a number of different companies will quickly come to the opinion that there is no magical value (e.g. one-to-one) that operates across all industries. For example, in retailing it is normal to find a level of around 0.4 to 1 cover for current liabilities. This is possible through cash trading, a high level of commitment from their suppliers and the fact that stock could be liquidated in time to meet maturing debts. Similar to the current ratio, if these companies maintained a higher level of cover for current liabilities there would be idle facilities.

3.4   Corporate ratios

In this section we focus upon corporate ratios which are particularly important to potential or actual investors. Our discussion will be based around the following three ratios:

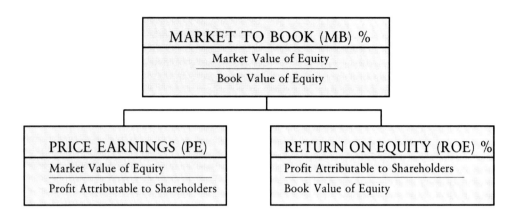

The MB % ratio is reliant upon balance sheet and market information about share price. To calculate the MB % ratio, the market value of equity is expressed as a percentage of the book value of equity.

The PE ratio and the ROE % relate to the MB % ratio because profit attributable to shareholders is common to both the PE and the ROE % ratios, and when cancelled out the MB % ratio remains.

These three ratios, MB %, PE and ROE %, give management an indication of what investors think of the company's past performance and future prospects. However, all three ratios are limited by the extent to which different accounting practices can be used to influence profit attributable to shareholders and book values, nevertheless, they are widely used and are important for you to understand.

3.4.1   Market to book (MB) % ratio

The market to book (MB) % ratio shows the extent to which the market value of a company exceeds the book value of the equity. Market capitalisation can be obtained by multiplying the market price of a share by the number of shares in issue during a period and the book value of owners' equity (shareholders' funds) is the sum of issued share capital plus reserves.

The MB % ratio is calculated as follows:

$$= \frac{\text{Market Capitalisation}}{\text{Book Value of Equity}} \times 100$$

$$= \frac{£153.6 \text{ m}}{£87 \text{ m}} \times 100$$

$$= 176.6\%$$

This ratio provides an indication of the company's financial position as perceived by the market, but it has to be viewed with caution because book value can be influenced by accounting policy, such as the treatment of intangible assets like goodwill. As you will recall from Chapter 1, the method by which goodwill is treated can have a considerable impact upon the book value of equity.

How should an MB % ratio be interpreted assuming no concern relating to accounting policy and the book value is realistic? A value of less than 100% would be worthy of attention because, by implication, the acquisition of such a company might be worthwhile simply for the purchase of its assets.

3.4.2. Price earnings (PE) ratio

The price earnings (PE) ratio, which you will find quoted daily in papers like the *Financial Times* is calculated by dividing the market capitalisation by the profit attributable to shareholders. As indicated earlier, a measure of market capitalisation can be obtained by multiplying the market price of an equity share by the number of shares in issue during a period. As an alternative the price earnings ratio can be calculated by dividing the market price of an individual equity share by the earnings per share. As shown in Chapter 2, earnings per share is quoted in UK and most other countries' annual reports, thereby making the PE ratio calculation very straightforward. You will recall that its calculation in the UK is based on profit after tax and interest, but before extraordinary items, divided by the number of ordinary shares ranking for a dividend. The supposed rationale for excluding extraordinary items is because of the distorting effect they have on year-by-year comparisons.

Using the information from *Table 3.1*, the price earnings ratio is:

$$= \frac{\text{Market Capitalisation}}{\text{Profit Attributable to Shareholders}}$$

$$= \frac{£153.6 \text{ m}}{£19.2 \text{ m}}$$

$$= 8 \text{ times}$$

or, using earnings per share information:

$$= \frac{\text{Market Price Per Ordinary Share}}{\text{Earnings Per Ordinary Share}}$$

$$= \frac{512 \text{ pence}}{64 \text{ pence}}$$

$$= 8 \text{ times}$$

PE ratios, such as those published in the financial press show the relationship between the market prices of shares and earnings from the most recent published accounts. The PE is a multiple, the magnitude of the ratio providing some indication of how the market values the future earnings potential of a share. The emphasis here is upon the word future. The market will form a view about the future quality of earnings which will be expressed in the share price from which a PE ratio may be calculated. However, increases in earnings may not always bring about increases in the share price and, earnings may rise but not be associated with a share price increase.

There is no 'normal' level for PE ratios which differ over time, within industry sector and between countries. For example, price earnings ratios in July 1990 for companies classified in Textiles ranged from 3 to 57, but with most falling in the 6 to 13 range, while in the Banks, HP and Leasing category, price earning ratios ranged from 4 to 50 but with most falling the 8 to 15 range.

One point which you should note in reviewing published PE ratios is that some are calculated after adjustments to published earnings figures have been made. This means that the results of your own calculations from published information may well be very different. So beware and always question the basis of any PE ratio calculation. For example, *Stag plc*, the furniture manufacturer's 1986, earnings were adjusted by the *Financial Times* in calculating the price earnings ratio. In effect the *Stag plc* earnings figure was lower than usual because of the absence of a tax charge. To ensure comparability this earnings figure was adjusted in calculating the published PE ratio.

3.4.3   Return on equity (ROE) %

The return on equity (ROE) % ratio is a measure of shareholder profitability. It is calculated by expressing the profit attributable to shareholders as a percentage of the book value of the equity, where the book value of equity is the sum of issued share capital plus reserves.

$$\text{ROE\%} = \frac{\textbf{Profit Attributable to Shareholders}}{\textbf{Share Price}} \times 100$$

In other words, the equity figure used in the calculation is limited to funds provided by ordinary shareholders and excludes those provided from long-term borrowing. In addition, as indicated, the relevant measure of profit is the amount available for ordinary shareholders, after interest on borrowings and any other prior claims have been satisfied. You should be aware that for quoted companies it is possible to use the market value of equity in calculating ROE% which is sometimes referred to as the 'earnings yield'. When calculated in this way the market value of equity is usually found by multiplying the share price by the number of shares in issue. Alternatively, the calculation can be undertaken per share using:

$$= \frac{\textbf{Earnings Per Share (EPS)}}{\textbf{Share Price}} \times 100$$

From the information provided in *Table 3.1*, ROE% using book value is:

$$ROE\% = \frac{\text{Profit Attributable to Shareholders}}{\text{Book Value of Equity}} \times 100$$

$$= \frac{£19.2 \text{ m}}{£87 \text{ m}} \times 100$$

$$= 22.1\%$$

While ROE% using market value is:

$$ROE\% = \frac{\text{Profit Attributable to Shareholders}}{\text{Market Value of Equity}} \times 100$$

$$= \frac{£19.2 \text{ m}}{£153.6 \text{ m}} \times 100$$

$$= 12.5\%$$

On every £1 of equity, the company has earned 22.1 pence using book value and 12.5 pence using market value. Differences of this order between book and market value are not unusual.

ROE% can be affected significantly by accounting policy which can influence both the numerator and/or the denominator in the calculation where a book value of equity is used. For example, we saw in Chapter 1 how profit and the book value of equity can be increased or decreased by differing treatments of goodwill.

3.5   A framework for financial ratios

We have discussed financial ratios from a profitability, liquidity, and corporate perspective. There is one other important perspective concerned with financial structure that we will consider in this section where we will draw together the ratios discussed so far within a single hierarchical framework. The basic components of this hierarchical framework is illustrated in *Figure 3.1*.

Figure 3.1   ROE%, Profitability and Gearing

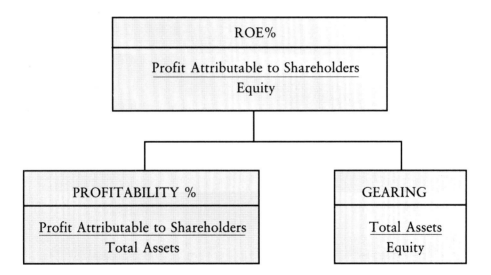

The key ratio in this hierarchical framework is ROE % which we saw earlier is calculated from the of profit attributable to shareholders expressed as a percentage of equity. But, at the business level it is usual in the UK to use an appropriate profit figure that equates to operating profit, i.e. profit before any deductions for financing or taxation, rather than profit attributable to shareholders. This means that the hierarchy in *Figure 3.1* to include ROTA % (which we discussed earlier) requires adjustments to be made to profit, as shown in *Figure 3.2*.

Figure 3.2   The link between ROE % and ROTA %

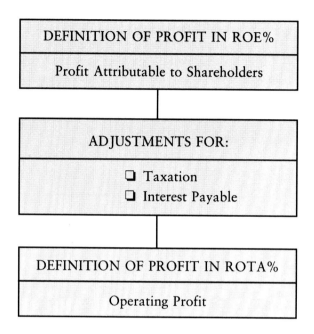

Operating profit can be obtained by taking the profit attributable to shareholders and adding back taxation and interest payable, an example of which is shown in *Table 3.4.*

Table 3.4   Adjustments for taxation and interest payable

	£'000
Operating Profit	32,000
less Interest Payable	2,000
Profit Before Taxation	30,000
less Taxation	10,800
Profit Attributable to Shareholders	**19,200**

You will recall that we have in fact discussed ROTA % earlier in this chapter, but not the second ratio, gearing, which completes the financial ratio framework. This is discussed in the next section.

3.6   Gearing and gearing ratios

The ratio of total assets/equity, is one measure of financial risk known as 'gearing' ('leverage' in the USA). Risk comes from two main sources: business risk and financial risk. Businesses within the same trade may vary in the general volatility of their profits, but the future flow of profits for all businesses which operate in the same sector will often be subject to similar economic influences. The degree of financial risk, on the other hand, is specific and relates to a particular company choice between debt and equity funding. This financial risk is typically measured using gearing ratios which are regarded by the both the stock market and financial directors as being an important indicator of corporate exposure.

Loan financing is preferable to equity because the interest on it is chargeable against pre-tax profit and for this reason is typically cheaper than dividend payments to equity shareholders made from post-tax profits. However, against this benefit there is a disadvantage to be taken into consideration because of increasing financial risk with higher levels of debt financing and gearing. The nature of this financial risk and how to measure gearing we consider in this section.

Gearing can be calculated with reference to one or more of the following:

❑   book values of capital employed and equity from the balance sheet;

❑   book values of borrowings and equity from the balance sheet;

❑   market values of borrowings and equity;

❑   the impact of interest charges upon earnings.

We illustrated the gearing ratio earlier in the ratio framework in *Figure 3.1*, as being represented by total assets divided by equity. The result of calculating the gearing ratio using this approach is:

$$\text{Gearing} = \frac{\text{Total Assets}}{\text{Equity}}$$

$$= \frac{£137 \text{ m}}{£87 \text{ m}}$$

$$= 1.58$$

You may often find this ratio inverted and expressed as a percentage. When calculated in this way the gearing ratio is:

$$= \frac{\text{Equity}}{\text{Total Assets}} \times 100$$

$$= \frac{£87 \text{ m}}{£137 \text{ m}} \times 100$$

$$= 63.5\%$$

Whilst this measure fits well within the ratio framework, it is only one of many, and is less popular in practice than others such as:

$$\frac{\text{Debt}}{\text{Equity}} \times 100$$

and/or,

$$\frac{\text{Total Debt}}{\text{Total Assets}} \times 100$$

The latter of these two, sometimes called the 'debt ratio', measures the percentage of total funds provided by creditors. Debt includes current and long-term liabilities. Creditors will tend to prefer low debt ratios, because the lower the ratio, the greater the cushion against their losses in the event of liquidation. The owners, on the other hand, will may prefer relatively high gearing up to a point because it will result in higher earnings per share or because the alternative of issuing additional equity would mean giving up some degree of control. The debt ratio in this case would be:

$$\textbf{Debt Ratio} \quad = \quad \frac{\textbf{Total Debt}}{\textbf{Total Assets}} \times 100$$

$$= \quad \frac{£50 \text{ m}}{£137 \text{ m}} \times 100$$

$$= \quad 36.5\%$$

This measure focuses upon total debt and total assets, whereas concern may often be more directed at the relationship between alternative long term sources of finance. As a consequence you will find debt as a percentage of equity is a widely used measure of gearing. The advantage of this measure is that it is easier to gauge the impact of changes in the balance between debt and equity.

$$\textbf{Gearing Ratio} \quad = \quad \frac{\textbf{Debt}}{\textbf{Equity}} \times 100$$

$$= \quad \frac{£10 \text{ m}}{£87 \text{ m}} \times 100$$

$$= \quad 11.5\%$$

A gearing ratio of 11.5% would not be viewed with concern, although the cautious analyst would look further to see whether any disguised debt existed.

Whatever measure of gearing is used, expansion through borrowing can be compared to the risks involved in stretching oneself to buy a new house. There is always a limit to a company's borrowing just as with an individual house purchase. A company's borrowing is typically limited by the value of it's assets and increases above a certain level will require shareholder approval together with the willingness of lenders to provide funds. Such restrictions can sometimes be overcome by regular asset revaluations and the inclusions of intangibles like brands, with the revised total asset base used to determine the amount of debt funding permitted. The inclusion of intangible assets while appearing to increase the total asset base, may not satisfy the shareholders nor the lenders.

Companies may also choose to seek shareholder approval to increase borrowing power. For example, in 1989 the UK half of *Unilever*, the Anglo-Dutch consumer products multinational, sought and gained shareholder approval that increased the company's borrowing limit from approximately two times adjusted capital and reserves to three times. In addition, for such borrowing purposes, the calculation was further boosted by allowing goodwill written off on all past and future acquisitions to be added back.

The *Unilever* proposal followed similar moves in 1989 by *Hanson* and *ICI*, whereby both companies successfully achieved the inclusion of acquired goodwill for calculating the borrowing limit. However, not all such pleas to shareholders have been successful. In the same year *Cadbury Schweppes*, failed in its attempts to raise its debt limit because of concerns expressed by *General Cinema*, an important shareholder.

Why is gearing an important consideration? In order to appreciate this you need to understand the effect of different levels of gearing on risk and return to shareholders.   By way of illustration we will use an example of two companies, both in the same business, each having sold the same quantity of goods and having achieved the same profit for a given period; the only difference between the two companies is the method by which they are financed.   As shown in *Table 3.5*, company A is financed £20 million from equity and £5 million from debt, while company B is financed £5 million from equity and £20 million from debt. The table also shows the gearing ratio in terms of debt expressed as a percentage of equity for the two companies.

Table 3.5   High and low gearing

	Company A £'000	Company B £'000
Equity	20,000	5,000
Debt	5,000	20,000
Gearing (Debt ÷ Equity %)	25% (low)	400% (high)

It can be seen that the gearing ratio for company A is 25% which would be considered low geared, while company B is highly geared at 400%. What is the problem of being highly geared? Whilst high gearing provides a potentially higher return to the shareholder, there is risk attached which is demonstrated in the profit and loss account for the two companies shown in *Table 3.6*. Both companies can be seen to have made an operating profit of £5 million. It has been assumed that the interest on debt is 10% per annum, and that a corporation tax rate of 40% is applied.

Table 3.6   Gearing and return on equity when the operating profit is £5 million

		Company A	Company B
		£'000	£'000
OPERATING PROFIT		5,000	5,000
less Interest Payable		500	2,000
PROFIT BEFORE TAX		4,500	3,000
less Taxation		1,800	1,200
PROFIT ATTRIBUTABLE TO SHAREHOLDERS	**(A)**	2,700	1,800
less Dividend		2,000	500
RETAINED EARNINGS		700	1,300
EQUITY	**(B)**	20,000	5,000
Return on Equity	**((A) ÷ (B) %)**	**13.5%**	**36.0%**

The results show that the return on equity for company B is almost three times that of company A, even though they both produce the same operating profit. The reason for this major difference is that company B deducts a larger amount for interest paid thereby producing a lower profit figure for assessing taxation payable. While it is acknowledged that there is a lower figure for profit attributable to shareholders, the number of equity shares is only a quarter the size of company A, therefore the profit is spread among fewer shareholders resulting in a larger overall percentage return.

So far, a higher level of gearing has been presented as being beneficial, but this is not always the case, as illustrated in *Table 3.7*.

Table 3.7   Gearing and return on equity

	Company A £'000	Company B £'000
OPERATING PROFIT	2,500	2,500
less Interest Payable	500	2,000
PROFIT BEFORE TAX	2,000	500
less Taxation	800	200
PROFIT ATTRIBUTABLE TO SHAREHOLDERS (A)	1,200	300
less Dividend	0	0
RETAINED EARNINGS	1,200	300
EQUITY (B)	20,000	5,000
Return on Equity ((A) ÷ (B) %)	6.0%	6.0%

In this case the operating profit has fallen to £2.5 million and the companies are paying no dividend. The fall in ROE% is far more marked for company B than company A. Company B still has to pay interest on its debt leaving a profit before taxation of £500,000 and a profit attributable to shareholders of £300,000. The result is therefore a fall in the return on equity from 36% to only 6%.

The risk associated with high levels of gearing is therefore evident when operating profits fall. A company with falling profits still has to service the interest on debt irrespective of the level of profitability. This creates a financial risk to the shareholders, whose dividends are paid subsequent to interest on debt. However, this should not be taken to infer that all levels of gearing are bad. Gearing up to a certain level offers substantial benefits because of the tax shield available against interest payments. Gauging what the appropriate level should be is a critical question and is dealt with later in Chapter 9.

An additional indicator on the financial risk to which a company is exposed can be gained by calculating the interest cover ratio: a comparison between the interest charges payable on debt and the level of profit from which that interest is funded. In *Table 3.8* the companies' profit before interest and tax for each of the profit scenarios is divided by interest payable on long-term borrowings. In the case of company A under both scenarios, the size of the interest cover indicates a very low level of risk to the equity investor. The company is able to meet the prior charges on debt and still have a healthy surplus available for retention or for distribution to shareholders. This is in stark contrast to company B.

Table 3.8   Calculation of interest cover

	Company A	Company B
	£'000	£'000
Profit Before Interest and Tax	5,000	5,000
Interest on Long-Term Borrowings	500	2,000
Interest Cover	= **10 times**	= **2.5 times**
Profit Before Interest and Tax	2,500	2,500
Interest on Long-Term Borrowings	500	2,000
Interest Cover	= **5 times**	=**1.25 times**

The number of times interest is covered is a ratio which is a very relevant indicator of corporate health. If the level of profits decreases in comparison with fixed interest charges, so proportionately less profits are available from which to provide a return on equity. In the long run, a low and deteriorating level of interest cover implies that the company is increasingly exposed to the risk of defaulting on interest payment, with the consequence threat of foreclosure.

For these reasons the level of interest cover will also be a matter of first importance to existing lenders - whether they be banks, debenture holders or unsecured loan stock holders. Just as importantly, it will be the first point of reference for potential lenders. Companies with already low levels of interest cover will find it increasingly difficult to borrow more money. If they do succeed in attracting funds, they will certainly have to pay higher rates of interest on them, in order to compensate lenders for the higher level of risk that attaches to their loan.

Please be aware that gearing may prove very difficult to measure in practice. We have considered two extreme forms of finance in terms of debt and equity, however, there are many in-between forms, like convertible bonds, which can cloud measurement. These, together with transactions 'off balance sheet' necessitate extreme caution on the part of the analyst.

3.7   Problems of applying financial ratio analysis

There are some potential problems of using financial ratio analysis in multi-division companies, which are frequently decentralised into divisions for organisational reasons. Often such divisions are defined as profit or investment centres, each with its own investment responsibility. Such investment responsibility for fixed and current assets and a share of general corporate assets like research laboratories and headquarters buildings, all form the base upon which a division is expected to earn an appropriate return.

For purposes of divisional control the term return on investment or ROI% is used. ROI% is typically expressed as a percentage of some measure of profit in relation to some measure of divisional investment. There is no universal standard for calculating ROI% and there are some factors that need to be taken into consideration. These are:

❏ *Depreciation.* ROI% is very sensitive to depreciation policy. If one division is writing off assets at a relatively faster rate than another, then its ROI% will be affected.

❏ *Asset life.* If a division is using assets that have been largely written off, both its current depreciation charge and its investment base will be low. As a consequence, its ROI% will be high in relation to newer divisions.

❏ *Transfer pricing.* The divisions in many multi-division companies trade with one another. Where this happens, the price at which goods are transferred between divisions will have a fundamental effect on divisional profits.

❏ *Divisional projects.* Divisions involved with projects having long gestation periods during which time expenditure is required upon research and development, plant construction, market development and the like, will often suffer an immediate increase in the investment base without an increase in profits for many years. During the life of such projects a divisions' ROI% can be seriously reduced and without proper constraints, its manager may be improperly penalised. If such companies have significant personnel transfers as a matter of course, then it is not difficult to see how the timing problem can keep managers from making long-term investments that are in the best interest of the company.

❑ *Industry conditions.* If one division operates in an industry where conditions are favourable in terms of earning high rates of return, while another is in an industry suffering from excessive competition, the differences may cause one division to look good and the other to look bad, even though the managers in both may be comparable.

Because of these factors, a division's ROI% is usually inadequate for evaluating performance. Some companies analyse comparative growth in sales, profits and market shares and adapt the use of ROI% to recognise the important differences between using ROI% in the measurement of a manager's performance, and in evaluating the worth of a past investment. A manager's performance can only be measured in relation to the assets under his/her control and a manager may have limited control over inherited fixed assets.

Appendix A

Return on net assets (RONA) %

In this chapter we have outlined the calculation for the key profitability using total assets as the denominator i.e.. ROTA.% We also showed the breakdown of ROTA % into the profit margin and the sales generation ratio.

In the UK, the ratio most commonly used is return on net assets (RONA)% i.e. profit before taxation and interest payable expressed as a percentage of net assets. Net assets is the sum of total assets minus current liabilities (or fixed assets plus net working capital).

It is important that we offer a word of caution about net assets.   If you extract the figures from a published balance sheet you should be able to identify a description   "total assets less current liabilities"   which is the same as net assets for the purpose of financial ratio analysis. However, we often find the practitioner extracting   "net current assets"   which is another name for net working capital and does not include fixed assets, and those described as net assets which, in published accounts, are after the deduction of long-term loans.

In what follows we will compare RONA% with ROTA% discussed earlier in this chapter.

Table 3.8   Basic data

		Col.1	Col.2	Col.3
Fixed Assets		5,000	15,000	15,000
+ Current Assets		45,000	45,000	45,000
= Total Assets	(A)	50,000	60,000	60,000
- Current Liabilities		30,000	40,000	30,000
= Net Assets	(B)	20,000	20,000	30,000
Operating Profit	(C)	6,000	6,000	6,000

Table 3.8 column 1, contains data extracted from a balance sheet. Column 2 and 3 both show the purchase of a fixed asset for £10,000, but in column 2, the purchase is financed through short-term borrowings (included in the £40,000) whilst in column 3 the purchase is financed using a long-term loan therefore, not included in current liabilities.

From the basic data in *Table 3.8*, the RONA% and ROTA% are:

	Col.1	Col.2	Col.3
(RONA)% ((C) ÷ (B) x 100	30%	30%	20%
(ROTA)% ((C) ÷ (A) x 100	12%	10%	10%

The most noticeable difference is in the absolute size of the ratios. Is it better to claim that the company is making a return on net assets of 30% or a return on total assets of only 12%?

On closer inspection we find with RONA % that the purchase of the fixed asset when financed through short-term borrowings has produced no increase in the profitability of the company, while with ROTA% there is a slight decrease. However, when long-term borrowings are used (i.e.. column 3) there is a significant reduction in RONA % (i.e. 30% to 20%) while ROTA % shows no movement.

This example serves to illustrate that RONA% can be affected significantly by the method of finance used. A company which uses short-term finance to purchase fixed assets and generate the same profits as in the preceeding period, RONA % will remain the same (the increase in fixed assets being off-set by the increase in short-term borrowings).

Consider the position of a company in poor financial health that uses short-term finance (just to keep things going). Its fixed and current assets are also declining. During the early stages, this company could produce an increase in profitability when using RONA %.

ROTA %, which is the method we recommend, is unaffected by the method of financing assets. This is evident from our example where the same percentage results irrespective of the method of finance used i.e. 10% in column 2 and in column 3.

Exercises

3.1 The following figures have been extracted from the accounts of RR Limited for the year ended 31st December 1990:

	£'000
Sales	3,500
Profit Before Taxation	200
Interest Payable	100
Share Capital	400
Reserves	800
Creditors	2,000
Bank Overdraft	800
Premises	300
Vehicles	200
Stock	2,100
Debtors	1,200
Cash	200

REQUIRED

1. You are required to calculate profitability, liquidity and working capital ratios for RR Limited.

2. Given the following ratios which reflect the averages for the same industrial sector, comment on the differences between the ratios calculated in above and the industry averages below.

Profit / Net Assets	32%
Profit / Sales	4%
Sales / Net Assets	8.00 to 1
Current Ratio	1.60 to 1
Liquid Ratio (or Acid Test)	0.60 to 1

3. Would there be any advantage in using total assets for calculating the profitability ratios for RR Limited?

3.2 The chairman of H.O. Ratio Limited has obtained figures from a comparison of a competitor.

Total Assets	£258,750
Current Liabilities	£125,000
Administration Expenses	£33,250
Current ratio	1.75 : 1
Quick ratio	1.05 : 1
Average age of outstanding customer debts (based on a 52 week year)	12 weeks
Net Profit/Net Current Assets %	20%
Gross Profit/Sales %	20%

REQUIRED

1. From the information above, prepare in as much detail as possible, a Profit and Loss account for the year ended 31st October 1990 and a Balance Sheet as at that date.

2. Comment on the limitations in using ratio analysis as a means of measuring the financial performance of a company.

3.3 1. From the Balance Sheet and Profit and Loss account data given on page 108, calculate profitability ratios using net assets and total assets as the denominator. For the purpose of this exercise, only calculate the final two years i.e. 1989 and 1990.

2. Provide a brief overview of what the ratios you have calculated in 1. reveal about the performance of the company.

The following Balance Sheet and Profit and Loss Account data should be used with question 3, and other questions which refer to its use.

CONSOLIDATED BALANCE SHEET DATA FOR FIVE YEARS (£000's)

	1986	1987	1988	1989	1990
Fixed Assets	26,000	70,000	80,000	96,000	135,000
Stock	50,000	50,000	51,000	52,000	58,000
Debtors	24,000	25,000	26,000	28,000	24,000
Current Assets	76,000	77,000	80,000	83,000	90,000
Creditors	52,000	50,000	52,000	55,000	65,000
Bank Overdraft	11,000	12,000	12,000	12,000	32,000
Current Liabilities	65,000	64,000	67,000	70,000	100,000
Share Capital	8,000	8,000	16,000	16,000	16,000
Capital Reserves	0	36,000	36,000	36,000	36,000
Revenue Reserves	10,000	13,000	15,000	28,000	40,000
Long Term Loans	19,000	26,000	26,000	29,000	33,000

CONSOLIDATED PROFIT AND LOSS ACCOUNT DATA FOR FIVE YEARS (£000's)

	1986	1987	1988	1989	1990
Sales	90,000	118,000	124,000	140,000	170,000
Raw Materials	38,000	60,500	58,500	59,400	76,500
Depreciation	4,500	5,500	6,000	6,000	6,500
Employee Costs	21,000	22,000	24,000	26,000	31,000
Other Costs	14,500	15,000	16,000	20,000	21,000
Interest Payable	3,000	3,000	3,500	3,600	10,000
Profit Before Tax	9,000	12,000	16,000	25,000	25,000

OTHER DATA

	1986	1987	1988	1989	1990
Earnings Per Share (p)	14.8	17.9	22.6	26.9	31.0
Dividend Per Share (p)	4.275	4.875	5.85	7.00	8.20
Market Value (p)	200	250	300	350	417
Nominal Value (p)	25	25	25	25	25
Employees: full time	1,350	1,370	1,400	1,400	1,900
part time	4,500	4,300	4,600	5,000	5,700

3.4 From the Balance Sheet and Profit and Loss Account data given in question 3, calculate liquidity ratios for the five years and provide a brief overview of what they reveal about the performance of the company.

3.5 From the Balance Sheet and Profit and Loss Account data given in question 3, calculate gearing ratios for the five years and provide a brief overview of what they reveal about the performance of the company.

3.6 From the Balance Sheet and Profit and Loss Account data given in question 3, calculate asset utilisation ratios for the final two years, 1989 and 1990 and provide a brief overview of what they reveal about the preformance of the company.

3.7   The following balances were extracted from the books of Goodpile Carpets Ltd at 27th April 1991.

	£m
Leasehold Property	2,755
Stock	98,662
Bank Overdraft	27,805
Accrued Expenses	16,108
Cash	1,121
Trade Creditors	75,926
Trade Debtors	92,757
Issued Share Capital	14,500
Prepayments	4,449
Motor Vehicles	20,278
Long-Term Loans	68,150
Share Premium	14,500
Profit and Loss Account	14,159
Plant and Equipment	11,126
Sales	522,000

REQUIRED

1.   Prepare a Balance Sheet as at 27th April 1991 in a format suitable to assist in the interpretation of the information.

2.   Calculate ratios to measure the following:-

a.   Liquidity or solvency

b.   Gearing

c.   Sales Generation

3.   Comment on the information disclosed by the ratios.

3.8   What is the PE ratio? What shortcomings, if any, does it have as an indicator of corporate performance?

3.9   Is an understanding of accounting policy important in interpreting financial ratios? Provide an explanation to a colleague who has limited knowledge of accounting and finance.

3.10   What are the main limitations of ratio analysis?

3.11   Distinguish between the following:

   1.   Return on equity %

   2.   Return on total assets %

   3.   Profit margin %

3.12   Your analysis of your company's financial statements has revealed:

   1.   a lower than average profit margin %.

   2.   a lower than average sales generation ratio.

   What further analysis could be undertaken to identify the reasons for such poor results?

WORKING WITH CORPORATE REPORTS AND PUBLISHED INFORMATION

LEARNING OBJECTIVES

When you have finished studying this chapter and completed the exercises you should be able to:

❏ Apply the concept of a diary of events to extracting data from published accounts.

❏ Prepare a hierarchical financial ratio analysis using data from published accounts or other source.

❏ Provide an interpretation of the results obtained from calculating financial ratios.

❏ Describe and apply Altman's 1968 ratio model.

❏ Describe the development and application of Robertson's 1983 ratio model.

❏ Describe and set in context the non-financial approach adopted by Argenti.

❏ Identify and use published sources of company information.

4.1 Introduction

We have considered the make-up of corporate reports and the general principles for their analysis using financial ratios in earlier chapters. However, financial ratio analysis is only one tool for interpreting published information much of which may be non-financial in nature.

In this chapter we consider how the published information provided in corporate reports of both a financial and non-financial nature may be analysed in a structured manner to permit useful interpretation. We also illustrate with reference to an example how the purely financial information provided in the published accounts may be analysed using the principles of financial ratio analysis discussed in the last chapter.

One problem of corporate reports is that the information they provide may well be long out-of-date or even incomplete. In fact there are many sources of additional company information which are available, we review a selection in *Appendix A*. Finally, research by academics over the last 25 years or so has revealed that statistical and non-statistical approaches can be used for analysing financial and non-financial data so as to be able to form a view about corporate financial health. What these approaches are and how they differ are considered in the final section of this chapter.

4.2 Diary of events

Corporate reports do in fact contain much useful information but it may not necessarily be (and is not usually) organised in the most appropriate way to permit analysis. All too often the inexperienced analyst will focus attention upon hard forms of analysis like the calculation of ratios without setting the scene appropriately.

In this section we will consider how to organise the information provided in a useful way via the diary of events. This you will find invaluable for both interpreting corporate reports in practice and for their analysis in business strategy.

A diary of events is a log of significant changes which have taken place in a company during the year under consideration. It should be directed both at financial and non-financial information obtained primarily from published accounts, but which may be supplemented with that from other sources.

What form should the diary of events take? We have provided an example of a checklist in *Table 4.1*.

Table 4.1   Diary of events

AUDIT REPORT
    Have the accounts been qualified?

DIRECTORS
    Any significant movements in key personnel e.g.
    resignations/appointments?
    Any non-executive directors?
    Who are the non-executive directors?

TRADING STABILITY
    Is the company losing its way e.g. diversification?
    Are there any statements on deterioration in the market-place?
    Are there statements referring to "Worst year in company's history"?
    Are there signs that the company is overtrading?

BORROWINGS
    Is there evidence that the company has agreed to a fixed and/or
    floating charge on all assets?
    How many banks does the company use?

FIXED ASSETS
    Is the company selling off key assets?
    Is there evidence of over-commitment to a big project which could
    cause the downfall of the company?

ACCOUNTS
    Is there evidence of delay in paying bills e.g. long creditor days?
    Is there evidence of a delay in publishing the annual report?

SALES BY ACTIVITY AND PROFIT BY ACTIVITY
    Is there any significant movements in sales or profitability by activity?

CAPITAL EXPENDITURE
    Is the company expanding from organic growth?
    Is there evidence of expansion by acquisition?

ACCOUNTING POLICY AND TREATMENT
    Has the company made any significant changes to its accounting
    policy and the treatment of key items e.g. goodwill and brands?

4.3   Financial ratio analysis - worked example

Once you have gained a feel for the company from compiling the 'Diary of Events' you then are ready to delve more deeply into the published accounts using financial ratio analysis. In this section we provide a worked example of financial ratio analysis using accounts in the format discussed in *Chapter 2* from which the ratios discussed in *Chapter 3* have been calculated and are explained.

CONSOLIDATED PROFIT AND LOSS ACCOUNT
for the year ended 31st January 1991

	Note	1991 £'m	1990 £'m
SALES		850	780
Cost of Sales	1	-780	-720
TRADING PROFIT		70	60
Net Interest Payable	3	-10	-10
PROFIT/(LOSS) ON ORDINARY ACTIVITIES BEFORE TAX		60	50
Taxation		-20	-15
PROFIT/(LOSS) ON ORDINARY ACTIVITIES AFTER TAX		40	35
Dividends	4	-15	-10
PROFIT RETAINED		25	25
Earnings per Ordinary Share (pence)	5	22.2	19.3

CONSOLIDATED BALANCE SHEETS
as at 31st January 1991

	Note	1991 £'m	1990 £'m
FIXED ASSETS			
Tangible Assets	6	230	190
CURRENT ASSETS			
Stocks		90	75
Debtors		120	100
Cash		25	60
		235	235
CREDITORS: amounts falling due within one year			
Borrowings		-30	-10
Other Creditors	7	-160	-130
NET CURRENT ASSETS/LIABILITIES		45	95
TOTAL ASSETS LESS CURRENT LIABILITIES		275	285
CREDITORS : amounts falling due after one year		-130	-115
NET ASSETS		145	170
CAPITAL AND RESERVES			
Issued Share Capital	8	50	40
Share Premium		30	30
Profit and Loss Account	9	65	100
SHAREHOLDERS' FUNDS		145	170

**CONSOLIDATED SOURCE AND APPLICATION OF FUNDS
for the year ended 31st January 1991**

	£'m	£'m
(1) SOURCES OF FUNDS		
Profit Before Taxation		60
Items Not Involving Movement of Funds:		
Depreciation		20
		80
(2) FUNDS FROM OTHER SOURCES		
Share Issue	10	
Premium on Shares	120	
Loans	15	145
		225
(3) APPLICATION OF FUNDS		
Acquisition	-240	
Taxation	-15	
Dividend Payments	-10	-265
		-40
(4) INCREASE/DECREASE IN WORKING CAPITAL		
Stock	15	
Debtors	20	
Cash	-35	
Borrowings	-20	
Creditors	-20	
		-40

Notes to the accounts

1. Cost of Sales

	1991 £'m	1990 £'m
Raw Materials	395	375
Employee Costs	195	180
Administration Costs	190	165
	780	720

2. Employees

	1991 £'m	1990 £'m
Wages and Salaries	172	159
Social Security Costs	15	13
Other Pension Costs	8	8
	195	180

Average number of employees during the year in the United Kingdom were 17,250 (1991 16,675)

3. Interest

	1991 £'m	1990 £'m
Interest Payable on Bank Loans and Overdrafts	13	12
less Interest Received	-3	-2
	10	10

4. Dividends on ordinary shares

	1991 £'m	1990 £'m
Interim Paid	4	3
Final Proposed	11	7
	15	10

5. Earnings per ordinary share

The calculation of earnings per ordinary share of 25p is based on profit (after minority interests but before extraordinary items) of £40m (1990 £35m) and on 180 million ordinary shares (1990 150 million) ranking for dividend, being the *weighted average* of shares in issue during the year

6. Fixed Assets

	Freehold property £'m	Plant and equipment £'m	Others £'m	Total £'m
Cost or Valuation:				
At 31 January 1990	97.3	175.0	31.5	303.8
Acquisitions	27.9	55.2	9.9	93.0
At 31 January 1991	125.2	230.2	41.4	396.8
Depreciation:				
At 31 January 1990	16.2	79.2	18.4	113.8
Acquisitions	9.9	19.6	3.5	33.0
Provided during the year	2.2	13.2	4.6	20.0
At 31 January 1991	28.3	112.0	26.5	166.8
Net Book Value:				
At 31 January 1991	96.9	118.2	14.9	230.0
At 31 January 1990	81.1	95.8	13.1	190.0

7. Creditors: amounts due within one year

	1991 £'m	1990 £'m
Bank Loans and Overdrafts	30	10
Others:		
Creditors	129	108
Corporation Taxes	20	15
Proposed Dividend	11	7
	160	130

8. Called up share capital

	1991 £'m	1990 £'m
200,000,000 Ordinary Shares of 25p (1990 £160 million)	50	40

The Authorised Share Capital is £70 million (1990 £70 million)

9. Share premium account and reserves

	Share premium £'m	Other reserves £'m
At 31 January 1990	30	100
Premium on Allotments	120	
Transfer from Share Premium	-120	120
Goodwill on Consolidation Written Off		-180
Profit Retained	—	25
At 31 January 1991	30	65

4.3.1   Extracting the figures

When extracting figures from published accounts or from other commercial sources (*e.g. Datastream or Extel),* we use a simple format to record the data for each year.   The format which is shown in   *Table 14.2*   can then be input into a computer spreadsheet developed to produce the financial ratios discussed in *Chapter 12.*

Table 14.2   Selected company financial information

	1991	1990
	£'m	£'m
Fixed Assets	230	190
Stock	90	75
Debtors	120	100
Current Assets	235	235
Creditors	125	105
Bank Overdraft	30	10
Current Liabilities	190	140
Share Capital	50	40
Capital Reserves	30	30
Revenue Reserves	65	100
Long Term Loans	130	115
Sales	850	780
Raw Materials	395	375
Employee Costs	195	180
Administration Costs	170	150
Depreciation	20	15
Profit Before Tax	60	50
Interest Payable	13	12
Market Value: (p)	320	270
Nominal Value: (p)	25	25

Note. The market value of a company's shares must be obtained from an external source. (e.g. Financial newspapers, *Extel, Datastream)*

4.3.2   Calculation of financial ratios

The output from the computer spreadsheet provided the financial ratios shown in *Table 4.3*.

Table 4.3   Financial ratio analysis

	1991	1990
BUSINESS LEVEL RATIOS		
PBIT / Total Assets %	15.70	14.59
PBIT / Sales %	8.59	7.95
Sales / Total Assets	1.83	1.84
PROFIT MARGIN RATIOS:		
Raw Materials / Sales %	46.47	48.08
Employee Costs / Sales %	22.94	23.08
Administration Costs / Sales %	20.00	19.23
FIXED ASSET UTILISATION:		
Sales / Fixed Assets	3.70	4.11
Sales / Land and Buildings	8.77	9.62
Sales / Plant and Equipment	7.19	8.14
Sales / Other Fixed Assets	57.05	59.54
CURRENT ASSET UTILISATION:		
Sales / Current Assets	3.62	3.32
Sales / Stock	9.44	10.40
Sales / Debtors	7.08	7.80
Sales / Other Current Assets	34.00	13.00
LIQUIDITY RATIOS:		
Current Assets / Current Liabilities	1.24	1.68
Liquid Assets / Current Liabilities	.76	1.14
CORPORATE RATIOS		
Market Value of Equity / Book Value of Equity (MB)%	441.38	254.12
Profit After Tax / Book Value of Equity (ROE) %	27.59	20.59
Market Value of Equity / Profit After Tax	16.00	12.34
BREAKDOWN OF ROE %		
Profit After Tax / Total Assets %	8.60	8.23
Total Assets / Book Value of Equity	3.21	2.50
GEARING RATIOS:		
Total Debt / Book Value of Equity	2.21	1.50
Total Debt / Market Value of Equity	0.50	0.59

4.3.3   Interpretation of financial ratios

The interpretation of financial ratios is often regarded as being the most difficult area to understand. These difficulties tend to arise because of the large number of financial ratios it is possible to calculate, and the inability of the analyst to arrive at a satisfactory conclusion.

The following interpretation will examine each sub-group of ratios in an effort to detect any changes which have taken place within the individual ratios year-on-year. In some cases e.g. the profit margin%, we will be able to examine the subsidiary ratios which should give clues to the underlying movements in the profit margin%. Comparison of ratios in this example will be restricted to trends, i.e. year-on-year. In practice, other comparisons should also be made against industry averages, or against a number of close competitors.

❑   **Business level ratios**

The key ratio, profit before interest and taxation as a percentage of total assets ROTA% shows a slight increase over 1990. This means that the company is obtaining a 15.7% return on its total asset base. As a general rule, the higher the better.

The profit margin%, profit before interest and taxation as a percentage of sales shows a similar increase to the key ratio. This means that the average profit margin has increased, and with reference to the third ratio in this section which has remained steady, leads us to conclude that it is the improvement in the profit margin% which has brought about the overall increase in the key ratio above. We will examine the subsidiary profit margin ratios in the next section.

The sales generation ratio, sales divided by total assets does not show any significant movement. We could conclude with this year-on-year comparison, that the company is still generating the same amount of sales from its total asset base. However, when we examine the fixed asset utilisation and the current asset utilisation we find that sales have fallen per £1 of fixed assets and increased per £1 of current assets, the net effect being zero. We will return to this shortly.

❑   **Profit margin ratios**

This group of ratios records the material costs, employee costs and administration costs as a percentage of sales. We can see that the most significant movement is the reduction in material costs from 48.08 to 46.47 percent of sales. This could be due to a reduction in material prices, material usage, or simply using cheaper materials.

❑ **Fixed asset utilisation**

The fixed asset utilisation ratios provide a breakdown of the sales generation ratio shown in the first section. In this group of ratios we can see that sales have fallen per £1 of fixed assets For example, the company increased its sales to land and buildings from £9.62 in 1990 to £8.77 in 1991. In this particular case we must consult the diary of events to determine whether the company has revalued its land and buildings, or if the reduction is simply due to additional fixed assets.

❑ **Current asset utilisation**

The current asset utilisation ratios provides a breakdown of the other part of the sales generation ratio, shown in the first section, and should be interpreted in conjunction with the fixed asset utilisation ratios above. In this group of ratios we see that sales have increased per £1 of current assets. However, when we examine the other ratios we see that both the stock and debtor ratios have fallen and conclude that the decrease is due to the significant increase in other current assets. In this case if we return to the balance sheet we find that other current assets are in fact cash. Cash has fallen from £60 million in 1990 down to £25 million in 1991.

❑ **Liquidity ratios**

The two most popular liquidity ratios are shown in this section. The first, the current ratio, current assets divided by current liabilities, gives an indication of the company's ability to meet short-term financial commitments. In 1990 current liabilities were covered once plus and additional 68%, whilst in 1991, the additional cover has fallen to only 24%. An examination of the figures contained in the balance sheet shows that the fall is due to an increase in creditors and bank overdraft.

The second ratio in this section, the liquid or acid test, liquid assets divided by current liabilities, gives an indication of a company's ability to meet its short-term obligations without having to liquidate stock. Here we find that the liquid ratio has followed the movement of current ratio, showing a movement from 1.14 down to 0.76. In the absence of industry averages a figure of 1.14 to 1 may indicate idle facilities in the working capital cycle. We should not feel uncomfortable with a figure of 0.76 to 1 although we should continue to monitor the situation.

❑ **Corporate ratios**

The first ratio, the market to book ratio (MB) % shows a significant increase over 1990, and generally speaking the higher the ratio the better. To find out the reasons for the increase we need to look at the movements in the subsidiary ratios i.e. ROE% and PE. Here we find that both ratios have increased. There is a higher percentage return to equity (ROE) % over the previous year and that investors are prepared to pay 16 times the earnings in 1991 compared to just over 12 times in 1990.

❏ **Breakdown of ROE%**

In this section we consider the breakdown of ROE% into profitability and gearing. The profitability ratio, profit after tax expressed as a percentage of total assets shows a slight increase. The gearing ratio, total assets divided by the book value of equity records an increase of just over 28%. This could be because total assets have increased and/or book value of equity has decreased. In examining the figures we find that total assets have increased by 9% while the book value of equity has decreased by nearly 15%. From note 9 to the accounts we find that book value of equity has decreased as a result of writing off goodwill on acquisition.

❏ **Gearing ratios**

In this section we examine two gearing ratios which enjoy more popular application than the gearing ratio described earlier. The first ratio, total debt divided by book value of equity, records an increase of just over 47%. In this case total debt as the numerator has increased by 25%, while the book value of equity has decreased by nearly 15%. From looking behind the numbers we find that the company has funded part of its acquisition through debt, and the proportion funded through equity has been eliminated due to writing off goodwill.

The second gearing ratio, total debt divided by the market value of equity, shows a smaller movement in the other direction. Clearly the market view differs from that portrayed in the financial statements.

4.4 Predicting corporate failure and measuring corporate health

We have demonstrated how to evaluate performance earlier in this chapter by calculating a number of financial ratios and exercising user judgement in interpreting the results. But there are alternatives to this approach that reduce the emphasis upon the exercise of user judgement. Approaches have been developed some of which are available from data services, like *Datastream*, but about which a basic understanding is important before being used. They can have tremendous user appeal because a single score can be calculated from information contained in the published accounts and notes plus the share price, and there is a benchmark against which to measure the result obtained. A major problem of interpretation in using a system of traditional ratios is therefore apparently removed. For example, the dilemma to the manager as to the conclusions to be drawn if profitability and liquidity ratios show conflicting movements is apparently no longer a problem. The combination of a statistical technique and ratios has made it possible to identify a number of ratios for measuring financial failure which have been proposed as providing an early warning about changes in a company's health.

4.4.1   Z scoring

Z scoring is an approach primarily associated with the work of *Professor Altman* in the USA. Since his first published research in 1968, *Altman* has developed ratio models designed to predict corporate failure using a statistical technique known as multiple discriminant analysis (MDA). His original work, which is most well known, determined five ratios each with its own weighting such that the sum of the products of the individual ratios and associated weights determined by the model yields a Z score predictor of failure. The format of *Altman's* 1968 model was as follows:

$$Z = 1.2X_1 + 1.4X_2 + 3.3X_3 + 0.6X_4 + 1.0X_5$$

where Z is the sum of the ratios times the weights and the individual ratios are defined as:

X_1 = Working Capital ÷ Total Assets

X_2 = Retained Earnings ÷ Total Assets

X_3 = Profit Before Interest and Tax ÷ Total Assets

X_4 = Market Value of Equity ÷ Book Value of Total Debt

X_5 = Sales ÷ Total Assets.

The model is applied as follows - individual ratios are calculated, then multiplied by the respective weights and added to produce a Z score for a company. A score of 2.675 was established by *Altman* as a practical cut-off point for potential failure, firms with a score of less than 2.675 are assumed to have similar characteristics of past failures. A band or range of scores between 1.81 and 2.99 was found to exist from the research study which fall in the 'zone of ignorance'. This zone represents the area where misclassifications can occur, i.e. a healthy company could in error be classified as a failure, and vice-versa.

This model, subsequently used by several other authors, has a very simplistic appeal insofar as it implies that all that is necessary is to calculate the relevant ratios, multiply them by the weights and then obtain a prediction of corporate failure.

Professor Taffler (1983) has produced a Z score model for the UK. Unlike *Altman*, he has not published the details of his model, but he has stated that:

1.   a 53 per cent contribution to the model is made by the 'profitability' measure:

$$\frac{\text{Profits Before Tax}}{\text{Current Liabilities}}$$

2.   a 13 per cent contribution is made by the 'working capital' measure:

$$\frac{\text{Current Assets}}{\text{Total Liabilities}}$$

3.   an 18 per cent contribution comes from the 'financial risk' measure:

$$\frac{\text{Current Liabilities}}{\text{Total Assets}}$$

4.   a 16 per cent contribution comes from the 'liquidity' measure or no credit interval i.e. the number of days a company can finance its operations from its immediate assets if it can no longer generate revenue.

In addition to developing this model for manufacturing companies, *Taffler* has developed another for distribution companies, which have different characteristics.

Why has there continued to be such strong interest in the prediction of corporate failure? The answer is that an accurate prediction of corporate failure can benefit a variety of parties. For example:

❏   Investors could seek to avoid losses associated with bankruptcy.

❏   Lenders could use bankruptcy techniques to help assess the risks of loan default.

❏   Auditors might use such a model as a warning signal about a company's vulnerability.

❏   Management might value such information to defend a proposed take-over bid.

❏   Employers or unions could use such a model to assess the risk of bankruptcy and the resulting threat to continued employment.

The practical potential of a technique which would provide an accurate prediction of bankruptcy is considerable. However, one major problem facing the interested user of such techniques is that numerous studies have indicated that further knowledge is needed in order to interpret and apply them. Whilst they may have all of the appearances of the panacea for the busy general manager wishing to form a view about corporate health there are some important difficulties which have to be borne in mind. These are:

❑   A single Z score cut-off for a specific industry group.

❑   The notion that practitioners can adjust this cut-off.

❑   Incorrect interpretation against a trend in Z scores.

❑   Using a single years results to predict failure.

❑   A strict single industry requirement.

❑   Using Z score models for purposes for which they were not intended, e.g. corporate turnaround.

4.4.2   Other approaches which measure changes in financial health

In addition to statistically oriented approaches others have been developed. First *Robertson (1983)* has developed a model which measures changes in financial health which:

❑   Suggests key elements (ratio categories) identifiable in failed companies and then constructs ratios to measure each element.

❑   Uses simple weights, to compensate for the natural differences in the individual ratio values, to arrive at a single score.

❑   Interprets the score by measuring changes in financial health from previous periods i.e. measuring changes in the score year-on-year; traditional interpretation follows this procedure.

❑   Identifies changes in financial health and allows examination of the individual ratio movements, in order that corrective action can be taken.

The financial change model

The final model comprised of the following ratios each of which have been described in the previous section. The ratios are referred to by using R_1 to denote ratio 1 through to R_5 to denote ratio 5.

R_1 = (Sales - Total Assets) ÷ Sales

R_2 = Profit Before Taxation ÷ Total Assets

R_3 = (Current Assets - Total Debt) ÷ Current Liabilities

R_4 = (Equity - Total Borrowings) ÷ Total Debt

R_5 = (Liquid Assets - Bank Borrowings) ÷ Creditors

The financial change model takes a similar form to *Altman's* 1968 model where the total score is found:

$$FCM = 0.3R_1 + 3R_2 + 0.6R_3 + 0.3R_4 + 0.3R_5$$

The model was developed using a systems approach. This required a statement of 'key elements' identifiable in failed companies, followed by the development of ratios which have individual meaning and will help to measure each of the elements; finally the provision for feedback (by observing the movements in the scores obtained from the individual ratios) to allow corrective action to be taken if necessary.

The identification of the key elements was produced using literature, especially *Argenti's* failure process (to be discussed later) also from a detailed examination of the data already collected for 8 failed companies. The 'key elements' identifiable in failed companies were:

❑ **Trading instability**

Most failing companies experience a fall in sales generated from an asset base. This is true of the declining product cycle and the rapid expansion or overtrading company.

❑ **Declining profits**

The conditions encountered in trading stability can erode a company's profit margins and when combined with other uncontrolled costs can result in substantial losses.

❑   Declining working capital

If not checked, declining profits can lead to a decline in working capital, accelerating if the company turns into a loss situation. Further reductions in working capital can be caused by continued expansion of fixed assets, especially when financed from short-term borrowings.

❑   Increase in borrowings

Instead of tackling the problem of trading instability and profitability, the failing company increases borrowings to maintain its required level of working capital. This has a double effect in that:

a   it further reduces profits through additional interest payments.

b   it increases the gearing of a company at a time when it is most vulnerable.

The selection of ratios to be included was considered to be the most important factor in the development of the model. Each ratio was selected to reflect the elements that cause changes in a company's financial health.

The ratios finally selected

❑   (Sales - Total Assets) ÷ Sales

This is a measure of trading stability. It highlights the important relationship between assets and sales. When a company increases it asset base it is looking for a corresponding increase in sales. Companies experiencing trading difficulties are unable to maintain a given level for this ratio. Deterioration indicates a fall in the sales generated from the asset base. If the ratio is maintained it can produce a stabilising effect even for a company that is failing.

❑   Profit Before Taxation ÷ Total Assets

Profit is taken after interest payable but before tax, because failing companies borrow more and suffer increases in interest payments in the years to failure. Total assets exclude intangibles and are used as the base because they are not influenced by financing policies and tend to remain constant or increase. Failing companies tend to show a decline in profits in the years to failure, often turning into a loss. The deterioration in profit is sufficient to cause this ratio to fall. However, many companies are involved in rapid expansion and this, if present, could cause a further decline in the ratio.

❑ **(Current Assets - Total Debt) ÷ Current Liabilities**

This is an extension of the net working capital ratio, and requires that long-term debt is also deducted from current assets. It measures a company's ability to repay its current debt without selling fixed assets. Total debt is taken in preference to the usual current liabilities because, when a company is in difficulty, it does not matter whether the debt is long-term or short-term it is the overall amount of the debt which matters. When compared over a number of years, failing companies show a marked deterioration in this ratio due to the current assets falling while total debt remains constant or even increases.

❑ **(Equity - Total Borrowings) ÷ Total Debt**

This is a gearing ratio. A low ratio indicates a high proportion of debt which means high gearing with associated high risk. Failing companies experience a drop in equity through a combination of losses in operations and reorganisation / extraordinary costs, while at the same time borrowings tend to increase. This can turn a healthy balance in favour of equity into a negative balance where borrowings exceed equity. Should a company not borrow but instead obtain additional funds from shareholders, then this will have a stabilising effect and reduce the risk of moving toward high gearing and associated interest expense. It will also help to reduce borrowings and improve liquidity ratios.

❑ **(Liquid Assets - Bank Borrowings) ÷ Creditors**

This ratio tests changes in immediate liquidity. After deducting bank borrowings from liquid assets it is then possible to measure the immediate cover for creditors. Increasing bank borrowings incurs additional financing costs for current and future periods and might require the company to agree to a fixed and/or floating charge over its assets.

The weights used were selected to adjust the natural values obtained from certain ratios. For example, the ratio of profit before tax divided by total assets could only, at best, produce a natural score of 0.20 (equivalent to a 20% return on total assets) while a liquidity ratio or a gearing ratio could easily produce a natural score of 1.00 or more. In this case the weights allow the profit ratio to be increased and/or the liquidity or gearing ratios to be reduced. Weights can also be used to increase the effect of one ratio and/or reduce the effect of another.

Given that a stated aim was that each ratio should contribute equally to the overall score it was then a series of simple arithmetic calculations to arrive at a set of weights applicable to a group of companies, or even a single company. It was also the aim that the resulting weights should be easy to use, so experiments were carried out by changing the weights (for example doubling and halving a ratio weight). This showed, contrary to expectations, that changes in individual ratio weights did not significantly affect the total score when comparing a company year-on-year.

Interpretation of the score

In traditional ratio analysis, the same ratios are used across 'industries' with ratio values being interpreted by observing the movements from previous periods or from an industry average. Given that the model was developed for use across 'industries', it is appropriate to use similar interpretation, i.e. observing the movements in the total (and individual) scores.

In testing the model it was found that, when the total score fell by approximately 40 percent or more in any year, then substantial changes had taken place in the financial health of a company. Immediate steps should be taken to identify the reasons for the change and all necessary action taken to stop the decline and restore the balance. If the score falls by approximately 40 percent or more for a second year running, the company is unlikely to survive, unless drastic action is taken to stop the decline and restore financial health.

In practice, the model should be used to identify all movements in the total score; further checks should then be carried out on the individual ratios contained in the model in order that action be taken to correct the situation.

4.4.3   Non-financial indicators of corporate distress

When companies fail they often are considered to display non-financial signs of deterioration as well as financial ones. These non-financial indications include some elusive matters, such items as 'bad management' and economic downturn, and others less elusive such as overtrading and excessive inventories.

Many individuals have considered the importance of non financial factors but one, *Argenti* (1976), is notable in his attempt to rank the items in some order of importance.

In contrast to the financial ratio approaches, *Argenti* proposes an A-score. The A-score is based on the assumption that, as a general rule, most companies fail for broadly similar reasons and in a broadly similar manner. The failure sequence is assumed to take many years, typically five or more, to run its course and to fall into three essential stages comprising:

❏ Specific *defects* in a company's management and business practices in particular at the very top.

❏ Subsequently, possibly years later, top management makes a major *mistake* because of the specific defects.

❏ Ultimately, signs and *symptoms* of failure begin to appear, manifest are financial and non-financial matters.

Argenti has discussed these three stages in more detail which we shall now consider.

The inherent defects

The inherent defects identified by *Argenti* relate to:

1. Management

2. Accountancy systems

3. Change

1. **Management.**

He identifies a major defect as being an autocratic chief executive, particularly where he or she is also the Chairman. Such an individual will tend to be viewed as being 'the company' and will be surrounded by people whose advice he/she has no intention of taking.

What are the other management defects. The Board may consist of passive, non-contributing directors, arguably a desirable situation for an autocratic leader, but not for the company. Second, the directors may lack all-round business skills. Third, there may be lack of strong financial direction. Poor working capital management is often good evidence of lacking financial direction. For example, there may be no substantial cash flow forecasting with clear difficulties for the management of future borrowing requirements. Finally, a lack of management depth below board level can lead to failure.

2. **Accountancy systems.**

Companies that fail are often found to have poor or non-existent accounting systems, a defect which can be related to poor financial direction. Other than working capital, budgetary control may be a particular problem. Either no budgets are prepared at all, or the budgets are prepared but are not followed by adequate variance reports. The consequence is that employees do not know what is required of them or, if they do, they do not know whether they have achieved it.

Within such a defective accounting system costing may be a particular problem. Managers may not know what each product or service costs and, if they do, they are not likely to be aware of the characteristics of reported costs, i.e. whether they are full costs or not.

3.   Change.

Many companies that fail are those which have either not noticed a change in their business environment, or have not responded to it. *Argenti* cites signs of such defects as being old-fashioned product, old-fashioned factory, out-of-date marketing, strikes attributable to outmoded attitudes to employees, an ageing board of directors, and no development of information management competencies, such as those associated with computerisation.

The mistakes

Three mistakes are identified by *Argenti* as being responsible for failure.
1. Over-gearing
2. Overtrading
3. The big project.

1.   Over-gearing.

Companies dominated by ambitious autocrats and not constrained by strong finance directors are particularly prone to taking on a higher level of gearing than a judicious review of the financial situation should allow.

2.   Overtrading.

Overtrading typically occurs when a company expands faster than its ability to generate funding. Expanding companies often overtrade and become prone to failure by relying upon loan finance often of a short term nature.

3.   The big project.

Some companies which have failed can be identified by having launched an unsuccessful project of such a size that its success is impossible as a consequence of its failure. A 'big project' can be physical, such as launching a major new product or service, but need not necessarily be tangible. The guaranteeing of a loan of a subsidiary company would fall within this category.

The symptoms

Argenti identifies a number of symptoms which can be observed as a company moves toward failure.

1.   Financial signs.

Financial signs of failure such as deteriorating ratios, we have discussed in some detail earlier in this chapter. Whilst of doubtless value their major shortcoming relates to their inability to indicate the likelihood of failure in a period of less than two or three years, unlike other non financial symptoms.

2.   **Creative Accounting.**

The prospect of failure has been known to encourage the accounting system to be used very imaginatively, particularly where financial information is required to be reported externally to outside parties. Such imagination, when not obviously exercised for reasons other than to mislead, is known as creative accounting. Such creativity may manifest itself in a number of areas. Extraordinary items and the treatment of depreciation are two fairly obvious examples, for which the exercise of creativity is likely to be severely constrained by the role of the auditor.

3.   **Other signs.**

A company heading for failure may exhibit numerous non-financial signs of distress as well as financial ones. Examples of those are management salaries are frozen, capital expenditure decisions are delayed, product quality or service deteriorates, market share falls, the chief executive is ill, staff turnover rises, morale deteriorates, rumours abound, and the dividend is not cut when there would seem to be sound reason for so doing.

At the very end of the process, when failure is imminent, all of the financial and non-financial signs become so severe that even the most casual observer can see them. These are referred to as terminal signs.

There is little general disagreement about the relevance of the *Argenti*-type approach. However, what is rather more contentious is the notion that individual defects, mistakes and symptoms can be scored to yield one total score indicative of potential failure or not. How does this scoring system operate? The scores given to each of the above items are weighted in accordance with their importance in the failure process and are as follows:

Defects

Autocrat		8
Chairman and Chief Executive		4
Passive Board		2
Unbalanced skills		2
Weak Finance Director		2
Poor management depth		1
No budgetary control		3
No cash flow plans		3
No costing system		3
Poor response to change		<u>15</u>
Total for defects	**(A)**	**43**

Mistakes

High gearing		15
Overtrading		15
Big project		<u>15</u>
Total for mistakes	**(B)**	**45**

Symptoms

Financial signs		4
Creative accounting		4
Non-financial signs		3
Terminal signs		<u>1</u>
Total for symptoms	**(C)**	**12**
Total overall possible score	**(A+B+C)**	**100**
Pass mark		**25**

Argenti recommends that the scores are given only if the observer is confident that an item is clearly visible in the company being studied. Only maximum or nil scores are allowed. This means that, for example, only if the observer is quite sure that the chief executive dominates the suspect company and has deliberately gathered around him a team of executives whose advice he does not intend to take, should the score of 8 for 'autocrat' be given, otherwise he should score nil.

The overall pass mark according to the system is 25. Scores above that level are considered to show so many of the well-known signs which precede failure that the observer should be profoundly alarmed. Within the overall score, the subscores are also noteworthy. If a company scores more than the pass mark of 10 in the defects section, even if it scores less than 25 overall, it is viewed as being indicative of a company in danger of making one of the mistakes that lead to failure.

Appendix A

Sources of company information

The following are examples of sources of company information which can be found in most college libraries, local reference libraries, and in certain local company libraries. The list is of necessity selective. However, you should experiment by using any library to which you have access, to find out details about a particular company or topic.

KOMPASS (Annual publication in four volumes)

Volumes I and II classify 35,000 U.K. companies according to their products and services. They provide the opportunity to identify companies in a similar industry sector.

Volume III, Company Information, arranges the companies by county and town. Most entries give name and address, list of directors, share capital, turnover, number of employees and product codes. This volume is useful in that it often provides entries for a number of limited companies which are part of a larger group. It is also useful from a geographic point of view.

Volume IV, Financial Data, provides some basic financial data for a three year period, together with three financial ratios. Like Volume III, it gives access to financial data for Limited companies which might be part of a larger group. However, the data is at least two years old.

WHO OWN'S WHOM (annual publication in two volumes)

Volume I lists the ultimate parent companies and gives an indented listing of the subsidiaries of each parent.

Volume II list over 100,000 subsidiaries on the left of a page, with the ultimate parent given in the right hand column.

DIRECTORY OF DIRECTORS (annual publication)

This is published in two sections. The first section is an alphabetical list of the directors of the principal public and private companies in the U.K., giving the names of the companies with which they are associated. The second section is an alphabetical list of the principal public and private companies in the U.K., giving the names of the directors.

It should be pointed out that there are a number of publications which list the names of the directors of companies. Due to the number of changes in directors, it is difficult to reconcile these lists.

KEY BRITISH ENTERPRISES (annual publication)

This is published in two volumes. The publication gives details of the top 20,000 U.K. companies, listed in alphabetical order and provides the address of each company, telephone, a statement on the principal activities of the company, trade names, parent company, date established, authorised capital, list of the directors, name of secretary, annual sales figure, number of employees and the Standard Industrial Classification (SIC) code. The indexes also arrange the companies by means of their products or services, and by county.

THE TIMES 1000 (annual publication)

This publication provides basic financial details of the top 1,000 UK public companies, the top 500 European companies, the top 100 US companies, etc. It also lists recent acquisitions and mergers, investment trusts, banks, building societies etc. Information is provided in list form on topics which are not available in other publications.

STOCK EXCHANGE OFFICIAL YEAR-BOOK (annual publication)

All London and provincial stock exchange listed companies are listed in some detail in this publication. Information provided includes, address of registered office, registrars, names of directors, secretary, auditors, solicitors, principal bankers, and brokers. Details of registration are also given, including registered number, a statement of the principal activities of the company, and principal subsidiaries. The majority of the entry for each company concentrates on the capital structure, including recent capital history, loan capital etc. The year-book is supplemented by the Stock Exchange Quarterly, which publishes articles on topical subjects.

EXTEL HANDBOOK OF MARKET LEADERS (published half yearly)

Detailed information is provided about companies constituting the Financial Times Actuaries All Share Index. Companies are listed in alphabetical order, one to each page. Each entry includes the nature of the business, the registrars, the address of the company's registered office. Details are also given for five years profit and loss figures, five years ordinary share record, together with selected figures from two years balance sheets. Graphs are also provided, and other general company information.

RESEARCH INDEX (published fortnightly)

The index is in two sections. The first section list topics in alphabetical order e.g. Trade Unions, and it lists details of news headings under each of the topics, together with the paper or magazine and page number(s). The second section provides similar information in alphabetic order of companies. The index is useful to locate newspaper articles, the problem arises when trying to obtain a hard copy. It is suggested that the user of this service should identify those items which can be traced using a newspaper microfilm facility e.g. Times or Financial Times.

McCARTHY COMPANY INFORMATION SERVICES

McCarthy sheets are produced for quoted and unquoted UK registered companies. They represent a collection of press cuttings which are accumulated for each company from relevant newspapers and journals. There is also an Industry Service which is based on subjects. This makes it possible to compare the performance and development of individual companies in their field of operation. The service provides cut-and-paste copies of write-ups, unlike the Research Index which only provides 'headings'.

EXTEL STATISTICAL SERVICES LTD

The service is essentially card based. The main services for UK companies are:

White cards. These give concise details of over 3,000 companies listed on the U.K. and Irish Stock Exchanges. For each company the annual card shows the address, structure of the company, list of the directors, authorised and issued capital and its history , director's interests, the dividend record, the profit and loss accounts (usually ten years), high/low share prices, and consolidated balance sheets (usually three or four years). The card also includes extracts from the Chairman's statement. Cumulative news cards are issued for each company on the announcement of dividends, interim and preliminary results, changes in directors, or on any other event of major importance concerning the company's finances.

Pink cards. These give similar details for over 2,000 UK unquoted companies. The service is usually for limited companies not required to provide such detailed information as public companies. The cards are therefore less comprehensive than the white cards. However, the service is useful for picking up subsidiaries of major UK public limited companies.

Blue cards. Those are the Extel Analyst's Service, and provide a ten year record for over 1,200 companies included in the UK quoted service. Details are provided for a ten year period for the main balance sheet items, capital issues and acquisitions, profit and loss account data, ordinary share record, dividend information and various ratios are also provided.

COMPANY REGISTRATION OFFICE

The company registration office holds certain information about companies on microfiche. Public limited companies are required to lodge their annual return not later than 7 months after their year end, limited companies 10 months.

The contents in a packet of microfiche contains general information about the company, including details of its incorporation, articles and memorandum of association, and details of movements of directors. It also includes financial information for a number of years which includes profit and loss account, balance sheet, source and application of funds, notes to the accounts, directors report and the auditors' report.

To obtain microfiche for a company, it is important to have the correct company name, and it is better still to have the registered number of the company. Access can be gained through visiting the Companies Registration Office at Cardiff or London (Edinburgh in Scotland), by post, or by using a company search agent.

Exercises

4.1 From the Balance Sheet and Profit and Loss Account data given below, apply Altman's 1968 ratio model and Robertson's 1983 ratio model. Comment upon what the results reveal.

BALANCE SHEET DATA FOR FIVE YEARS (£000)

	1986	1987	1988	1989	1990
Fixed Assets	1,600	1,700	2,310	3,350	4,900
Stock	900	850	1,220	1,240	1,850
Debtors	930	910	1,000	1,150	1,200
Current Assets	2,020	2,340	2,500	2,700	3,550
Creditors	720	700	760	890	920
Bank Overdraft	120	140	250	450	780
Current Liabilities	1,000	1,070	1,280	1,660	1,850
Issued Share Capital	550	570	580	590	600
Profit and Loss Account	1,200	1,400	1,650	1,800	1,850
Long Term Loans	870	1,000	1,300	2,000	4,150

PROFIT AND LOSS ACCOUNT DATA FOR FIVE YEARS (£000)

	1986	1987	1988	1989	1990
Sales	4,000	4,500	5,500	7,500	9,900
Interest Payable	100	150	180	210	250
Profit BeforeTax	560	600	450	630	400

OTHER DATA (pence)

	1986	1987	1988	1989	1990
Market Value	200	220	250	300	180
Nominal Value	25	25	25	25	25

4.2   B. Clumsy Limited have been successful in manufacturing home computers and until recently were able to show a modest profit.

However, due to increasing inflation the company has not been able to reflect increased costs in selling prices and, on a number of occasions, has sold at a loss.

The company is also currently developing a revolutionary micro computer. Development costs are continually rising and no target date has been set for trials. There has also not been any financial evaluation undertaken, nor any budgets set for the project.

The following information is available, having been extracted from the accounts for the year ended 31st October 1990.

	£'m
Stock	1,500
Vehicles	2,500
Bank Overdraft	1,000
Debtors	3,000
Share Premium	20
Turnover	27,200
Plant and Machinery	15,000
Profit and Loss Account	-500
Creditors	4,000
Profit/(Loss) Before Tax	-150
Issued Share Capital	500
Land and Buildings	3,000
Interest Payable	2,500
Long Term Loan	20,000
Cash	20

Directors:

B. Clumsy (Chairman/Managing)

S.O. Soft (Production)

A. Blunder (Research)

I. Clumsy (Shareholder)

REQUIRED

1.   Prepare a Profit and Loss Account and Balance Sheet from the financial data provided.

2.   Calculate appropriate ratios to show how the company has performed for the year.

4.3   Obtain the published accounts for a company of your choice and produce a diary of events for a two year period. Calculate profitability and liquidity ratios, and use the diary of events.

4.4   Explain the differences in methodology, analysis and interpretation between Altman's 1968 ratio model and Robertson's 1983 ratio model.

4.5   Describe and evaluate Argenti's defects, mistakes and symptoms approach.

4.6   Under what circumstances could Argenti's non-financial method identify possible failures at an earlier date than either the traditional ratios or ratio models.

4.7   A colleague has informed your managing director about the value of ratio models for measuring corporate financial health. Produce a brief overview of such models in relation to traditional ratio analysis.

INTERNATIONAL DIFFERENCES IN FINANCIAL REPORTING

LEARNING OBJECTIVES

When you have finished studying this chapter and completed the exercises you should be able to:

❏ Discuss the attempts made to classify international financial reporting practices.

❏ List the discriminating factors of international financial reporting which may constitute long-run fundamental differences between countries.

❏ Comment on the observable differences in financial reporting between EC member states.

❏ Outline the steps which have been taken towards the harmonisation of financial reporting within the EC.

❏ Identify the differences in financial reporting between the UK and USA.

❏ Comment on the present position of international standard setting for financial reporting.

5.1   Introduction

Considerable international differences in financial reporting are a fact of life which have really come to the fore with the growth of multinational corporations. This growth highlighted the need for accountants to know about accounting and financial reporting practices other than their own and encouraged support for a set of standardised accounting practices that would cross national frontiers. However, many differences still remain, the implications of which are that caution must be exercised in attempting to analyse and draw conclusions about the published results provided by companies from different countries.

To some extent events like the moves towards legal harmonisation in the European Community (EC) have helped to reduce some differences, but much still remains to be done even to achieve substantial comparability between EC member states. In this chapter we commence with a review of the attempts that have been made to classify financial reporting practices and to identify the main areas in which differences in practices seem to exist. Thereafter, we focus specifically upon practices and developments within the EC, and the USA. It is important to recognise the enormity of this subject area and hence the reason for focusing attention upon two key geographic areas. However, the harmonisation of accounting and financial reporting practices has not only been localised to specific geographic areas like the EC. International initiatives that have been undertaken are reviewed in the final section of this chapter.

5.2   International financial reporting classifications

There have been many attempts at classifying financial reporting practices with a view to revealing underlying structures and sources of difference. First, a number of subjective classifications have been suggested. For example, *Mueller (1967)* proposed the following four group classification:

1. Accounting within a Macroeconomic Framework. In this case, the development of accounting is as an adjunct to national economic policies (e.g. Sweden).

2. The Microeconomic Approach. This is most relevant to a market-oriented economy with individual private business as the focus of economic affairs (e.g. the Netherlands).

3.   Accounting as an Independent Discipline. In this case the system develops in response to solutions adopted for various problems faced. Theory plays a minor role and may only be used to justify practical solutions (e.g. UK and USA).

4.   Uniform Accounting. In this case, systems develop as part of the administrative control of business. As a consequence, accounting can be used to measure performance, allocate funds, assess the size of industries and resources, control prices, collect taxation, manipulate sectors of business, and so on. It typically involves standardisation of definitions and measurements (e.g. France).

Various other subjective classifications have also been proposed such as that focusing upon zones of influence (the *American Accounting Association, 1977*) identified the following zones:

❏ British
❏ Franco-Spanish-Portuguese
❏ Germanic-Dutch
❏ United States
❏ Communistic

This classification includes the influence of different political ideologies by recognising the communistic zone, however no classification, subjective or otherwise, has been acknowledged as being totally comprehensive. For example, in considering zones of influence the place of religious ideology cannot be ignored particularly with recent events in the Middle East.

In addition to purely subjective approaches, others have produced classifications based upon statistical techniques. Following the publication of a worldwide survey of accounting principles and reporting practices by *Price Waterhouse International* in 1973, 1975 and 1979, a number of researchers used clustering techniques to develop classifications. Both subjective and statistical classification approaches have been criticised for a lack of:

❏ precision in the definition of exactly what is to be classified;
❏ hierarchy and any clear relationship between the groups classified;
❏ judgement in the selection of important discriminating features, and;
❏ a model against which to compare any statistical results.

An alternative classification concerned with overcoming the criticisms of earlier approaches has been proposed by *Nobes (1980)*. His research was directed specifically at:

❏ public companies;
❏ chosen from the developed Western world, and;
❏ reporting practices concerned with measurement and valuation.

Nobes produced a hypothetical classification which was based upon fourteen countries which included all countries viewed as being important in achieving international comparability i.e. France, Japan, Netherlands, UK, USA and West Germany. His hierarchy used labels borrowed from biology and was tested by him against the following nine discriminating factors of financial reporting practices, which he considered may constitute long-run fundamental differences between countries:

1. Type of users of the published accounts of the listed companies.

2. Degree to which law or standards prescribe detail and exclude judgement.

3. Importance of tax rules in measurement.

4. Conservatism/prudence, e.g. valuation of buildings, stocks, and debtors.

5. Strictness of application of historic cost (in the historic cost accounts).

6. Susceptibility to replacement cost adjustments in main or supplementary accounts.

7. Consolidation practices.

8. Ability to be generous with provisions (as opposed to reserves) and to smooth income.

9. Uniformity between companies in the application of rules.

Nobes found very strong support for the primary 'micro/macro' split and considerable support for the more detailed groupings.

More recent research based upon accounting practices in the USA and Switzerland by *Pratt and Behr (1987)* has attempted to explain external reporting systems in terms of the costs of transactions in capital markets. They argue that the size, complexity, and diversity of capital transactions, the wide distribution of ownership, the ratio of owners to managers, and the opportunistic nature of the market participants in the USA underlie the creation, implementation, and maintenance of extensive and costly controls on managerial reporting behaviour. Such controls reduce transaction costs by leading managers to provide unbiased reports and therefore generate a flexible and dynamic standard-setting process, an extensive set of reporting regulations, high levels of auditor liability and standards, and many legally enforceable contracts among capital market participants. By contrast, Switzerland has a relatively small, closely held, and centrally controlled companies which are owned and managed by individuals who value co-operation and loyalty. The incentive is insufficient in Switzerland to expend the resources required for an extensive external reporting system. The consequence is that there is a slow and cumbersome standard-setting process, poorly specified reporting standards leaving much to the manager's discretion, limited emphasis on audit quality, very little auditor liability, and virtually no legally enforceable contracts among capital market participants.

It cannot be ignored that the accounting practices adopted by countries and therefore differences in international practice are influenced significantly by political change. As we will discuss in the next section, the creation and development of the European Community (EC) has had a significant influence upon the financial reporting practices of member states. Similarly the changes which have taken place, and which are still occurring in Eastern Europe, will have implications for the accounting practices of these countries. There, with the movement towards a free market economy approach significant changes will be necessary, the pace of which will doubtless be accelerated by the development of business relationships between Western and Eastern European companies.

As you will doubtless appreciate from this brief review of international financial reporting classifications, the international accounting scene is very complex and in a chapter such as this it is only possible to provide an overview. In fact, this overview is also of necessity focused and directed. Particular attention is given in the next section to differences within the European Community and thereafter a comparison of UK with USA practices. However, there have also been an important part played by various international bodies with implications far wider than Europe and the USA, which is discussed in the final section of this chapter.

5.3 Financial reporting in the European Community

*N*obes' classification of international accounting and financial reporting practices was undertaken prior to the implementation of European Community (EC) directives concerned with legal harmonisation among member states. As we will demonstrate, such directives have had, and will continue to have, an important influence upon accounting practices by EC member states, but there are substantial obstacles which cannot be ignored in gauging the likely immediacy of their impact. Obstacles that have been reviewed can be grouped under the following main headings:

❑   The legal system.

❑   Share ownership patterns.

❑   The influence of taxation.

❑   The strength, size and competence of the accounting profession.

5.3.1   The legal system

There are two primary systems of law in the EC. First, much of continental Europe is reliant upon Roman law (or codified law) which emanated from the Roman Empire and was transported to its conquest countries. It involves a detailed scheme of laws and penalties with a basic stance that there should always be a law on any matter and for all eventualities. This includes company law and therefore accounting such that specific rules are typically prescribed for matters like income measurement, asset valuation and the formats of financial reports.

The second system in use is common law where the law effectively legalises actions which are in common usage. The UK operates such a system and, in terms of accounting and financial reporting, the implications are that businesses have greater flexibility in publishing annual reports. However, as we will see in a later section of this chapter, the UK has moved closer to the rest of Europe in terms of financial reporting, thereby closing the gap between the two distinct legal systems to some extent.

Nevertheless it is important to be aware of and to understand the differences between the two legal systems which have important implications for accounting. The common law approach permits far more judgement than Roman Law with a consequent view of the discipline as being more of an art form than a science. The adoption of common and Roman Law has differed between European countries, such that in a number of EC countries (like France and West Germany) accounting is just another part of the law requiring detailed rules from the state, whereas, in some other EC countries (like the UK or the Netherlands), accounting is a mixture of art and science, in which the highly trained professional is left to exercise judgement.

5.3.2 Ownership, the raising of finance and business control

A second source of accounting differences is that the providers of finance and the users of accounting information differ markedly between EC members, thus necessitating different publication requirements. In West Germany, the banks are the most important providers, whilst in France and Italy the providers are a combination of bankers, family businesses and the government, but in the UK private and institutional shareholders are the primary source of company finance.

A good appreciation of the difference between the member states can be obtained by comparing the UK with West Germany. Whereas in the UK there is a well established   equity market providing the majority of corporate finance, in West Germany the majority of financing emanates from the banks. Furthermore, whilst the very large West German companies seek capital on their own (and foreign) stock exchange(s), the West German stock market is fairly under-developed, despite considerable encouragement in recent years by the government.

In West Germany the domination of the financial market by the banks can be linked to significant historical economic crises, like the inflationary periods in the 1920's and 1940's, when many businesses were put at considerable risk. The intervention by the banks at these times in the form of loans was important in preventing many business failures, but there was a price in the form of providing seats on the boards of the companies and in some cases control. One other important service of control by the banking fraternity in West Germany is the use of 'bearer shares' rather than 'registered shares'. Such bearer shares are typically kept at the bank for security purposes and it is normal practice for banks to be allowed to use a proxy vote on shareholders' behalf. This in effect means that banks without necessarily owning the majority of shares can have effective control. It should not, therefore, be too surprising that financial reporting in West Germany is heavily orientated towards creditors rather than shareholders, since the largest creditors are the banks themselves. Of course because the bank and its representatives usually have additional knowledge of the performance of a company, the financial reports may not always provide the most detailed information. However, in view of the creditor orientation, profits are generally calculated in a conservative manner and heavily reserve based to avoid making any dividend payments which might adversely affect creditors.

The impact of the differences between member states in terms of ownership and the raising of finance and business control is marked, with the UK and West Germany providing good examples of two extremes. However a better EC-wide appreciation can be gleaned when we consider that the UK with more than 2200 companies listed on its Stock Exchanges, has a much greater number of listed companies than other EC countries. Second, whilst there is a tradition of outside shareholders and published audited information in other EC countries, there is far greater reliance upon 'insiders' such as banks, the family and government representatives as main board directors.

5.3.3   The influence of taxation

A third source of difference can be attributed to the importance of taxation in determining accounting rules. In the UK by the time tax on business income first became important, there was a fully operational system of accounting and auditing already in place, such that taxable profit was based on accounting profit with adjustments. By contrast in much of continental

Europe many of the rules of accounting were determined by tax acts, because a coherent system of financial reporting was lacking.

The different rules for tax assessment within EC member states has important implications for financial reporting. Whereas in the UK tax computations are dealt with outside the accounts, many EC countries require that expenses like depreciation claimed for tax purposes must be the same as those in the accounts. One good example of the difference this can cause is the necessity to show any accelerated capital expenditure allowances for tax purposes in the accounts, which would not be permissible under the 'true and fair view' concept applied in the UK. West Germany represents a good example of an EC country in which the 'legal and correct view' as opposed to the 'true and fair view' is applied in accounting and financial reporting.

5.3.4   The accounting profession

The number of accountants working in the EC recognised by the Federation of European Accountants (FEE) varies markedly between member states. For example, the UK (including Northern Ireland) has over 165,000 of the 265,000 total number of accountants in the EC, followed by Italy with 46,000 and France with 19,000. However, West Germany with a broadly similar population size to France and the UK, has only 4,800 accountants.

This can be explained partly because a far stricter definition is applied to the definition of the professional accountant in most European countries than is the case in the UK. Those specialist areas of the accounting profession, like management accountancy, would not be included within the definition of an accountant in West Germany and in fact professionally qualified West German accountants (Wirtschaftsprufers) transferring to industry may not use their title. This is not to say that there is no such specialisation in these countries, rather it is dealt with outside the realms of the accounting profession, eg. by graduates of business economics. One other important source of difference for the number of accountants relates to the companies required to be audited. Whereas in the UK all limited liability companies irrespective of size must be audited this has not always been the case elsewhere. In fact as a result of EC legislation being implemented in West Germany a significant increase in the number of accountants is anticipated to deal with the tens of thousands of private limited companies now required to be subject to audit.

5.4 Observable differences between EC member states

The results of the diverse influences upon the development of accounting systems in individual EC member states are that many differences in accounting and financial reporting practices exist. Important differences are summarised below:

1. The adoption of a 'true and fair' as distinct from a' legal and correct view'. The low degree of legal intervention and the dominance of outside shareholders as financiers has been instrumental in the adoption of a true and fair view approach in the UK and the Netherlands. By contrast, the much higher level of legal intervention and the much lower reliance upon outside finance in some continental member states, like West Germany and France, has encouraged the development of a legal and correct approach. Even the moves towards legal harmonisation to be discussed in the next section have done little to bring greater uniformity in the calculation of accounting numbers in financial statements. Rather, the response has been to increase the level of and consistency in disclosure.

2. The relative influence of taxation rules and accounting principles. In some member states taxation rules have a substantial influence upon depreciation charges, bad debt provisions and asset valuations. This is in contrast with practices in the UK and the Netherlands where accounting values and measurements are not seriously affected by taxation requirements.

3. The relative emphasis upon accounting principles. In some EC countries like West Germany, conservatism plays a much greater role than matching, whereas in the UK the opposite is the case. Such conservatism is observable from the lack of capitalisation of development expenditure, the strictness of the application of historic cost accounting, the use of replacement cost when it gives the lowest valuation of stocks, the establishment of statutory reserves, and the maintenance of significant provisions for contingencies. An example of the lower emphasis upon accruals accounting in practice is the omission of proposed dividends in German balance sheets.

4. The use of provisions and reserves. This is a significant feature of continental EC countries, where, as discussed with reference to West Germany provisions for contingencies are not unusual.

5. The valuation bases adopted and the quantity and quality of supplementary information provided. This varies markedly between member states.

For example some EC countries with detailed legal and tax rules comple-
mentary with commercial accounting practices, like West Germany, have
valuation systems permitting a minimum of human judgement. The reason
is that such judgement and any resulting flexibility would make it difficult
for auditors to determine whether the law had been obeyed and might lead
to arbitrary taxation demands. For example, in West Germany the
required method of valuation is a very strict form of historical cost which
extends to the use of book values rather than fair values for the
consolidation of subsidiaries' assets. By contrast, in the Netherlands some
companies have published replacement-cost financial statements since the
early 1950s.

The quantity and quality of supplementary information varies considerably between EC member countries. Earlier we discussed how ownership
and control serves to influence the quantity and quality of information
provided in West Germany. These countries with a wide distribution of
ownership, and where the suppliers of finance do not have inside
information, like the UK, are far more likely to require a greater quantity
of good quality supplementary information than in countries such as West
Germany.

6. Consolidation practices vary considerably. In the UK consolidation has
   been a feature of practice since the early decades of this century, because
   of the predominance of shareholders, the complex structures of businesses
   and the absence of inflexible laws. By contrast, in West Germany and
   France substantial moves towards consolidation have only occurred
   during the 1980s and in yet other member states consolidation is still a
   relative rarity. However, moves towards comparability in practice are
   likely to occur with the gradual implementation of the 7th Directive (which
   is discussed later).

7. The degree of uniformity of practice within EC countries. At one extreme
   France has operated a uniform system of accounting since 1957 when the
   Plan Compatible General (PCG) was first implemented. PCG operates via
   a chart of accounts which is prescribed in law not only as to description
   but also through a decimalised numbering system, to the ordering,
   grouping and summarisation of accounts. This system was modified in
   1983 for implementation in 1984-85 as the PCG-R ('Plan Compatible
   General Revise') to achieve compliance with the 4th Directive (which is
   discussed in the next section).

The PCG-R is designed to serve the French fiscal authorities. It requires
a profit and loss account, together with back-up schedules for fiscally
important reserve movements, to be forwarded to the tax office three
months after the year end. Furthermore, this return is required on standard
preprinted forms, or their precise equivalents. As a consequence of such
requirements to comply with the tax law many companies under the old

PLG plan used to economise their effort by limiting their accounts to the fiscally required format. An opposing influence was created by PCG-R which required a change from a 'regular and sincere' view to one which is 'true and fair'.

Thus, the influence of anglo-saxon accounting practice has been marked in recent times in France with the implementation of a 'true and fair view' and the requirement to provide expanded information such as that typically available in the notes to the accounts. However, a requirement for uniformity still exists in France which is not to be found in other EC countries. Consider the UK for example which, as shown in Chapter 2, has a regulatory framework with no uniformity requirements.

8. The presentation of financial statements. Most UK companies adopt the vertical format which allows net working capital, net assets and shareholders' funds to be shown, whilst the typical West German two-sided double-entry format does not permit this. Furthermore, a West German balance sheet may also show current profit at the base of the liabilities side, current losses as an asset, and bad debt provisions as a liability. The double-entry logic is beyond question but does not help in providing a clear portrayal of the company's financial position.

5.5   EC harmonisation

The removal of different business practices between EC member states has been in increasing evidence. This has included efforts to harmonise accounting practice via EC directives as a small part of an overall programme directed at company law. Directives are a means of effecting the same degree of protection to members and third parties, such as creditors, in all EC member countries.

It is vital to understand that investor protection is not the primary objective of harmonisation and its scope extends way beyond company members and the companies themselves. Furthermore, harmonisation affects all companies, not simply those which are listed or which have made a public issue of securities. Thus, the harmonisation endeavours must be distinguished from the capital market approach used as the basis for setting accounting standards in other parts of the world.

As indicated, the instrument used for harmonising company law is the directive. A directive can be considered to be a legal instrument addressed to EC member states which is binding as far as the result to be achieved is concerned, but individual member states are free to determine the form and method for its implementation. However, once a directive has been transposed into national law it is binding for all companies covered by it. Furthermore, national provisions which have been enacted must be interpreted in the light of the directive and it is insufficient to apply only national law. The key point is that the rules introduced by a directive should be interpreted in the same way throughout the EC and, if necessary, an interested party can request that a case is referred to the European Court of Justice to obtain a preliminary ruling.

Member states are given several years to implement directives. It must be borne in mind that harmonisation takes place in an environment which may be quite different between member states. For example, differences are observable in terms of the means by which corporate finance is raised, the relationship between accounting rules and tax rules, and the size of the home market. As a consequence, different implementation time-scales may be applied to different member states, with the potential for intervention by the EC for non-compliance. In most cases the accounting directives have established minimum requirements but companies or member states may go beyond these.

Five accounting directives have so far been adopted by the EC the following three of which have been implemented in the UK:

1.   The Fourth Directive concerned with the annual accounts of limited liability companies.

2.   The Seventh Directive concerned with consolidated accounts.

3.   The Eighth Directive concerned with the approval of persons responsible for carrying out the statutory audit of accounting documents.

The Fourth Directive has had the most impact within the EC. This directive provides the basic structure of accounting within the EC and deals with the preparation of annual accounts, which must give a true and fair view of companies' assets, liabilities, financial position and profit or loss. It introduced harmonised layouts for the balance sheet and profit and loss account.

In terms of the balance sheet two formats, horizontal and vertical, are permitted by the Fourth Directive and member states may prescribe one or both and even allow companies to choose between them. The laws of the member states who have implemented this directive currently require or permit the following balance sheet layouts:

Figure 5.1   Balance sheet layouts permitted in EC

HORIZONTAL	VERTICAL OR HORIZONTAL
France	Luxembourg
Germany	Netherlands
Belgium	United Kingdom
Greece	Ireland
	Denmark

Source: European Survey of Published Financial Statements in the Context of the Fourth EC Directive, FEE, 1989.

With regard to the profit and loss account layout, the directive allows presentation by:

❏ type of expenditure, or

❏ type of operation.

Each of these can be presented horizontally or vertically.

A 1989 survey of EC member state profit and loss account requirements found the following methods of analysis to be used:

Figure 5.2   EC Profit and loss account requirements

Analysis by Type of Expenditure:	France (Horizontal and Vertical) Germany (Vertical) Belgium (Horizontal and Vertical)
Analysis by Type of Operation:	Germany (Vertical) Greece (Vertical)
By Type of Expenditure or Type of Operation:	Luxembourg Netherlands United Kingdom Ireland Denmark

Source: FEE Survey, 1989.

The Fourth Directive also lays down valuation rules based upon the historical cost principle, but which also allow member states to introduce alternative valuation methods (periodic revaluation, replacement value method, inflation accounting). It also deals with the notes to the accounts, the preparation of the annual report, the publication of the accounting documents and the audit of the accounts. Member states can relieve small and medium-sized companies of certain obligations under the directive. Such relief relates to the amount of information to be published and to the audit requirement, but not the valuation rules.

The Seventh Directive has been implemented in the UK as a result of the 1989 Companies Act. The directive deals with the preparation, publication and audit of consolidated accounts, and an important part deals with the conditions for their preparation. As indicated in Chapter 2, the concern of the directive is with establishing the principle of legal power of control in the preparation of published consolidated accounts. The legal principle of control underpinning consolidated accounts represents a significant change in UK practice but is far less alien to other member states where legal influences are more important.

Finally, the 1989 Companies Act has also implemented the EC Eighth Directive in the UK concerning the regulation of auditors. The rules within the Act, which are expected to be effective from 1991, will be a move towards the harmonisation of the qualifications of those people entitled to carry out company audits in the EC. It deals with qualifications and regulations to ensure that auditors are independent and that they carry out their audits properly and with integrity.

5.6   Financial reporting in the USA

Insofar as the UK and USA have apparently similar legal systems, wide private ownership of shares, tax systems which are to a large degree distinct from accounting, and a strong professional body of accountants there is considerable similarity between UK and USA accounting and financial reporting practices. One important area of difference to be aware of concerns legal influences. Other differences do exist as regards the setting of standards but these appear to be decreasing as a result of recent changes in standard setting in the UK.

5.6.1   Legal influences

One respect in which the legal system is not similar is that unlike the US, the UK legal system is not federal. This means that most companies are incorporated under state laws which are generally vague in regard to accounting requirements and do not specify the form or content of the books and accounts that a company must maintain. State laws do not usually require a company to publish or file financial statements with state authorities. In fact, unless a company operates in a regulated industry (banking, public utilities, insurance and transportation), or offers securities for sale to the public, it can avoid compulsory publication and audit requirements. Those registered with the Securities Exchange Commission (SEC) are subject to rigorous disclosure requirements and whilst many not registered do 'volunteer' to be audited, the vast majority of over 2.5 million US corporations face no compulsory legal constraints. This contrasts dramatically with the UK, where the smallest business that has limited liability has to comply with the majority of the extensive legal requirements including statutory audit.

Companies, whose securities are publicly traded and held by more than a specified number of shareholders, must submit quarterly and annual reports, including audited financial statements to the SEC. The SEC, created in 1934 after the Wall Street crash, has the statutory power to prescribe accounting and reporting standards and, as will be demonstrated, it has permitted the private sector to establish accounting standards.

5.6.2   Federal Accounting Standards Board (FASB) and Governmental Accounting Standards Board (GASB)

The Financial Accounting Standards Board (FASB), and the Governmental Accounting Standards Board (GASB) are recognised by both the SEC and the accounting profession as the authorities for determining Generally Accepted Accounting Principles (GAAPs) in the United States.

FASB Statements of Financial Accounting Standards and Interpretations provide the GAAPs which must be complied with. Technical Bulletins are issued by the FASB staff to provide guidance for applying existing accounting standards and for resolving issues not directly addressed in published standards. The GASB issues similar types of documents that establish standards for financial accounting and reporting by state, county, and municipal government entities.

Standard setting in the USA is distinct from the USA accounting profession and has been so since 1973 when FASB was set up with a substantial annual budget with a small full-time board, a large research staff and formal independence from the profession. It has issued more than 90 standards, which tend to be far more detailed than UK SSAPs and which have long enjoyed legal enforcement via the SEC.

USA GAAP produced by FASB and its predecessors require that assets are valued at depreciated historic cost, which contrasts with the common UK practice of reporting periodically revalued land and buildings. Another important difference is the use of the last-in-first-out (LIFO) method of stock valuation, which is virtually prohibited by the relevant UK accounting standard (SSAP 9).

There are areas of difference in reporting practice between the UK and the USA. Those really noteworthy are differences in profit and loss account and balance sheet layouts. Moves towards EC harmonisation since the implementation of the Fourth Directive account in part for some of the observable differences. Such differences are also exacerbated by differences in terminology for both the statements and their contents. A comparison of some important terms is provided in the following illustration:

Figure 5.3   *Examples of differences in key accounting terms*

UNITED KINGDOM	UNITED STATES OF AMERICA
Balance Sheet	Statement of Financial Position
Profit and Loss Account	Statement of Earnings
Stock	Inventories
Debtors	Accounts or (Current) Receivables
Creditors	Accounts Payable
Ordinary Shares	Common Stock
Share Premium Account	Paid-in Surplus

One other important difference is the publication of a Statement of Cash Flows which was discussed earlier in Chapter 2, and others noteworthy is the tradition of more detailed segmental reporting, the inclusion of two years as past comparatives in USA income and cash flow statements, and the prohibition of capitalising development expenditure in the USA.

Standard setting in the United States is not without its critics. For a number of years the Business Round Table, an association of chief executives of 200 of the biggest USA companies, has been complaining that FASB has been issuing standards that are incomprehensible and extremely expensive to implement. A good example of one such standard is that which came into effect in 1989 requiring all subsidiaries to be consolidated, thereby having the potential for very substantial effects upon the size of company balance sheets. Companies with large finance subsidiaries, such as *Ford*, *General Motors* and *General Electric* have been particularly affected.

5.7   International standardisation

Worrld-wide, there are in excess of twenty national financial accounting standard-setting organisations or boards with relatively little synchronisation of activities between them. From a political perspective, national financial accounting standard setting the world over arises as a result of:

1. Purely political action to be found predominantly in France and West Germany, where national legislative action decrees accounting standards.

2. Private professional action to be found in Australia, Canada, and the UK (until very recently) whereby accounting standards are set and enforced by private professional actions alone.

3. A mixture of public and private action typified by the USA and which countries like Japan seem to be emulating, whereby standards are basically set by private sector bodies. These bodies behave as though they are public agencies and their standards are enforced through governmental actions.

4. Broadly mixed action, like that in the Netherlands, where not only accounting professionals and governmental agencies but also trades unions, industry and trade associations take an active direct hand in setting and enforcing accounting standards.

In an effort to reduce differences in national practices the following standard-setting efforts have been taking place:

1. International political bodies like the United Nations (UN), the Organisation for Economic Co-operation and Development (OECD), the European Community (EC) and the African Accounting Council (AAC), have sought to formulate various financial and non-financial reporting requirements in a purely political manner. Representation on their accounting committees or working groups is by treaty, and the selection process to choose an individual to represent a country is not necessarily based on accounting expertise but, rather, on political considerations.

2. International professional accounting organisations that deal with various professional issues such as auditing standards, educational requirements and ethical standards for the profession in the international setting. Included within such organisations are the International Federation of Accountants (IFAC), the Federation of European Accountants (FEE) and the Associacion Interamericana de Contabilidad (AIC).

One other international accounting organisation which plays an important role is the International Accounting Standards Committee (IASC). This body, with its headquarters in London, was formed in 1973 to formulate accounting standards to be observed in the presentation of financial statements. The IASC is closely linked with the IFAC by virtue of common membership and financial support. How these two bodies differ is generally not well understood but in essence the distinction is in terms of the breadth of their respective objectives. Whilst IFAC's broad objective is to develop and enhance a co-ordinated worldwide accountancy profession with harmonised standards, the IASC is concerned specifically with international standard setting. It is accepted by IFAC, which recognises the complete authority of the IASC in the setting of international accounting standards and has undertaken to support its work and not to establish any other committee to work in the area of accounting standard setting.

It is important to realise that the IASC has no legitimate legal or political power. Its role is of an advisory nature and its recommendations must be adopted at the national level before any real implementation is possible. For example, international standards have no direct application in the UK. However, the provisions of international standards are, as far as possible, incorporated into UK standards, so that only one document needs to be consulted i.e. the UK standard. The Stock Exchange requires UK companies to comply with UK SSAPs and foreign companies with a listing in the UK to comply with the IASC standards.

Finally, there are three really noteworthy political organisations- the UN, OECD, and the EC. Developments within the EC have already been reviewed, but a complete picture of the international scene is incomplete without a brief review of the work of the UN and the OECD.

The UN has been at work since 1977 promulgating accounting standards at the committee level. Technical papers have been developed which contain many specific accounting standards regarding the substance of corporate annual reports as well as rules for such issues as consolidation. Much of the UN effort has been directed towards multinational enterprises, where the concern has been to extract data which developing nations do not feel powerful enough to extract via national controls. These data are primarily oriented toward employment information and technology transfers. The UN is powerless to enforce its recommendations.

The OECD began its involvement with international accounting standards in 1976. Because it is made up of developed countries it represents a different view from that adopted by the UN. This can be seen from the standards recommended by the OECD which ignore the recommendations of the UN to expand the data set contained in corporate annual reports. They tend to be distillations of national standards already used in the countries represented and is not generally considered to have broken any new ground with any of its recommendations. Similar to the UN, but in contrast to the EC discussed earlier, the OECD is powerless to enforce its recommendations.

APPENDIX A

International accounting standards

IAS Number	Title
1	Disclosure of accounting policies
2	Valuation and presentation of inventories in the context of historical cost system
3	Consolidated financial statements
4	Depreciation accounting
5	Information to be disclosed in financial statements
6	Accounting responses to changed prices
7	Statement of changes in financial position
8	Unusual and prior period items and changes in accounting policies
9	Accounting for research and development activities
10	Contingencies and events occurring after balance sheet data
11	Accounting for construction contracts
12	Accounting for taxes on income
13	Presentation of current assets and current liabilities
14	Reporting financial information by segment
15	Information reflecting the effects of changing prices
16	Accounting for property, plant and equipment
17	Accounting for leases
18	Revenue recognition
19	Accounting for retirement benefits in the financial statements of employers
20	Accounting for government grants and disclosure of government assistance
21	Accounting for the effects of changes in foreign exchange rate
22	Accounting for business combinations
23	Capitalisation of borrowing costs
24	Related party disclosures
25	Accounting for investments
26	Accounting and reporting by retirement benefit plans
27	Consolidated financial statements and accounting for investments in subsidiaries

Exercises

5.1 What classifications have been suggested for international financial reporting and are any of particular use in accounting for international differences in practice?

5.2 What do you understand by European Community harmonisation in financial reporting? What part do directives play in achieving harmonisation?

5.3 What is meant by international standardisation in financial reporting practices? How does EC harmonisation fit within such standardisation?

5.4 Describe major obstacles which prevent consistency in financial reporting in the European Community.

5.5 Describe how financial reporting in the EC differs from that in the UK.

5.6 Describe how financial reporting in the USA differs from that in the UK.

MANAGEMENT ACCOUNTING: BUDGETING AND BUDGETARY CONTROL

LEARNING OBJECTIVES

When you have finished studying this chapter and completed the exercises you should be able to:

❏   Identify the diverse range of organisations to which budgeting is appropriate.

❏   Outline the activities which can be identified as being an integral part of the budgeting process.

❏   Comment on the effect of human behaviour with regard to budget setting and budgetary control.

❏   Prepare and interpret cash budgets.

❏   Prepare the main budget financial statements including profit and loss account, cash flow forecast and balance sheet.

❏   Understand the key elements in budget administration.

6.1   Introduction

In earlier chapters we have discussed accounting and financial reporting with reference to the published accounts required to be produced by quoted companies in the UK, other European Community countries, and the USA. Rather than the popularly held view of accounting as being a science with distinct and clear-cut rules and procedures we have seen that it involves considerable human judgement, choice, and discretion. As you will see in this chapter the problem of judgement, choice and discretion feature very strongly in determining the form that accounting procedures used internally will take.

This chapter provides an introduction of what has come to be termed management accounting. You will find that it includes much with which you have gained some familiarity in earlier chapters. For example, in our discussion of budgeting you will encounter profit and loss accounts, cash flow forecasts and balance sheets. However, their form may well be different. Such differences are commonplace because organisations develop internal accounting procedures to suit their own individual needs which are not subject to no mandatory requirements. Unlike financial reporting, there is no formalised regulatory framework, however, you will find that the practices adopted by professional accountants will be similar. This is because of professional training and also the need for the internal accounting system to relate to the published accounts and auditing requirements.

One other key point worthy of note is that the orientation of internal management accounting is necessarily different. It is not backward looking but forward looking in meeting the needs of managers to run the business, rather than reporting results to shareholders and other interested parties, it serves a different purpose. To manage current and future events various members of the organisation will be reliant upon accounting information which, because it is prospective and deals with uncertainty, is usually less accurate. Timeliness of information may well be traded off against precision, something that clearly is not possible in published accounts which have to be audited and must be precise, if out-of-date.

This is not the only chapter about management accounting. In fact this and the two subsequent chapters are concerned with management accounting issues. The distinction between these three chapters is that the focus of attention in the first is upon more routine issues in management accounting like budgeting and budgetary control, whereas the others are concerned with the use of management accounting for responding to decisions that will usually have to be analysed and taken on a more ad-hoc basis.

Before we consider the main focus of attention in this chapter in the form of budgeting and budgetary control it is appropriate to introduce one important area of management accounting, cost accounting. Pick up most books on management accounting and you will usually find a substantial section devoted to cost accounting. In fact management accounting has its origins in cost accounting and whilst the subject area is important in its own right, it is only reviewed briefly here simply because its detailed study is of most relevance to the professional management accountant and not the professional manager.

To what does cost accounting relate? At its simplest the concern with cost accounting is to determine what it costs to produce a good or provide a service. This can be very straightforward in a one product or one service organisation where all costs can be clearly identified with the product/service being provided. However, very few such organisations exist and in a multi-product or multi-service environment procedures have to be found and used if costs are to be identified with that which is provided. If you refer to cost accounting texts you will discover that procedures have been developed primarily in manufacturing organisations to deal with the cost accounting problems of different types of operation. Thus, you will encounter descriptions and discussions about cost accounting techniques and approaches for organisations producing bespoke one-off products, and those dealing with batch operations, process operations and long-term contracts. These techniques will focus upon the various elements of cost like labour and materials and the problems of accounting for raw materials, work in progress and finished goods.

What is important for you to understand about cost accounting is that it is also not a science, considerable judgement necessarily has to be exercised. The reliance upon judgement in dealing with an uncertain future means that most organisations have devices for checking and tracking progress. Such devices are often manifested in a system of budgetary control whereby expectations about the future are formally expressed in a short-term plan, usually known as a budget, against which progress is regularly monitored. Actual deviations from the budget known as variances will often be calculated and reported to individuals responsible for their achievement.

6.2   Budgeting

The result of budgeting we will illustrate as being a set of financial statements in the form of a profit and loss account, balance sheet and cash flow forecast. These statements prepared and approved prior for a defined future period of time, for the purpose of attaining specific objectives.

Budgeting is used in organisations of all types to assist in the development and co-ordination of plans, to communicate these plans to those who are responsible for carrying them out, to secure co-operation of managers at all levels and as a standard against which actual results can be compared. You will find budgeting used in a diverse range of organisations and activities including:

❏ Central and local government.

❏ The health service.

❏ Education.

❏ Large companies.

❏ Small businesses (such as the local garage).

❏ Churches.

❏ Charities.

❏ Television and radio networks.

❏ Local clubs.

❏ The family.

The analogy of our discussions with the family budget may be helpful for you to bear in mind. For example, a budget could be compared with the preparation of a shopping list. In its preparation we would be able to make changes to the list to ensure that personal objectives were met both in terms of goods obtained and money spent. During the actual shopping activity, regular comparisons of actual spend against budget could be undertaken and, if necessary, changes could be made to attain our objectives.

Why budget? Consider the alternative of shopping without making a mental or written list. The outcome might be that many of the important items would not be bought and/or a situation of overspend reached, a feature of many bankrupt companies!

Successful budgeting is not always easy to achieve particularly in large complex organisations. To achieve success attention has to be paid to a number of activities which can be identified as being an integral part of the budgeting process, these are:

❑ Defining objectives.

❑ Planning.

❑ Organising.

❑ Controlling.

❑ Co-ordinating.

❑ Communicating.

❑ Motivating.

6.2.1   Defining objectives

The budgeting process cannot be seriously undertaken until top management has defined the objectives of the business to be achieved during the period of the budget. Such objectives should be stated in terms in which they can be measured. Objectives might include:

❑ To achieve a specified percentage return on capital employed.

❑ To reduce borrowing by a specified amount.

❑ To increase market share by a specified percentage.

❑ To introduce a specified number of new products.

❑ To reduce labour turnover by a specified figure.

The above are only a few examples of possible business objectives and you will doubtless be aware that they will usually relate to a range of activities within a company and not necessarily be restricted to purely financial or profit orientated objectives.

Once top management has agreed overall company objectives then particular areas of responsibility can be assigned to lower levels of management and the budgetary process can commence.

6.2.2   Planning

Planning within the budgeting process typically takes place by the expression of departmental, functional or cost centre activities for the forthcoming year within individual budgets. These budgets will relate to the business objectives set by or agreed with top management for the year and will usually be a part of the overall budget, commonly called the 'master budget'.

The advantage of good planning is that it provides the opportunity to evaluate available alternative proposals designed to achieve the best utilisation of resources to meet the objectives specified.

Planning, by its very nature, requires an in-depth examination of possible future events. It offers the means to evaluate alternative proposals and should reduce uncertainty and risk. Is current or past information relevant? Planning is essentially about the future, such that results and information from the past is usually only relevant as the basis from which to forecast.

There are many different types of plans and budgets which will need to be developed, examples of which are:

❑   Sales plans.

❑   Purchasing plans.

❑   Manpower plans.

❑   Research and development plans.

❑   Capital expenditure plans.

❑   Marketing plans and business plans.

Alternative scenarios can be analysed via what is commonly referred to as a master budget which is illustrated in *Figure 6.1*. This consists of a profit and loss account, balance sheet and cash flow forecast. Once approved the master budget allows management to plan and co-ordinate the future direction of the business.

Figure 6.1   Master budget and individual budgets

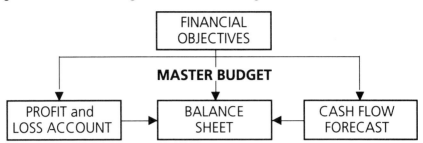

6.2.3   Organising

It is important to realise that a budget will not happen on its own. The more physical and human resources that are involved the less likely is it to be conceived or achieved without good organisation.

Organising necessitates an understanding of the organisational structure, the tasks, the processes and systems, and the people involved if any agreed budget is to have any chance of success. In particular its success requires the following characteristics which you can probably relate only too well to budgeting within your own household:

❑   The definition of the organisation structure so that possible areas of overlap can be identified and removed or at least reduced.

❑   The identification of tasks, responsibilities and the methods by which individuals will be measured.

❑   The means by which the budgeting activities will take place, including any training and/or documentation required.

❑   The recognition that budgeting can only be achieved through people and that they are an integral part of the process and any systems developed.

6.2.4   Controlling

There has to be a means of monitoring performance so that actual results are continuously compared against budget, any deviations recorded and fed back in order that corrective action can be taken if considered necessary. Control is best achieved by comparing actual performance with expectations via a process known variance analysis, and by using management by exception such that managers only pay considerable attention to those items in their budgets which are exceptional.

Feedback from the plan, after the event or before the event, is an essential ingredient to the control process. An example of after the event feedback would be where the result of actual overspending is recorded and reported. As a consequence of this feedback the manager responsible may be able to take corrective action either to adjust future spending so that it conforms to the agreed budget, or request additional resources.

Of at least equal importance is before the event feedback whereby proposed spending would be measured against the budget.

6.2.5   Co-ordinating

Co-ordinating is an integral part of the budgeting process. Having organised, as discussed earlier, there is the need to look at the sequencing and inter-relationship of the individual budget components.

It is difficult to view any process without considering its effect on other processes. Therefore, co-ordinating can be seen as a balancing activity. It is a procedure which seeks to allocate priorities based on some predetermined agreement, and attempts to unite a number of individual activities into a whole.

The different viewpoints of the co-ordinating process are usually apparent when agreeing company objectives. The activities will take into account the overall balance within the company, also such things as competitors and customers, economic political and social change, and if there is a need to change the future direction of the company.

6.2.6   Communicating

Within any budgeting system involving more than one person communication is important. For successful budgeting it is essential that relevant details are communicated to those managers who are responsible for carrying out certain tasks. Communicating is another integral part of the budgeting process to ensure that:

❏   objectives;

❏   guidelines;

❏   completed budgets and revisions;

❏   actual results;

❏   deviations from budget;

❏   corrective action to be taken, and;

❏   revisions to be included into forecasts are provided to relevant management in an appropriate form.

If the communication process is to be successful it is essential that managers are provided with suitable documentation which describes just how the budgeting system works. This should be offered in 'jargon free' terms because jargon hinders communication.

6.2.7   Motivating

A key part of the budgeting process hinges upon the motivation of the individual involved. The most successful budgeting systems will be those that achieve a 'fit' between individual and organisational objectives. Unfortunately, all too often benefits can be achieved for individuals rather than the organisation and, for the organisation at the expense of the individual, rather than for both the individual and the organisation.

The problem is how can we know that if we take certain actions individuals will respond in a particular manner? For example, why do some managers like the budgeting process? Is it the challenge? Is it the power that information gives? Is it the 'games' they can play? Is it because they understand the system? Is it because they can see the purpose of the budgeting system? Is it because they are winning?

If there are two key 'strands' to be developed from these pre-requisites they are that successful budgeting is dependent upon a well developed administrative system and should encourage human behaviour beneficial to both the individuals involved and the organisation.

6.3 Budgetary control

We have reviewed the key facets of the budgeting process, however, as we have indicated a plan alone is usually quite inadequate and there must be a means of monitoring and keeping it on the required course. We have alluded to this being achieved by budgetary control which specifically is concerned with:

❑ the comparison of actual results against budget;

❑ the identification, recording and communication of controllable differences, and;

❑ the taking of corrective action either to maintain budget levels or to replan to meet recent developments.

The comparison of actual against budgeted performance requires that the budget is divided into twelve monthly periods or 13 four weekly periods against which data collected about actual results for each period may be compared.

It is important to ensure that the comparison of budgeted and actual performances matches like with like. For example, if actual sales volumes are higher, then certain items in the budget which move in line with sales will have to be increased. If this process was omitted a simple comparison would show an overspending on certain items (e.g. sales commissions) the result of which would be to record an unrealistic difference from budget. It is also important that only controllable items should be included for purposes of analysis. For example, items outside the company's control such as a strike at a suppliers factory should be omitted. Any corrective action required should be geared towards the achievement of revisions to the annual budget which have been required to meet changing circumstances and targets for the current budget period. How is this achieved? Let us assume that a company compares actual against budget every four week period. At the end of the first period a comparison is made against budget. Budget holders are required to forecast the effect any deviations from budget will have on the year end position and this is incorporated into a years forecast or out turn. At the end of period six, budget holders will have six periods of actual results and will be asked to forecast for the remaining six or seven periods. As the number of actual periods increase the importance of the original budget is reduced and the years forecast takes on a higher level of significance.

Budgetary control procedures are reliant for their satisfactory operation upon the actions of employees and managers. The best designed system can and will not work unless the effect of human behaviour is recognised.

Ideally a budgetary control system should be designed and operate in such a way as to enable corporate objectives to be achieved more effectively. How can this be achieved? A number of studies of budgeting have shown that the more participative is the process of setting budgets, the more effective they are likely to be in committing personal motivation towards their achievement. These studies develop the work undertaken in the 1950s by the American psychologist *Argyris*, who demonstrated the ineffectiveness of budgetary control upon line management where at least the following conditions prevailed:

❏ only results were reported with no comment as to reasons for their occurrence;

❏ the existence of inflexible budget officers, and;

❏ increased pressure was caused by increasing targets, always set unrealistically high.

From these research studies and others certain key points have been identified which we have summarised for you by way of a checklist. You might care to think about each of these in relation to your own budgetary control system with a view to identifying areas for improvement:

❏ When setting budgets real participation should be sought from those involved.

❏ Information flow should be downwards (to subordinates), sideways (to relevant peers) as well as upwards to superiors.

❏ Managers should know exactly for what costs and revenues they are responsible.

❏ Communication should be encouraged in the language of those involved, e.g. graphs and charts, or numbers to be sold this week to meet a target may be more appropriate to some members of the workforce.

❏ Misunderstanding caused by the presentation of information should be minimised whenever possible. Financial reports by accountants are often misunderstood, a situation which should be resolved by 'encouraging' explanations by accounting staff.

❏ The control system should be as supportive as possible rather than relying upon it as a policing mechanism.

❏ Budgets set should be attainable and not just an ideal, far too tight to make them truly achievable.

6.4 Zero based budgeting

I n many organisations, budgeting is typically an incremental activity whereby adjustments are made to the most recent budget upon the basis of future expectations. In many cases this involves making some adjustment for different levels of activity and for expectations about inflation. However, sometimes such an approach is inadequate to achieve the desired degree of cost control because, for example, the adjustments made to the budgets over the years no longer correspond sufficiently with the costs of the operations being supported.

Concern about the ability of conventional budgetary control systems to move away from realistic requirements over time encouraged the development of what is termed zero based budgeting (ZBB) and its more recent derivative priority based budgeting (PBB). ZBB adopts a different stance by requiring that a budget is developed from scratch according to what is required to provide a specified level of service. This bottom-up as apposed to incremental approach is relatively demanding in terms of the time and resources required to develop the budget, but may yield substantial financial benefits.

6.5 The mechanics of budgeting

W e will now work through the preparation of a cash budget together with an interpretation of the results. This example will be followed by one which requires the preparation of the main financial statements.

6.5.1 Cash budget

A cash budget records the estimated cash inflow / outflow resulting from budgeted activity and shows monthly balances for the period under review. Therefore, the principal purpose for the preparation of a cash budget is to identify periods where there will be a shortage of cash and periods where there will be a surplus of cash.

The preparation of a cash budget requires assumptions to be made with regard to the phasing of the cash flows. In reality there is often substantial timing differences between the physical transaction and the cash transaction. The question is not "when did we sell the goods"?, but "when do we expect to be paid"? Similarly, not "when did we purchase these goods"?, but "when do we expect to pay for them?"

Preparation of a cash budget

From the following information prepare a cash budget for the six months to 30th June 1992. The estimated cash balance at 1st January 1992 is £4,000.

	Sales £	Purchases £	Wages £
1991			
November	40,600	24,500	
December	48,000	23,200	
1992			
January	34,200	16,600	5,600
February	36,400	18,900	6,200
March	38,500	20,300	6,350
April	42,500	22,100	6,500
May	43,400	24,400	6,650
June	47,100	27,200	6,800

a. Credit allowed to customers: 60% pay in one month
   40% pay in two months

b. Suppliers are paid one month in arrears

c. Other payments: £

January	Taxation	20,000
March	Equipment	40,000
June	Dividend	10,000

The steps to be taken in the preparation of a cash budget are provided in (*1 to 4*) which follow. The completed cash budget statement is shown in *Table 6.1.*

Step

1   Enter the opening cash balance in January which is given i.e. £4,000.

2   Calculate the receipts from debtors, 60% pay in one month, 40% pay in two months following the month of sale, therefore:

Cash received	60% of sales in	40% of sales in
January	December	November
February	January	December
March	February	January
April	March	February
May	April	March
June	May	April

3   Payment to creditors is delayed by one month. Therefore purchases in December will not be paid until January.

4   Complete the cash budget by entering the remaining figures and then calculate the monthly and cumulative balances to establish the cash flow picture.

Table 6.1   Cash Budget for the six months to 30th June 1992

	Jan £	Feb £	Mar £	Apr £	May £	Jun £
Part A						
Receipts						
Sales	45,040	39,720	35,520	37,660	40,900	43,040
Subtotal A	45,040	39,720	35,520	37,660	40,900	43,040
Part B						
Payments						
Creditors	23,200	16,600	18,900	20,300	22,100	24,400
Wages	5,600	6,200	6,350	6,500	6,650	6,800
Taxation	20,000					
Equipment			40,000			
Dividend						10,000
Subtotal B	48,800	22,800	65,250	26,800	28,750	41,200
Part C						
Balance (A-B)	-3760	16,920	-29,730	10,860	12,150	1,840
Part D						
Balance b/f	4,000	240	17,160	-12,570	-1,710	10,440
Balance c/f (C+D)	240	17,160	-12,570	-1,710	10,440	12,280

In this case there will be a cash shortage in March and April and we can use the statement to help identify the problem areas and possible courses of action. The main problem is in fact the purchase of the capital equipment in March. As an alternative we could:

❑   delay the purchase of the capital equipment;

❑   negotiate terms for delayed payment;

❑   negotiate finance for the capital equipment;

❑   arrange hire or lease;

❑   obtain additional bank finance;

❑   reduce credit period allowed to customers, and/or;

❑   increase credit period allowed by suppliers.

Each course of action involves the consideration of an additional set of variables before arriving at a decision. For example, the last two items on the list above both affect the trading environment. If a company attempts either, it could lose customers and/or suppliers.

In February, May and June the statement shows that there will be a surplus of cash. In this case a company should take steps to transfer funds into other activities which will generate interest. These include:

❑   bank deposit or building society;

❑   short-term money market. (Many large companies have departments whose function is to forecast closing cash positions on a daily basis and then negotiate terms on the overnight market).

6.5.2   Example: Preparation of main financial statements

In this example we start with an opening balance sheet and a number of budget assumptions and show the preparation of monthly trading accounts, monthly cash budget, budgeted profit and loss account for the period and a closing balance sheet.

The executives of Rusty and Dusty Musty Ltd are preparing budgets for the six months July to December 1991. They have produced the following financial objectives as guidelines for the assessment of the budget:

❑ To increase working capital by £150,000.

❑ To reduce borrowings (overdraft and long term loans) by £300,000.

❑ To achieve a 7% return on total assets.

❑ To reduce the gearing ratio by 0.15 to 1.

Estimated Balance Sheet as at 30th June 1991

	£'000	£'000	£'000
FIXED ASSETS	Cost	Depn	
Land and Buildings	650		650
Plant and Machinery	1,760	500	1,260
	2,410	500	1,910
CURRENT ASSETS			
Stock - Goods for resale		950	
Debtors		1,650	
Cash		70	
		2,670	
less CURRENT LIABILITIES			
Creditors	650		
Bank Overdraft	1,100		
		1,750	
Working Capital			920
Net Assets			**£2,830**

Financed as follows:	
Issued Share Capital	400
Profit and Loss Account	930
Shareholders' Funds	1,330
Long Term Loan (12% per annum)	1,500
	£2,830

a. The board has approved the purchase of a new machine in August 1991 costing £250,000

b. Salaries, assume to be 10 % of monthly sales
    Fixed costs estimated at £60,000 per month (all cash payments)

c. Depreciation to be charged at £24,000 per month

d. Interim dividend of £50,000 payable 15th July 1991

e. Sales and closing stock estimates:

	July £'000	Aug £'000	Sept £'000	Oct £'000	Nov £'000	Dec £'000
Sales	600	760	840	1000	680	520
Closing stock	1000	900	800	800	700	650

f. Creditors at 30th June 1991 are for purchases:

May	£270,000
June	£380,000

Debtors at 30th June 1991 are for sales:

April	£500,000
May	£600,000
June	£550,000

Assume the same credit periods will continue, i.e. two months for creditors and three months for debtors.

g. Gross profit to sales is budgeted at 30%.

Assume purchases to be the balancing figure for the preparation of the Monthly trading accounts

Monthly trading accounts

The monthly trading accounts record the physical transactions and balances. In this example we have been given a gross profit percentage and monthly forecast of closing stock. Purchases, are the balancing figure. Later we will use the summary when preparing the budgeted profit and loss account.

The following steps should be taken during the preparation of the monthly trading accounts. You can check the results in *Table 6.2*.

Step

1   Enter the sales and closing stock from note (e), then calculate the gross profit e.g. 30% of sales (30% of £6000 in July).

2   Enter the opening stock for July (£950) which is taken from the opening balance sheet, then enter the remaining opening stock figures, i.e. previous month's closing stock.

3   Cost of sales is the sum of sales less gross profit, e.g. for July: (£600 - £180) = £420.

4   Purchases will be the balancing figures and calculated as follows:

cost of sales + closing stock - opening stock, e.g. for July (£420 + £1,000 - £950) = £470.

Table 6.2. Monthly trading accounts
— for the six months ending 31st December 1991

	July £000	Aug £000	Sept £000	Oct £000	Nov £000	Dec £000	Summary £000
Sales	600	760	840	1,000	680	520	4,400
Opening Stock	950	1,000	900	800	800	700	950
Purchases	470	432	488	700	376	314	2,780
	1,420	1,432	1,388	1,500	1,176	1,014	3,730
Closing Stock	1,000	900	800	800	700	650	650
Cost of Sales	420	532	588	700	476	364	3,080
Gross Profit	**180**	**228**	**252**	**300**	**204**	**156**	**1,320**

Monthly cash budget

The preparation of the monthly cash budget follows a similar pattern to the earlier cash budget example *(see Table 6.1)*. At each stage, check the figures against *Table 6.3*.

Step

1   Enter the opening cash balance which is taken from the opening balance sheet.

2   Enter income from debtors. The example states a three month delay; therefore:

Sales	Cash received
April	July
May	August
June	September
July	October
August	November
September	December
October	
November	} closing debtor figure
December	

3   Enter payments to creditors which are delayed for two months. Therefore purchases from May to October will be paid for in July through to December. November and December purchases will remain unpaid and represent the closing creditor figure.

4   Complete the cash budget by entering the remaining figures then extract the monthly balances.

Table 6.3 *Monthly cash budget*
— *for the six months ending 31st December 1991*

	July £000	Aug £000	Sept £000	Oct £000	Nov £000	Dec £000	Summary £000
Part A							
Receipts							
Sales	500	600	550	600	760	840	3,850
Subtotal A	500	600	550	600	760	840	3,850
Part B							
Payments							
Creditors	270	380	470	432	488	700	2,740
Salaries	60	76	84	100	68	52	440
Dividend	50						50
Capital Expenditure		250					250
Fixed Costs	60	60	60	60	60	60	360
Subtotal B	440	766	614	592	616	812	3,840
Part C							
Balance (A-B)	60	-166	-64	8	144	28	10
Part D							
Balance b/f	70	130	-36	-100	-92	52	70
Balance c/f (C+D)	130	-36	-100	-92	52	80	80

Budgeted profit and loss account for the six months

Step

1 The figures for the first section of the profit and loss account (from sales down to gross profit) are taken from the summary column of the monthly trading accounts, *Table 6.2*.

2 There is no delay in the payment of wages or fixed costs therefore the totals can be taken from the summary column of the monthly cash budget, *Table 6.3*.

3 Calculate the interest payable for the six months (1,500 x 12% ÷ 2).

4 Enter depreciation then add salaries, fixed costs, interest payable and depreciation the sum of which should be deducted from gross profit to find the profit for the period (1,320 - 1,034 = 286)

Table 6.4 *Budgeted profit and loss account*
for the six months ending 31st December 1991`

	£'000	£'000
Sales		4,400
Opening Stock	950	
Purchases	2,780	
	3,730	
Closing Stock	650	
Cost of Sales		3,080
Gross profit		1,320
Salaries	440	
Fixed Costs	360	
Interest Payable	90	
Depreciation	144	
		1034
Profit for the Period		286
Dividend		50
Retained Profit		236

Budgeted closing balance sheet

The simplest way to prepare the closing balance sheet is to take each figure in turn from the opening balance sheet and

❏ if no change has occurred then enter the same figure in the closing balance sheet, or

❏ if change has occurred make the necessary adjustment then enter the revised figure in the closing balance sheet.

You will find that the preparation of the closing balance sheet helps to 'tie up' a number of figures which, until now have apparently been ignored. The closing balance sheet is illustrated in *Table 6.5* and the figures included were calculated as follows:

Step

1 Land and buildings - No change.

2 Plant and machinery: in this case additional capital has been spent and the provision for depreciation increased. Therefore the calculation is (£1,260 + £250 - £144) = £1,366.

3 Stock - This is the closing stock at December, i.e. £650.

4 Debtors - Sales for October, November and December will remain unpaid at the end of the period (£1,000 + £680 + £520 = £2,200)

5 Cash - This is the closing cash position at December, i.e. £80.

6 Creditors - Purchases for November and December will remain unpaid at the end of the period (£376 + £314 = £690).

7 Bank Overdraft - No change.

8 Interest payable - We calculated the interest payable and entered £90 into the profit and loss account. A similar entry is required in the closing balance sheet to recognise the liability.

9 Share Capital - No change.

10 Profit and Loss Account - This is found by taking the figure from the opening balance sheet and adding the profit for the period (£930 + £236 = £1,166).

11 Long-term Loan - No change.

Table 6.5   *Budgeted closing balance sheet as at 31st December 1991*

FIXED ASSETS	Cost £'000	Depn £'000	£'000
Land & Buildings	650		650
Plant & Machinery	2,010	644	1,366
	2,660	644	2,016
CURRENT ASSETS			
Stock - Finished Goods		650	
Debtors		2,200	
Cash		80	
		2,930	
less CURRENT LIABILITIES			
Creditors	690		
Bank Overdraft	1,100		
Interest Payable	90		
		1,880	
			1,050
Net Assets			3,066
Financed as follows:			
Issued Share Capital			400
Profit and Loss Account			1,166
Sharholders' Funds			1,566
Long Term Loan (12% per annum)			1,500
			3,066

Interpretation of budget statements

The cash budget, *Table 6.3* produces a satisfactory result if taken for the whole six month period. However, there is a period in the middle when the company will not be able to meet its cash commitments. The main problem is the purchase of capital equipment in August and we considered possible courses of action when reviewing the cash budget.

Further interpretation can be carried out by calculating a number of ratios to cover profitability, liquidity and gearing then comparing against the budget objectives stated earlier.

	Opening Balance Sheet	Closing Balance Sheet
Profitability	n/a	7.6%
Current ratio	1.53	1.56
Liquid ratio	0.98	1.21
Gearing ratio	1.13	0.96

To increase working capital by £150,000

The current ratio shows a slight increase by contrast with the much larger increase in the liquid ratio. This indicates that the company may have idle resources, that is, it either has too much in liquid assets (current assets minus stock), and/or is not stretching itself in terms of shortterm liabilities.

An examination of the net working capital position between the opening and closing balance sheets clearly shows an increase in working capital of £130,000 which does not meet this budget objective.

Reduce borrowing by £300,000

The assumptions contained in this budget revision do not meet this budget objective. There is no change in shortterm or longterm debt financing.

To achieve a 7% return on total assets for the period

The profitability ratio, i.e. profit before interest and taxation expressed as a percentage of total assets, shows a return of 7.6% for the period.

To reduce the gearing ratio by 0.15 to 1

This budget objective has been met. However, it will be achieved through retaining the profit for the period which in turn will increase equity.

Appendix A

Budget administration

What are the key elements in administering a budget? We recommend that you review those we provide and compare them with practice in your own organisation. See if you can identify possible areas for improvement.

Budget guidelines

Budget guidelines are a means of conveying important budget assumptions to budget holders. They should be prepared at least annually and should include various percentages for budget holders to apply expense items. They might also include information relating to overall movements in sales volumes, the increase/reduction in certain sectors of the business, or the requirement to implement a particular aspect of health and safety.

Budget manual

A budget manual should contain sufficient information to enable managers to operate the budgeting system within a particular business, division or department. It should explain all the terms which are used in the budgeting system and provide worked examples of the main documents. A budget manual should not only deal effectively with the detail that a budget holder requires, but also provide an overview of the total system.

Budget period

The main budget period within business is usually one year. However, many companies consider their three year plan to operate within the budgeting system. The usual method of operating such a three year plan is that the annual budget represents the first year of a three year plan. The second year is usually shown in less detail, with the third year simply taking a broad overview.

Budget factor

In any business there can be a number of factors which restrict its potential growth, a common one being sales volume. Whatever the factor that restricts potential growth it should be identified and made explicit. For example, if sales are considered to be such a factor then all other budgets should be prepared in an attempt to maximise sales. Other budget factors could include a shortage of skilled labour, shortage of materials, storage of material, storage space or a specific item of plant within the manufacturing process.

Budget timetable

In many large organisations budget preparation will often extend over the six months prior to the budget period. The complex nature of budget preparation demands that a detailed timetable be produced to ensure that each component within the overall activity will be completed in time for input into other components of the system.

Budget timetables should be produced to meet a number of key dates which relate to divisional and group board meetings.

Budget training

If the budgeting system is to succeed it is important that the budget administration should include management training in the processes and techniques appropriate to a particular business. Such training should involve guided in-company instruction by staff familiar with the system and the specific responsibilities. It is not desirable to leave an individual with the manual and the responsibility - the training should precede the responsibility.

Exercises

6.1 E. Tee Ltd. prepares cash budgets on a monthly basis. The following forecasts are available for the four months ending 31st March 1992.

	Purchases £000	Sales £000	Overhead expense £000	Wages £000
December 1991	90	270	33	57
January 1992	60	180	31	60
February	120	165	36	51
March	30	150	30	52

Other information is available as follows:

a   All purchases are on monthly credit terms - the suppliers being paid, less 2.5% cash discount, in the month following purchase.

b   20% of all sales are made on a cash basis, the remainder being sold to credit customers who pay in the month following the month of sale.

c   Overhead expenses include depreciation amounting to £4,500 each month. Payments are made in the month following the month in which expenses are incurred.

d   Wages are paid for in the month that they are incurred.

e   A new computer installation, costing £37,500, is to be paid for in February 1992. During March 1992, old fixtures and fittings, which originally cost £27,000 are to be sold for £1,500 cash.

f   The bank balance at 1st January 1992 is expected to be £30,000.

REQUIRED

1   Produce a cash budget in tabular style for the quarter ending 31st March 1992 showing the bank balance at each month end.

2   Comment on the results of your analysis, and suggest ways to deal with cash shortages and cash excesses.

6.2 Dream Ltd. is planning to open, on 1st January 1992, a new factory to manufacture tables.

Estimates for the first six months are as follows:

a   Sales will be £40,000 per month for the first three months and £60,000 per month thereafter. Payment for one half of these sales will be received in the month following the sale, the remainder will be received two months after the sale.

b   Production each month will equal that month's sales, i.e. no stocks.

c   Raw materials will cost 30% of sales value and will be paid for in the month following purchase.

d   Wages and salaries will cost 20% of sales value and will be paid in the month they occur.

e   Rent will be £40,000 per year, payable quarterly in advance.

f   Heat and light will cost £20,000 per year, payable at the end of each quarter.

g   Other expenses will cost £10,000 per month and will be paid at the end of each month.

h   Plant and machinery for the factory will be purchased on 1st January 1992 at a cost of £50,000 and will be paid for in ten equal instalments.

i   The company's rate of depreciation for plant and machinery is 25% per year.

j   The new factory will be provided with a bank balance of £25,000 at 1st January 1992.

REQUIRED

1   Prepare a monthly cash budget for the factory for the six months ending 30th June 1992.

2   Prepare a budgeted profit and loss account for the six motnhs ending 30th June 1992 and a balance sheet as at that date.

3   Advise management on any action which might be required from the information disclosed by the cash budget.

6.3   Alastair Dryant is planning to commence business as a manufacturer on the 1st January 1992. The business is to be financed from capital of £25,000 provided by Dryant on the 1st January 1992 and an overdraft limit of £15,000 agreed with the bank. Estimates of costs and revenues for the first six months are as follows:

a   Sales: January £9,000, February £12,000, March £18,000 and £20,000 per month thereafter. Half of the sales are expected to be for cash, the balance will be on one month's credit.

b   Production will take place during the month of sale, but raw materials are to be purchased in the month before production, except for the first month when two months' stock will be obtained. Raw materials are 40% of sales value. Payment is made for raw materials in the second month following their purchase.

c   Direct wages and other direct expenses are expected to be a further 30% of sales value per month, they will be paid for in the month incurred.

d   Fixed expenses are budgeted at £2,200 per month, paid for in the month incurred.

e   During December 1991 machinery will be delivered, the cost of which has been quoted at £48,000. It has been decided to depreciate this machinery at 10% per annum on cost, and allowance for depreciation has been included in fixed expenses. Payment for the machinery will be in four equal instalments commencing February 1992.

f   Dryant will draw a managers salary of £2,000 per month.

REQUIRED

1   A cash budget for the first four months.

2   Comment on the situation revealed by the cash budget.

6.4   The executives of P.C Ltd are preparing budgets for the six months July to December 1991.

The budgeted Balance Sheet as at the 30th June 1991

	£		£
		Fixed Assets	
Share Capital (£1 shares)	50,000	Land and Buildings	100,000
Profit and Loss Account	115,000	Plant and Machinery	160,000
Loan stock 12%	250,000		
Current Liabilities		**Current Assets**	
Creditors	65,000	Stock	220,000
Bank Overdraft	150,000	Debtors	150,000
	630,000		630,000

a   The board has approved the purchase of a new machine in August 1991 costing £40,000.

b   Wages, assume 10% of monthly sales.

Fixed costs estimated at £5,000 per month (all cash payments).

c   Depreciation is to be charged at £3,000 per month.

d   Interim dividend of 20p per share, payable 15th July 1991.

e

	Jul	Aug	Sep	Oct	Nov	Dec
	£000's	£000's	£000's	£000's	£000's	£000's
Sales	50	70	80	100	60	40
Closing Stock	200	190	180	170	170	160

f   Creditors at 30th June 1991 are for purchases: May £40,000 and June £25,000. Debtors at 30th June 1991 are for sales: April £70,000, May £40,000 and June £40,000. Credit periods are expected to be the same during the second half of 1991 i.e. two months for suppliers, and three months for customers.

g   Gross profit to sales is budgeted at 30%. Assume purchases to be the balancing figure.

REQUIRED

1   Prepare a cash budget for the six months to 31st December 1991.

2   Describe the principle purposes of a cash budget.

6.5   The executives of Thrust Limited are concerned about possible cash shortages arising from a number of large payments due in the third quarter of 1991.

a   The cash balance on 1st July 1991 is forecast to be £30,000.

b   A new machine is to be installed in August 1991 costing £40,000 and will be paid for in September 1991.

c   A sales commission of 2% on sales is to be paid in the month following the sale.

d   Taxation of £110,000 is to be paid in August 1991.

e   In July 1991 and interim dividend of £50,000 is to be paid to ordinary shareholders (ignore taxation).

f   Production costs are paid as incurred. The average delay in paying administration costs is one month.

g   The average delay in paying wages is one week, with research and development costs averaging two weeks.

h   To encourage payment of invoices, the company allows a cash discount of 5% if payment is made within the month of the sale, and 2% if payment is made in the month following the sale. It is estimated that 20% of the debtors pay within the month of the sale, and a further 50% of the debtors pay in the month following the sale. The remaining debtors are expected to pay their invoices in full, within two months.

i   The period of credit allowed by suppliers averages three months.

j   An issue of loan stock is expected to be made in August 1991 which will result in £30,000 being received during that month.

A forecast of costs and revenues produced the following:

	Apr	May	Jun	Jul	Aug	Sep
			£'000			
Sales	190	240	290	245	180	170
Purchases	60	55	80	50	40	45
Labour	50	45	65	40	30	35
Production Costs	20	18	20	25	20	18
Administration Costs	20	20	25	30	25	20
Research and Development	6	7	8	10	15	12

REQUIRED

Prepare a cash budget for the three months to 30th September 1991.

6.6   Findings Ltd are about to negotiate with the bank the short-term financing of a new venture until it has concluded arrangements for permanent finance.

Budgeted Profit and Loss account to 30th April 1991

	January £'000	February £'000	March £'000	April £'000
Credit Sales	120	130	84	132
Materials	40	42	28	46
Labour	34	34	26	36
Costs:				
Production	7	8	7	8
Administrative	8	8	8	8
Selling and Distribution	8	9	6	10
Net Profit	23	29	9	24

The following additional information is available:

a   There are no stocks of finished goods.

b   Cost of materials has been arrived at as follows:

	January £'000	February £'000	March £'000	April £'000
Opening Stock	-	22	30	42
Purchases	62	50	40	50
less Closing Stock	22	30	42	46
Cost of Raw Materials	40	42	28	46

c   The period of credit allowed by suppliers of materials is one month.

d   To encourage early payment of invoices, Findings Ltd. allows a cash discount of 10% if payment is made within the month of sale. It is estimated that 10% of the debtors each month will take this discount, and a further 50% of the debtors of each month will pay in the following month. The remaining 40% are expected to pay their invoices in full, two months after the month of sale.

e   The overhead costs include the following items which have been allocated on an equal monthly charge but which are payable as follows:

	Monthly charge	Amount and date of payment
Costs		
Production	£1,000	£4,000 in January
Administration	£800	£2,000 in January
Selling and distribution	£500	£1,500 in March

f   Depreciation has been charged and included in production overhead at £1,500 per month.

g   The capital budget indicates that capital payments will be made as follows:

January £180,000

March £ 20,000

h   Unless stated otherwise, items can be treated on a cash basis.

REQUIRED

1   Prepare a monthly cash budget to determine the finance required.

2   Discuss the importance of cash budgets in a system of budgetary control.

6.7   'Our business is too complex for a budgeting system to work.' Discuss

6.8   'Why prepare budgets when costs and revenue assumptions change within a few months.' Discuss.

6.9   Outline the main benefits of preparing a cash flow forecast.

6.10   Discuss the key requirements of a successful budgeting system.

6.11   The executives of PVY Plc are preparing budgets for the year to 31st December 1992.

The Budgeted Balance Sheet as at 31st December 1991

	£ Cost	£ Depn.	£ N.B.V.
Fixed Assets			
Land and Buildings			130,000
Plant and Machinery	1,000,000	200,000	800,000
			930,000
Current Assets			
Stock - Finished Goods		145,000	
Stock - Materials		220,000	
Debtors		90,000	
Cash		30,000	
		485,000	
less Current Liabilities			
Creditors	290,000		
Taxation	20,000		
		310,000	
			175,000
Net Capital Employed			1,105,000
financed as follows:			
Issued Share Capital			200,000
Profit and Loss Account			905,000
			1,105,000

		Product A	Product B
a.	**Sales:**		
	Volume	Units	25,000	70,000
	Selling Price	per Unit	£45	£35
b.	**Finished Goods:**		
	Stock at Beginning	Units	3,000	2,000
	Stock at End	Units	2,500	6,000
c.	**Materials:**		**101**	**102**
	Stock at Beginning	Kilos	70,000	10,000
	Stock at End	Kilos	90,000	15,000

	Direct Costs:	**Price/Rate**	**Product A**	**B**
d.				
	Material 101	£3.00 per Kilo	2 Kilos	4 Kilos
	Material 102	£1.00 per Kilo	1 Kilo	2 Kilos
	Labour	£6.00 per Hour	3 Hours	2 Hours

e.   Overheads: are absorbed on the basis of Direct Labour Hours.

e   Factory Overheads:

	£
Consumable Materials	80,000
Indirect Labour	100,000
Wages and Salaries	100,000
Electricity	40,000
Maintenance	40,000
Depreciation	50,000
Rates	20,000
Insurance	5,000
Supervision	70,000
Stores and Handling	10,000
Miscellaneous	5,000

f   Selling and Administration Costs:

	£
Sales Commission	80,000
Advertising	20,000
Sales Salaries	50,000
Distribution	10,000
Administration Costs	50,000
Personnel	5,000
Administration Salaries	80,000
Management Services	15,000

g   Provide for Taxation for year £100,000

h   Budgeted Cash Flows are as follows:

	Quarter 1 £	2 £	3 £	4 £
Receipts from Debtors	700,000	750,000	750,000	950,000
Cash Outflows For:				
Materials	250,000	300,000	350,000	300,000
Other Costs	40,000	60,000	65,000	45,000
Wages and Salaries	360,000	400,000	400,000	480,000
Current Taxation	20,000			
Capital Expenditure			90,000	

REQUIRED
Prepare budget schedules for the year ending 31st December 1992.

EVALUATING NON-ROUTINE DECISIONS

LEARNING OBJECTIVES

When you have finished studying this chapter and completed the exercises you should be able to:

❏ Describe the main differences between variable and fixed costs, and relevant and irrelevant costs.

❏ Use cost, volume, profit (CVP) analysis and understand the advantages and disadvantages of its application.

❏ Prepare statements to show whether a company should continue with apparently unprofitable products, divisions, branches.

❏ Apply the concept of relevant costs to identify the best use of scarce resources.

❏ Apply the concept of relevant costs to the make or buy decision.

❏ Apply the concept of relevant costs to the decision to accept or reject a special order.

7.1   Introduction

Not all managerial action can be pre-planned and handled within a budgetary context. The reality of management is that periodically events will arise on a non-routine or ad-hoc basis which require a decision to be taken. What tends to make such events difficult to deal with is that rarely are they the same, however, there are some guidelines that are generally applicable which can be summarised as:

❑   Establish the exact nature of the issues requiring a decision to be taken.

❑   Identify the alternative courses of action.

❑   Identify the most appropriate data, irrespective of its source.

❑   Measure data correctly and logically analyse it.

❑   Ensure that financial and non financial data is presented well so as to facilitate information sharing and its correct interpretation.

In this chapter we are primarily concerned with decisions directed towards the short-term, which is frequently defined as one year or less, and the accounting information required to make these decisions. Decisions with implications greater than one year are discussed in the next chapter, however, it must be emphasised that much of the discussion about organising and analysing short-term decisions is relevant to dealing with long-term decisions.

What sorts of events might such short-term decisions include? The following are some illustrations:

❑   Whether to expand certain business activities.

❑   Whether to continue with apparently unprofitable products, divisions, branches.

❑   The best use of scarce resources.

❑   Whether to make internally or buy outside.

❑   Competitive tendering.

❑   Whether to accept a special order.

❑   Pricing.

As we will illustrate, dealing with short-term decisions requires a sound understanding of the economic issues of each situation to ensure an appropriate action is taken. In particular, use of the right data in the right way for each decision is critical for making good decisions. Unfortunately, there can often be confusion concerning the correct data to use because of a temptation to rely upon systems developed and currently operating to provide data for routine accounting purposes, such as budgetary control. Such systems will often have been developed for specific purposes relating to the control of activities and the information provided by it is often inadequate for answering the key question for managing decisions which is:

'How do costs and revenues differ if one
course of action is adopted rather than another?'

Answering this key question requires the ability to identify costs and revenues which are likely to change as a consequence of the decision, irrespective of their source. For example, in a decision whether to discontinue an operation or not, the historical cost of the stock from the accounting system may often be irrelevant. The crucial question is what alternative uses are there for the stock. If the only alternative is to sell the stock, the relevant information is its resale value which may be totally different from its historical cost. It also should not be ignored that there will often be non-financial information to be taken into consideration which may have a significant impact upon a particular situation, such as the effect on labour relations in the case of discontinuing an operation. Once all relevant points have been considered, it is critical that the resulting information is presented in the most appropriate form to ensure it is interpreted and correctly acted upon by the parties involved.

In this chapter we will consider the evaluation of non-routine decisions with the aid of a number of illustrations which represent the subtle differences in emphasis as to the type of data required. We first focus upon those decisions which require the analysis of cost behaviour and its application in what is now popularly called *cost-volume-profit* analysis. This type of approach can be useful for studying such issues as what is the effect on profit when a new product range is introduced. It is also relevant to managers in not-for-profit organisations, mainly because knowledge of how costs fluctuate in response to changes in volume is valuable regardless of whether profit is an objective. No organisation ever has unlimited resources!

Following cost-volume-profit analysis we consider specific categories of short-term decisions with the objective of developing an approach that will aid decision making in any situation.

7.2   Cost-volume-profit relationships

good understanding of how cost, volume and profit relate to one
another can be invaluable in dealing with certain types of short-term
decisions. Consider for example a request by a customer to provide a
large consignment of standard product at a substantial discount. In order to
establish the viability of such a request one issue likely to be of importance
is the profitability that will result. We will illustrate how using cost-volume-
profit (CVP) analysis such a request can be readily evaluated but, before then,
it is important to be aware of some basic terminology associated with its use.

7.2.1   Fixed and variable costs

At its simplest, cost-volume-profit analysis is reliant upon a classification of
costs in which fixed and variable costs are separated from one another. Fixed
costs are those which are generally time related and are not influenced by the
level of activity. For example, the rent payable by a manufacturer for factory
space will not be related to the number of items produced. Whether times are
good or bad the cost will have to be incurred and the same will apply to any
other costs which are contractually incurred. Of course if activity is to be
increased beyond the capacity of the premises additional rent would have to
be incurred, but within what is known as the 'relevant range' of activity the
cost is fixed. Variable costs on the other hand are directly related to the level
of activity; if activity increases variable costs will increase and vice versa if
activity decreases.

Fixed and variable costs can be readily understood when portrayed graphi-
cally as illustrated in *Figure 7.1.*

Figure 7.1   Illustration of fixed and variable costs

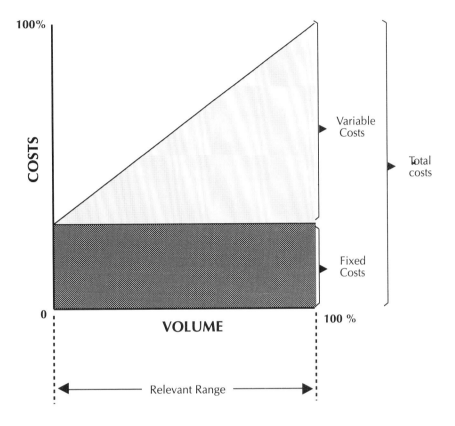

Fixed costs are shown to be constant for all levels of activity within the relevant range, whilst variable costs can be seen to increase in proportion to the level of activity. The sum of the fixed and the variable costs equals the total costs to be incurred over the level of activity within the relevant range.

In considering cost-volume-profit relationships it is usual to consider cost behaviour within the context of a model comprising only straight lines. This assumption can, of course, be relaxed to accommodate non-linear relationships, but it does make the analysis more difficult and in considering whether so to do, it is important to determine whether the benefit derived from greater accuracy of the input data will warrant the effort required to be expended.

Finally, you should not ignore the fact that costs may be simultaneously affected by more than one activity base. For example, labour costs associated with road haulage may be affected by both the weight and the number of units handled.

7.2.2   Cost-volume profit example

In what follows we shall assume that any costs may be classified as either variable or fixed, that a given variable cost is associated with one measure of volume, and that all cost behaviour relationships are linear. As indicated this approach is an abstraction of what might be found in practice, nevertheless via such a simple example the basis of the technique and the analytical power of cost-volume-profit analysis can be appreciated.

The profit and loss account of H.A.D. (Henley Alcohol-free Drinks) Ltd. for the previous 3 months is as detailed below. The cost-revenue relationships for the coming 3 months are expected to follow the same pattern as in the preceding 3 months. The company currently produces single-size bottles of only one sought after alcohol free lager and is operating at full capacity.

Table 7.1   H.A.D. Ltd – Profit and loss account

	£	per bottle £
Sales Revenue	800,000	1.00
Variable Costs	480,000	0.60
CONTRIBUTION	320,000	**0.40**
Fixed Costs	**240,000**	
Profit		
	80,000	

In *Table 7.1* an important accounting term is illustrated. This is the 'contribution', which represents the difference between sales revenue and variable costs. Its use in evaluating non-routine decisions will become evident from the discussion which follows in this chapter.

The study use of cost-volume-profit relationships is often called *break-even analysis*. Use of the latter is to be avoided because the break-even point, the point of zero net profit, is often only incidental to a planning decision at hand.

However, knowledge of the break-even point does provide an insight into the possible riskiness of certain courses of action. What is the break-even point for H.A.D. Ltd for the coming 3 months?

$$\text{Break Even Point (units)} = \frac{\text{Fixed Costs}}{\text{Contribution Per Unit}}$$

$$= \frac{£240,000}{40 \text{ pence}}$$

$$= 600,000 \text{ bottles}$$

Since cost-revenue relationships for the coming 3 months will be the same as those for last 3 months the break even point must correspond with a position where the fixed costs of £240,000 are covered after meeting variable costs. Where the contribution (sales less variable costs) equals fixed costs there will be zero profit for the period and the company will break even. From knowledge of this break even point corresponding with £240,000 we can calculate what this means in terms of the number of units. From *Table 7.1* it can be seen that each bottle contributes 40 pence, therefore the number of bottles corresponding with £ 240,000 (600,000) can be found as illustrated above by dividing the fixed costs by the contribution per unit.

We can extend the analytical technique described to calculate the break-even point and explore other aspects of cost-volume-profit relationships For example, there is a proposal to increase capacity by 30% in order to raise profit to £120,000 which will necessitate an extra £56,000 of fixed costs. How many bottles must be sold to break even and achieve the desired level of profit once capacity is increased? If we assume no change in the unit contribution as a result of the increase, the number of bottles can be calculated following a similar approach.

$$\text{Sales volume required} = \frac{(\text{Fixed Costs} + \text{Required Profit})}{\text{Contribution Per Unit}}$$

$$= \frac{(£296,000 + £120,000)}{40 \text{ pence}}$$

$$= 1,040,000 \text{ bottles}$$

7.2.3   Uses of costvolumeprofit analysis

The ability to analyse and use costvolumeprofit relationships is an important management tool. The knowledge of patterns of cost behaviour offers insights valuable in planning and controlling short and longrun operations. The example of increasing capacity is a good illustration of the power of the technique in planning. The implications of making changes upon profit can be determined as well as the requirements to achieve a given level of profit.

The technique can be used to work forwards or backwards and, as should be only too obvious, it is ideal for spreadsheet analysis, whereby the effects of all sorts of modifications and assumptions can be evaluated.

The technique is also useful within the context of control. The implications of changes in the level of activity can be measured by flexing a budget using knowledge of cost behaviour, thereby permitting comparison to be made of actual and budgeted performance for any level of activity.

7.2.4   Limitations of costvolumeprofit analysis

A major limitation of conventional CVP analysis that we have already identified is the assumption and use of linear relationships. Yet another limitation relates to the difficulty of dividing fixed costs among many products and/or services. Whilst variable costs can usually be identified with production services, most fixed costs usually can only be divided by allocation and apportionment methods reliant upon a good deal of judgement. However, perhaps the major limitation of the technique relates to the initial separation of fixed and variable costs. This can often be difficult to achieve with any sort of precision because many costs do not fall neatly into one or other of the two categories, and methods for separating fixed and variable costs may be required for the technique to be used. If this is the case, then you should be particularly mindful about applying a great deal of sophistication to any analysis because this may serve to cloud the key issue which is the quality of the data input.

The quality of input data is an important point and one you will find we often emphasise. In our opinion too much emphasis has been placed upon how to make techniques more sophisticated without sufficient consideration of the quality of the data to which such sophisticated techniques will be applied. With this in mind let us consider briefly how fixed and variable costs can be separated.

First, judgement can be applied to the data in an attempt to separate those costs which can be considered as being wholly fixed or wholly variable. Bearing in mind that we are considering a defined range of activity, examples of fixed costs would be salaried staff and occupancy costs, such as rents and rates, whilst materials costs and sales commissions are illustrative of typical variable costs to a commercially oriented manufacturing operation.

Of course, the likelihood of separating a substantial proportion of total costs in this way is often very low and the remainder will fall somewhere between the two extremes of wholly fixed and wholly variable costs. This remainder, known as semi-fixed, or semi-variable costs, need to be separated in order to make cost-volume-profit analysis operable.

A number of methods are available to make such a separation possible ranging from comparing costs at high and low levels of activity, to regression analysis, whereby using statistical analysis a line of best fit is found from available cost data. Irrespective of the method applied, the result will only be an approximation! Yes, it is possible to minimise the approximation but you should weigh the cost of so doing against the relative likely benefit that will be achieved.

7.2.5   An example of cost-volume-profit analysis

The following data relates to a new product due to be launched on the 1st May 1991.

Selling Price	£20.00 per unit
Forecast Volume	120,000 units
Variable Costs	£16.00 per unit
Fixed Costs	£300,000

In the following we will apply the principles to CVP analysis to the following five situations in which each is treated as being independent of the other:

1 Break even point in units.

2 Break even point in units if variable costs per unit increase to £17.00.

3 Break even point in £ sterling if the fixed costs increase to £336,000.

4 Minimum selling price to meet a profit target of £120,000.

5 Volume of sales required at a selling price of £19.00 per unit.

The first step in tackling such a problem is to calculate the total contribution and the contribution per unit.

	£	£ per unit
Sales	2,400,000	20.00
less Variable Costs	1,920,000	16.00
CONTRIBUTION	480,000	**4.00**
less Fixed Costs	**300,000**	
Profit	180,000	

1. Using this information we calculate the break-even point by dividing the costs to be incurred irrespective of the level of activity (i.e. fixed costs) by the contribution each unit will generate.

$$\text{Break Even Point (units)} = \frac{\text{Fixed Costs}}{\text{Contribution Per Unit}}$$

$$= \frac{£300,000}{£4.00}$$

$$= \quad 75,000 \text{ units}$$

2. Where the variable costs per unit change, so too will the contribution per unit:

	£ per unit
Sales	20.00
Variable Costs	17.00
Contribution	3.00

With an unchanged £20.00 selling price and a revised variable cost of £17.00 a contribution per unit of £3.00 will result. Assuming that the fixed costs remain unchanged at £300,000, the break even point in units is 100,000 (£300,000/£3.)

3. Break even always arises where total cost equals total revenue. To find the break even point in value rather than volume, we first calculate the break even point in units and then multiply it by the selling price.

In this case where fixed costs are £336,000 (with no other changes), the break even point in units will be £336,000 divided by £4.00, which equals 84,000 units. Break even in value can be found by multiplying 84,000 by £20.00, which equals £1,680,000.

4. The minimum selling price to meet a target profit is found from the sum of the contribution per unit plus the variable cost per unit. The contribution per unit in this situation can be found by dividing the required units into the sum of the fixed costs and the profit target. For example, we are told that the profit target is £120,000 which added to the fixed costs of £300,000 gives £420,000 (i.e. the contribution in value). The contribution per unit can now be found by dividing £420,000 by 120,000 units to give £3.50. Therefore, the minimum selling price is £3.50 plus the unit variable cost of £16.00 which equals £19.50.

5. The calculation of total volume to cover fixed costs and meet the target profit is similar to the approach used to determine the break even volume. The only difference is that the profit target is added to the fixed costs in order to calculate the number of units (volume) required to cover fixed costs and to cover the profit target from a given contribution per unit.

In this case the requirement is to identify the volume to cover fixed costs and profit assuming that the selling price per unit is decreased to £19.00. Where the selling price is £19.00, the unit contribution falls to £3.00, i.e.

	£ per unit
Sales	19.00
Variable Cost	16.00
Contribution	3.00

The volume of sales under those circumstances is found by adding the fixed costs of £300,000 to the profit target of £180,000 and then dividing the result by £3.00, to give 160,000 units.

7.2.6 Contribution margin and gross margin

We have shown the contribution margin to be the excess of sales over all variable costs. It can be expressed as a total amount, a unit amount, and a percentage.

You should be aware of the potential for confusion about the difference between contribution and gross profit. Gross profit is a widely used concept, particularly in the retailing industry and is the excess of sales over the cost of goods sold. However, the cost of goods sold will usually be very different in nature and amount from the contribution. The cost of goods sold relates solely to the direct costs associated with those items sold and any attributed overhead. It, therefore, usually contains elements of both fixed and variable costs unlike the contribution margin which is calculated with sole reference to variable costs.

What costs are relevant?

The application of the principles of CVP analysis does suffer one major limitation for many decisions, other than those discussed earlier. In situations where there are different potential courses of action, relevant data for evaluating the alternatives is required and the cost behaviour information used in CVP analysis is unlikely to meet all of its requirements. What must be identified in such circumstances is the amount by which costs will change if one course of action is taken rather than another.

Surely, you must be thinking, this is simply an extension of cost-volume-profit analysis, but this need not be so. In discussing and applying cost-volume-profit analysis we did not question the relevance of the input data used to the decision in question. Questioning cost relevance is an important part of choosing between alternative courses of action.

As a manager, you must avoid using irrelevant information for evaluating alternatives no matter how impressive it may appear to be. The problem is, how do you avoid the use of irrelevant information and identify that which is relevant?

First, the accounting information used in any decision must relate to the *future*, not the past. It is essential that only costs and revenues yet to be incurred are used for purposes of decision making. This is because they alone will be incurred as a result of taking the decision in question. Past costs and revenues, which are often referred to as 'sunk' costs and revenues, are irrelevant to decision making, apart from their use in helping to forecast the future.

Second, where you are faced with a decision, the only relevant costs or revenues are those which are different under the alternative courses of action. Such costs are often referred to as *differential* costs. An understanding of how to use differential costs is important because most decisions will require at least two courses of action to be considered, given that one course of action may merely be to confirm current practice!

We will now consider the importance of these two relevant cost characteristics with the following simple light-hearted example which will also draw upon material covered earlier concerning cost behaviour analysis. We have deliberately related the example to more personal matters because our experience has shown its benefit in discussing the important concepts we will consider.

Example of cost relevance

E. Tee, an aspiring manager, recently hit by the increase in interest rates upon his newly acquired mortgage, has a problem with the financial arrangements for his golf. He can either pay £5.00 every time he plays, or £80.00 for a non-refundable season ticket plus £1.00 for every round played. Which should he choose? This you should immediately recognise as being similar in principle to the earlier discussion of cost-volume-profit analysis. In order to make a decision between these two alternatives we can work out how many times E. Tee would have to play so that he is indifferent between either of the two. This point of indifference where he is no better or worse off is like the break-even point discussed earlier. It is found by taking the cost of the annual season ticket and dividing it by the savings (the differential cost/benefit) achieved each time E. Tee would play.

$$= \frac{\textbf{Annual season ticket}}{\textbf{Saving on each round}}$$

$$= \frac{£80.00}{£\ 4.00} = 20 \text{ times}$$

E. Tee would have to play more than 20 times in the year before a season ticket and £1 payment for each round would be a worthwhile decision. Because E. Tee likes golf and intends to play twice a week for the whole year he purchases an annual season ticket for £80.

Simple so far, but true to life complications arise. One month later, he identifies another problem which he cannot solve. He has visited another golf club which is nearer to his home. There is a single payment of £200.00 for membership with no additional green fees. The course is not heavily used, and it takes approximately three hours to complete a round compared to the four hours at the present club. What should he do? What about the £80.00 he has recently paid for his annual season ticket? The £80.00 is not relevant to this decision. It has already been paid, is not refundable and it will be the same irrespective of the decision he takes. Only the additional costs (incremental costs) and the additional savings (incremental receipts) are relevant to this new decision, i.e. those costs which will change as a result of making the decision.

The incremental costs in this case would be the £200.00 membership fee, and the incremental savings would be the £1.00 per round he has to pay at the present club.

$$= \frac{\text{Incremental Costs}}{\text{Incremental Savings}}$$

$$= \frac{\text{£200.00}}{\text{£ 1.00}} = 200 \text{ times}$$

Therefore, E. Tee would have to play four times a week in order for it to be financially worth his while joining the other golf club. If, on the other hand, E. Tee could save £1.00 on travel by joining the other golf club (which is nearer to his home), break-even would be achieved after 100 rounds (£200 divided by [£1+£1]). However, there are a number of other aspects not necessarily of a financial nature which should be considered in making a decision to change to another club. Examples are:

❏ The time taken to play, and travel.

❏ The possibility of sharing travelling.

❏ Who else plays.

❏ The amenities and social aspects.

❏ The quality of the facilities.

The problems of choice which we have related to E. Tee are common to many decisions. Many decisions in business can and do become clouded by seemingly plausible but incorrect information. You only have to consider the £80 already paid for the annual season ticket and relate this to a decision to cease production and switch operations to another product where stocks of raw materials costing £10,000 are still on hand. It is not inconceivable that this £10,000 sum would be brought into the conversation even though it may be totally irrelevant. What was paid for the stock is history and not relevant to a future decision, which should be concerned with determining the real value of the stock in this situation either from re-sale or re-use. Do not worry if you find this elusive from this simple illustration, we consider a number of examples in the next section of this chapter.

In addition to considering financial information the E. Tee example served to show the need for judgement to be exercised about other matters, not necessarily of a financial nature. This will often also be the case in business.

7.3   Applying relevant cost analysis to short-term decisions

We have introduced the characteristics of financial information required for short-term decision making which must be differential as between alternative choices and relate to the future. We will reinforce these two requirements and, where appropriate, apply the principles of CVP analysis with reference to five common applications of short-term decision techniques. These are:

❏   Whether to continue with apparently unprofitable products, divisions, branches.

❏   How to make the best use of available scarce resources.

❏   Whether to make or use internal resources or buy from outside.

❏   Whether or not to use competitive tendering.

❏   Whether or not to accept a special order.

7.3.1   Whether to continue with apparently unprofitable products, divisions, branches.

This application of short-term decision making techniques we will consider using the following example:

> T.O. Wood Ltd manufactures and sells three products, X, Y and Z. The internally prepared product profitability statement for the company is shown in *Table 7.2*. Fixed overhead costs are absorbed as a percentage of labour costs and have been rounded to the nearest £100,000. Products X and Z are machine intensive while Product Y is labour intensive. Management is considering whether to drop Product Y because it is making a loss, the assumption being that they could increase the total profit of the company by £100,000 by dropping Product Y. Do you agree?

Table 7.2   T.O. Wood Ltd - Product profitability statement

	X	Y	Z	Total
	£'000	£'000	£'000	£'000
(a) Sales	1,500	1,600	800	3,900
(b) Materials	500	400	100	1,000
(c) Labour	400	800	300	1,500
(d) Fixed Costs	300	500	200	1,000
(e) Total Costs	1200	1700	600	3,500
(f) Profit/(Loss)	**300**	**-100**	**200**	**400**

With reference to line (d) Product Y is absorbing 50% of the total fixed costs many of which may not be avoided even if the company were to drop Product Y. In such a situation where there is a limited differential effect upon fixed costs in continuing or dropping Product Y, they are not really relevant in making the decision.

On the assumption that fixed costs are not avoidable in the short-term we have re-arranged the contents of *Table 7.2* to show a distinction between those costs likely to be avoidable and those that are not:

Table 7.3   T.O. Wood Ltd - Product contribution and profitability statement

	X £'000	Y £'000	Z £'000	Total £'000
Sales	1,500	1,600	800	3,900
Materials	500	400	100	1,000
Labour[1]	400	800	300	1,500
Total Variable Costs	900	1,200	400	2,500
Contribution	600	400	400	1,400
Fixed Costs				1,000
Profit				400
Contribution/Sales %	40	25	50	

[1] *Labour costs are usually considered to be variable costs because they do respond to changes in the level of activity, albeit that this response may not be immediate.*

In the re-arranged *Table 7.3* the value of retaining Product Y is shown assuming that no fixed costs are avoidable. Product Y can be seen to contribute £400,000 towards the fixed costs. If dropped, T.O. Wood Ltd would lose this contribution, with the result being a reduction in the total contribution by £400,000. Furthermore, this £400,000 reduction in contribution would completely wipe out the £400,000 profit currently obtained from making all three products.

This example illustrates one issue which must be considered in short-term decision analysis that arises from the allocation of fixed costs. Where fixed costs have been identified with products, as in this example, it is tempting but usually wrong to assume that they will necessarily disappear when a product is dropped. In fact, in many organisations all that is known with any certainty is the total fixed costs likely to be incurred, their allocation across products or services is frequently heavily dependent upon judgement.

T.O. Wood Ltd is a useful illustration of CVP analysis. This technique can frequently be usefully extended by relating the contribution per product to the sales revenue to produce what is known as the contribution to sales (C/S) ratio. The contribution to sales ratio is potentially useful when costs have been separated into fixed and variable categories. This is because the effect on total profit of a given volume change for any product(s) can be assessed using knowledge of the contribution to sales ratio. Let us consider the calculation and application of the C/S ratio.

The contribution to sales ratios for X,Y and Z, are found by expressing the contributions of £600,000, £400,000 and £400,000 as a percentage of the sales revenues of £1,500,000, £1,600,000 and £800,000, respectively. The resulting contribution to sales ratios are 40%, 25% and 50%. The effect on profit of an extra £1,000,000 of sales revenue being generated by each of the products assuming that fixed costs would remain the same would be £400,000, £250,000 and £500,000, for X, Y and Z, respectively. Therefore, given the potential to increase sales revenue by £1,000,000 the first product to be selected would be Z which has the highest contribution to sales ratio. Thus, the assumption that fixed costs are time related and remain unchanged for such an increase in activity, and that there is no differential effect between products, then the highest profit will be generated from increasing sales of Product Z.

You will note that we have been able to consider the potential financial benefits of an increase in sales revenue by considering the C/S ratio alone. Given that the relationships in the model are understood it is not necessary to undertake lengthy calculations to gauge the benefit.

Of course we have assumed no resource constraints. Where these exist the contribution to sales ratio is not a useful distinguishing mechanism between alternative products, as we will see in the next section.

7.3.2   How to best use available scarce resources

In some production and distribution decisions, management may be confronted with the question of how best to allocate the firm's limited resources. Where demand for the product is greater than the production or distribution capabilities available, a company should seek to maximise its total contribution margin from these limited resources.

Limited resources can arise from one, or a combination of the following:

❏   Shortages of raw materials or purchased goods.

❏   Shortage of certain labour skills.

❏   Restricted space for production, in the warehouse or in a retailing outlet.

❏   Maximum machine capacities.

It may not only be on the supply side that limitations prevail. It is also quite possible that a firm will face limitations upon the amount it can produce and/ or sell because of:

❏   Customer demand for one or more products or services.

❏   Government restrictions.

In such circumstances the challenge is to obtain the maximum possible benefit from the market opportunities and the resources available.

Where there is one single constraint, it is possible to carry out an analysis to determine the best mix of products to maximise total contribution margin. At its simplest the analysis requires the contribution margin for a product to be divided by the unit of scarce resource, i.e. the limiting factor. That product or service with the highest contribution per unit of the scarce resource is the most desirable whilst the resource constraint operates. The application of the contribution per unit of scarce resource will be demonstrated with reference to T.O. Wood Ltd, where management is considering the most desirable mix of products to incorporate into their annual budget.

Market research information has produced the estimated sales of T.O. Wood's present products together with further estimates of two new products, P and Q. There is no sales constraint, but there is a constraint on machine capacity of 4,800 hours and, given this constraint, management needs to know the mix of products which should be produced so as to maximise total profit margin. The product data which has been summarised in *Table 7.4* is available:

Table 7.4   T.O. Wood Ltd - Possible alternative products

	Existing products			New products	
	X	Y	Z	P	Q
Machine Hours	2,000	800	2,000	800	1,000
	£'000	£'000	£'000	£'000	£'000
Sales	1,500	1,600	800	700	1,000
Materials	500	400	100	200	400
Labour	400	800	300	200	200
Total Variable Costs	900	1,200	400	400	600
Contribution	600	400	400	300	400
Contribution to Sales Ratio	40%	25%	50%	43%	40%

Unfortunately, as we will illustrate, the current product analysis is inadequate for selecting the appropriate product mix to maximise profit. What is required is an analysis of the contribution yielded per machine hour for each product. This we have provided in *Table 7.5* which has been used to rank the products from those which show the highest contribution per machine hour through to the lowest.

Table 7.5   Best use of scarce resources - ranking

	Existing products			New products	
	X	Y	Z	P	Q
(a) Machine Hours	2,000	800	2,000	800	1,000
	£'000	£'000	£'000	£'000	£'000
(b) Contribution	600	400	400	300	400
	£	£	£	£	£
Contribution Per Machine Hour [(b) ÷ (a)]	300	500	200	375	400
Ranking	4	1	5	3	2

The analysis shows that Product Y ranked first, provides the highest contribution per machine hour. Each unit requires less of the scarce resource than the other products, and it contributes £500 per machine hour.

The ranking illustrated in the table provides the order which will result in the best use of scarce machine hours. Given the total constraint of 4,800 hours and the selection of Product Y which requires 800 hours, the remaining 4,000 hours would be allocated to products Q, P and X. This allocation to the four products does not exhaust the 4,800 hours available and 200 hours still remain unused. This 200 hours spare capacity could be used to ease production scheduling, or it might be used to produce a proportion of Product Z.

Assuming that the 200 hours are retained to ease production scheduling, the following revised product income statement shows the results of maximising total contribution per machine hour available.

Table 7.6   *Product contribution and total profit statement*

	Y	Q	P	X	TOTAL
Machine Hours	800	1,000	800	2,000	4,600
	£'000	£'000	£'000	£'000	£'000
Sales	1,600	1,000	700	1,500	4,800
Materials	400	400	200	500	1,500
Labour	800	200	200	400	1,600
Total Variable Costs	1,200	600	400	900	3,100
Contribution	400	400	300	600	1,700
Fixed Costs					1,000
Profit					700

You will have doubtless noted by selecting the product mix using contribution per machine hour, Product Z with the highest contribution sales ratio is the least desirable. Whilst it may produce the largest effect on contribution for a given increase in sales, it suffers from being inefficient in terms of machine hour use. Hopefully, you will be thinking why not buy or lease a new machine or investigate sub-contracting production. This line of thinking is entirely appropriate as is questioning whether T.O.Wood should focus more heavily on Product Y. However, your attention would not have been so readily directed at these questions in the absence of the analysis we have outlined.

Where more than one constraint exists the problem will be reliant upon operations research methods like linear programming for its solution. Such techniques are beyond the scope of this book.

7.3.3 The decision to make or buy

If you are not involved in a manufacturing environment, you may be tempted to skip this section on the grounds that make or buy decisions will be irrelevant to you. Nothing could be further from the truth! This we will demonstrate in the next section which is concerned with the evaluation of providing internal services against the use of outside contractors, and represents a good illustration of an application of make or buy principles.

Stated very simply, in a make or buy decision, buying is preferable on economic grounds when the relevant costs for making are greater than the price quoted by the supplier. As with many decisions, what often confuses the analysis is the distinction between those costs that are relevant to making the decision and those that are not. The distinction between relevant and irrelevant costs for make or buy decisions is exactly the same as described earlier insofar as relevant costs are future orientated and differential. However, to aid your understanding of their applications to make or buy decisions we will relate it to the following example.

> The purchasing manager of T.O. Wood Ltd has been investigating the possibility of buying a certain component from an outside supplier. L. Driver Ltd is prepared to sign a one year contract to deliver 10,000 top quality units as needed during the year at a price of £5.00 per unit. This price of £5.00 is lower than the estimated manufacturing cost per component of £6.00, which is made up as follows:

	Unit cost
Direct Materials	1.20
Direct Labour	1.80
Factory Variable Cost	0.60
Annual Machine Rental	0.40
Factory Fixed Costs - Specific	0.50
- Allocated	1.50
	£6.00

It appears at first sight that it will make better economic sense to buy rather than to make, however, let us consider whether all of the items within the product cost breakdown are relevant, i.e. 'If the decision is made to buy, which of the costs will be avoided?' An investigation of the components reveals that direct materials, direct labour, factory variable costs, annual machine rental and factory fixed costs - specific would all be avoided. As the total of these relevant costs amounts to £4.50, which is less than the price of £5 quoted by the supplier, the decision should be to continue making the component. The remaining £1.50 of costs relating to allocated fixed costs would presumably have to be borne elsewhere in the company and because they do not differ, irrespective of the course of action, are irrelevant.

Even if the analysis had indicated it to be more desirable to buy on economic grounds, there would still be factors to be considered other than purely the financial ones. For example loss of know-how in producing this component, the loss of certain skilled labour, not being able to control future cost increases and, therefore, final product prices, the ability to fill up capacity in slack times, and the possibility of finding it difficult to obtain supplies at a reasonable price during boom times, must all be taken into consideration.

7.3.4   Competitive tendering

As indicated, the principles used in the make or buy decision can also be applied to an evaluation of services to answer the question – 'Do we provide a service using our own resources or do we invite outside suppliers to compete to provide the service?'

There are many examples of organisations using competitive tendering in an attempt to obtain savings in the services they provide. These include, local authorities with refuse collection, health authorities with domestic, catering and building maintenance services, and even the Royal Navy with ship repair.

What is the basis used to determine whether an organisation should provide a service in-house or accept an offer from an outside supplier? The financial criteria are exactly the same as the make or buy decision, such that an organisation should provide an in-house service when the relevant costs associated with its provision are less than the price quoted by outside suppliers. These relevant costs are once again those costs which would be avoided if the provision of the service were to cease, and would tend to include materials consumed and wages. However, you must be constantly aware of irrelevant costs like historical as opposed to future values of stocks and other assets, and allocated costs which can often cloud a decision. A thorough review of all costs associated with such a service must always be undertaken.

Once again please do note that our discussion has been concerned with financial criteria only. As we have emphasised on a number of occasions there will always be non-financial issues often of equal importance to take into consideration before a decision can realistically be taken.

7.3.5 The decision to accept/reject a special order

One issue likely to be appropriate to all managers at some time in their careers is whether to accept what we will refer to as a special order. By this we mean, 'Are there circumstances in which it might make sense in financial terms to sell products or services at a lower price than normal, or, alternatively to provide a service internally at less than its full cost?'

In considering such decisions it is most important to be quite clear about the meaning of the term *full cost*. In many organisations external and internal prices for products and services are generated with reference to the full or total cost of its provision plus a percentage profit margin, a practice known as *cost-plus pricing*. Within the full cost there will usually be allocated and apportioned fixed overheads required to be covered irrespective of whether a special order is accepted. Such irrelevant costs must be ignored. The criterion for accepting a special order must only consider whether the direct benefits which result exceed those costs that could be avoided by not taking it.

Such evidence as exists from surveys of pricing reveals that some organisations do accept special orders using some form of the contribution analysis, although the bias towards its use is not as significant as many textbooks would imply.

You should be aware that the acceptance of a special order with reference to direct costs and benefits can be problematic if it generates a special order 'culture'. If all orders are priced as special how will fixed overheads ever be recovered!

There are also other considerations to be taken into account that may have financial consequences. For example, if it became widely known that special orders were negotiable then the subsequent marketing and selling of products, or services, may be far more difficult, and require a good deal more effort to be expended than currently.

As a general guideline then, in these types of decisions a company must consider:

1   Whether the acceptance of a special order will tie up capacity which could be used for profitable orders at some time in the future. If it does so then it should avoid the special contract.

2   Whether the acceptance of a contract will affect the regular sales of the product and ultimately the future pricing structure of that product. Generally speaking a special contract should not be accepted if it will affect consumer behaviour adversely within the same market place. General knowledge of the availability of special orders may well lead to consumer games with the supplier.

7.4   Structuring decision analysis

Clear thought and the application of certain key principles is critical for making sound decisions. We have offered these key principles by way of a number of applications which you may be able to apply to your own circumstances. All too often a major barrier to decision making is a lack of structure and we offer the following as a guideline:

❏   Clearly define exactly what the problem is for which a solution is sought.

❏   Consider all possible alternative courses of action which could lead to a solution.

❏   Discard those alternatives which on a common sense appraisal are 'non- starters' for one reason or another.

❏   Evaluate the cost differences between each of the remaining courses of action.

❏   Weigh up the non-financial factors related to each course of action.

❏   Take into account both financial and non-financial factors important to the decision.

All common sense you might be thinking? We would agree, but in our experience it is all too easy to overlook, underestimate, or evaluate incorrectly one or more of the steps.

Exercises

7.1   The following data has been extracted from the budget of Hogan Ltd., for the six months ending 30th June 1991.

Sales (at £30 each)		£210,000
Costs:		
Variable Costs	140,000	
Fixed Costs	40,000	
		180,000
		£30,000

REQUIRED

1.   Calculate the break even point in units.

2.   Assuming that each of the following are independent of one another, calculate the breakeven point assuming an increase in:

   a Fixed costs by 10%.

   b Variable costs by 5%.

   c Selling price by 4%.

   d Sales volume by 8%.

7.2 The following data relates to a new product due to be launched on the 1st March 1992.

Selling Price	£25.00	per unit
Forecast Volume	30,000	units
Variable Costs	£15.00	per unit
Fixed Costs	£200,000	

REQUIRED

Assuming that each of the following are independent of one another, calculate the

1. Break even point in units and £ sterling.

2. Break even point in units if variable costs per unit increase to £16.00.

3. Break even point in £ sterling if the fixed costs increase to £235,000.

4. Minimum selling price to meet a profit target of £70,000.

5. Volume of sales required at a selling price of £23.00 per unit.

6. Additional units required to cover an advertising campaign of £40,000.

7.3   A business makes and sells a single product from a plant with a capacity of 60,000 units per year.

The results for the six months ended 31st December 1990 are shown below:

	£'000	£'000
Sales (20,000 units at £300 per unit)		6,000
Costs:		
Direct Materials	2,200	
Direct Labour	640	
Production Overheads (90% fixed)	1,600	
Selling and Administration Overheads (all fixed)	1,960	6,400
		-400

The directors agree that this result is unsatisfactory. They propose cutting the price by £20, which they believe will stimulate sufficient sales to utilise all of the capacity during the six months to 30th June 1991.

REQUIRED

1. Calculate the break-even point in units for the six months to 31st December 1990.

2. Calculate the break-even point in units for the six months to 30th June 1991.

3. Calculate the profit for the six months to 30th June 1991 assuming that the increase in sales can be achieved.

4. Calculate the profit and break-even point for the next financial year if market conditions do not allow the price to be increased from the new level set by the directors, but fixed costs do increase by 10% and variable costs by 4%.

7.4 Memory Incorporated have been appointed sole agents to market and sell a low priced scientific calculator through the retail trade.

A profit plan has been developed on a forecast volume of 1,000,000 units.

	£	£
Sales		4,000,000
Costs:		
Purchase	1,500,000	
Packaging	500,000	
Variable Selling Overheads	200,000	
Administration Overheads	500,000	
Marketing and Selling Overheads	300,000	
		3,000,000
Profit		1,000,000

REQUIRED

You are asked to evaluate each of the following separately.

1. Calculate the break-even point in units.

2. Given an increase in marketing and selling overheads of £300,000 and a required target profit of £1,500,000:

   a Calculate the minimum selling price on the forecast volume of 1,000,000 units.

   b Calculate the volume required assuming that the selling price remains at £4 per unit.

3. Using the original data:-

   a Calculate the minimum selling price required to achieve a profit/sales ratio of 20% on a volume of 1,000,000 units.

   b Calculate the volume required to achieve a profit/sales ratio of 20% assuming that the selling price remains at £4 per unit.

7.5 E. Tee Ltd., manufactures three models of electric powered golf trolleys, standard, super, and deluxe.

Budgeted fixed costs for the year ending 30th November 1991 are £1,000,000.

The following data shows the selling prices and volumes together with the costs per unit for each of the models.

| | **Models** | | |
	Standard	**Super**	**Deluxe**
Sales Volumes	4,000	3,000	1,000
Selling Price	£300	£375	£550
Direct Materials	£ 90	£120	£160
Direct Labour	£ 45	£ 45	£ 90
Variable Overheads	£ 20	£ 30	£ 50

The Deluxe model has not been selling due to a cheaper import which has obtained an increased share in that market. E. Tee Ltd., has a choice, to drop their selling price of the Deluxe model by £75 which they feel will increase sales volume by 50%, or to drop the Deluxe model from their range.

The extra labour, which is currently employed on the Deluxe model could be transferred to increase the production of the Standard or the Super model, or of both models equally.

REQUIRED

1. State what the profit would be if E. Tee Ltd., continued with their budget plan.

2. Evaluate the choices available to E. Tee Ltd., and state which choice you would recommend.

7.6   A company making a single product has a factory in Swindon and distributes its production through three depots situated in Swindon, Bristol and Reading.

It is estimated that during the coming year 99,000 units will be manufactured and sold at a price of £22 per unit, the sales being spread as follows:

Swindon	67,000 units
Bristol	22,000 units
Reading	10,000 units

Standard costs of production are:

Direct Materials	£6.50 per unit
Direct Labour	£3.40 per unit
Variable Production Overheads	150% on direct labour
Fixed Production Overheads	£250,000 per year

The cost of selling and distribution incurred by the depots are estimated as follows:

Fixed costs

Swindon	£70,000 per year
Bristol	£60,000 per year
Reading	£60,000 per year

Variable costs

Swindon	8%	of Sales Revenue
Bristol	10%	of Sales Revenue
Reading	12%	of Sales Revenue

Management is considering closing the Bristol and/or Reading depots. If this is done it is expected that all sales in these areas will be lost, but the sales in Swindon will not be affected.

REQUIRED

1.   From the figures provided prepare a statement indicating why management is thinking of closing the depots in Bristol and Reading.

2.   Present additional information to help management make a decision in regard to this problem, and make recommendations from your figures.

7.7 A meeting has been arranged of the executives of W.E. Look Ltd., to consider the budget for the coming year. They are not convinced that the products they produce and the products they sell are giving the optimum profit. Until they move into the new factory in two years time there will be severe restrictions on capacity.

The current machine capacity is 160 hours per week with no other major restrictions (i.e. materials, labour etc.)

The following information has been collected for the products the company is able to sell per week with no seasonal trends.

Products	A	B	C	D £'000	E	F	G
Sales	7.0	2.0	2.0	4.0	6.0	2.0	4.0
Materials	4.0	0.8	0.7	2.5	3.0	0.6	0.6
Labour	2.0	0.6	1.0	1.0	1.0	0.6	2.0
Machine Hours	40	20	20	60	80	20	120

Fixed costs will remain constant at £115,440 per year, regardless of product mix.

REQUIRED

1. Prepare a statement showing which products should be produced to give the optimum profit from available capacity.

2. From the information obtained in above, prepare an income statement for a single week.

7.8   The company accountant of L. Driver Ltd has drawn up the following statement to assist production management in their decision on product production during the coming year.

Product	A	B	C	D	E	F
Selling Price (£)	<u>420</u>	<u>570</u>	<u>510</u>	<u>480</u>	<u>540</u>	<u>570</u>
Materials	190	160	130	205	240	150
Labour	40	90	90	50	70	90
Variable Overheads	50	25	25	40	35	55
Fixed Overheads	<u>60</u>	<u>135</u>	<u>135</u>	<u>75</u>	<u>105</u>	<u>135</u>
	<u>340</u>	<u>410</u>	<u>380</u>	<u>370</u>	<u>450</u>	<u>430</u>
Profit Per Unit	80	160	130	110	90	140
Ranking for Production	6	1	3	4	5	2
Estimated Maximum Sales per annum (units)	400	1000	300	800	500	300

Specialist labour is required to produce the products and earns £8.00 per hour; the company can hire only 25,000 labour hours during the coming year. All other resources can be obtained in the desired quantities. Fixed overheads are charged at 150% of labour cost under the company's costing system.

REQUIRED

1.   Produce an alternative method of ranking the company's products to make the best use of the shortage of specialist labour.

2.   What other factors should be taken into consideration?

7.9   AMILL is a chemical used in the production of XZX Ltd's range of fertilisers. Because of a fire at the chemical works, supply is restricted to 12,000 kg per month, at a cost of £6 per kg.

Before supplies were restricted XZX's budget was:

	A	B	C	D
Sales (in kgs)	18,000	21,600	18,000	28,800
Selling Price (per kg)	£3.24	£4.92	£4.62	£6.00
Variable Costs per kg of output:				
Amill	£0.90	£1.44	£1.08	£2.40
Other Direct Materials	£0.30	£0.48	£0.48	£0.72
Direct Labour	£0.48	£0.66	£0.60	£0.84
Production Overhead	£0.12	£0.18	£0.12	£0.24

Fixed Costs £30,000 per month.

REQUIRED

Calculate the maximum profit possible, per month, while Amill is in short supply.

7.10   Mars Packers Ltd has its own internal department which produces a standard size carton for packaging of the company's products. 360,000 of these cartons are used annually and the detailed budgeted costs of production are as follow

	£
Direct Materials	84,000
Direct Labour	18,000
Electricity (power costs)	4,500
Depreciation of Plant	13,500
Repairs to Plant	3,000
Fixed Production Overheads	15,000

An outside supplier has quoted to supply all the cartons on a regular basis throughout the year at a price of £325 per 1,000. In the event of accepting this offer the section will be closed and the specialist plant sold for £18,000. The company will also incur additional fixed costs of £9,000 per year for inspection and storage of the cartons.

REQUIRED

1.   Prepare a financial statement to assist management to decide whether they should buy in the cartons.

2.   Identify any other factors which should be taken into consideration.

7.11 Whines Ltd., manufactures and assembles small electric motors. 32,000 units of part 1790 are manufactured each year to which the following production costs apply:

	£
Direct Materials	16,000
Direct Labour	24,000
Variable Production Overheads	16,000
Fixed Production Overheads	32,000

Wedge Ltd., has offered to sell Whines Ltd., 32,000 units of part 1790 at £2.50 per unit. If the company accepts the offer, £12,000 of fixed overheads applied to part 1790 could be eliminated. Additionally, some premises used during the manufacture of part 1790 could be rented to a third party at an annual rental of £8,000.

REQUIRED

1. Explain whether Whines Ltd. should accept the offer from Wedge Ltd. or not.

2. What other factors might the management of Whines Ltd. wish to consider before arriving at a decision.

7.12 Dymond Ltd. manufactures specialist jewellery for fashion shops. For the last year the company has been operating at 60 percent of its capacity and its results were as follows:

	£
Sales (300,000 units at £8 each)	2,400,000
Variable Costs (at £4.8 per unit	1,440,000
Fixed Costs	600,000
Profit	360,000

A major retailer has offered to purchase the output from the excess capacity for the next three years at a price of £5.60 per unit.

REQUIRED

1. Evaluate the offer from the major retailer.

2. Re-evaluate the offer if acceptance involves the company in additional fixed costs of £80,000.

3. Identify any other factors that the company should take into consideration before reaching a final decision.

LONG-TERM DECISION ANALYSIS

LEARNING OBJECTIVES

When you have finished studying this chapter and completed the exercises you should be able to:

❏ Understand the need or organisations to identify and invest in high quality capital projects.

❏ Prepare a list of the main financial variables required for project appraisal.

❏ Identify the main points to consider when assessing the quality of input data.

❏ Evaluate capital projects using traditional methods of investment appraisal and discounted cash flow methods.

❏ Illustrate the important differences which can arise in evaluating projects when using net present value (NPV) and internal rate of return (IRR).

8.1   Introduction

A key ingredient in achieving business growth success is the exercise of sound investment judgement in business related activities, as opposed to the investment of funds in the financial securities of another organisation. By investing wisely in the business to achieve returns in excess of the associated costs involved, growth must occur, but of course as we know only too well from managing personal investments, uncertainty about the future makes it difficult to ensure that such a result is achieved. This is also a problem encountered by businesses which need to be able to identify potential investment opportunities that relate to the future, but about which there must therefore be some uncertainty?

In considering this problem the following two questions are typically asked:

❏   Are there any tools or techniques available from the realms of accounting and finance to help marshal views about the desirability of particular investments?

❏   Are there any differences between these tools and techniques, if so what are they?

We will consider these questions and other important issues in this chapter in relation to the evaluation of investments within the business. The evaluation of investments can be seen to be very closely related to the decision by a private individual to purchase a car. In making such a decision he or she would have probably considered the relative priority of purchasing a car, but having made the decision would investigate the alternative models available, evaluate them making some reference to the financial benefit of the main alternatives, make the purchase, and then (probably subconsciously) evaluate the quality of the purchase. The process we will show to be the same for companies but there is one major difference of which you should be aware, the activities associated with the financing of capital expenditure decisions are usually omitted from the evaluation. Whereas for most personal capital expenditure decisions, the decision to buy and how to finance such a purchase go hand in hand, for business capital expenditure the two are usually treated as being distinct issues for consideration.

8.2 Organising investment decisions

A major stimulus for much investment is often the concern about the future performance of the business if investment does not take place. However, in practice many businesses actually consider investment requirements according to the particular needs to be addressed. Let us consider such needs with reference to the following four categories of investment:

❑   Asset replacement.

❑   Cost saving.

❑   Expansion.

❑   Reactive.

8.2.1   Asset replacement

If a company fails to replace those assets which currently generate its cash flow and profit, then in the absence of any other investment, its performance will as a matter of course decline, whether quickly or slowly. If the current profile of activities are appropriate to future long term plans then, in order to continue to generate adequate cash flows and profit, the business must replace assets as they become worn out or obsolete. However, the key point to be stressed is that in the case of any investment, including replacement decisions, the following important questions must be asked: "Do we really need this asset?" and "Are there any better alternatives?" Under no circumstances should any investment decision be taken automatically.

8.2.2   Cost saving

Cost saving projects are critical to companies which have products or services where sales revenues have reached the maximum level that can be absorbed by the market. Irrespective of whether this maximum is temporary because of depressed economic conditions, or more permanent because the maximum achievable share of a mature market has been reached, a reduction in the firm's cost structure is possible by improving the efficiency with which existing assets are employed. Ratio analysis, focusing upon sales generation ratios as described in Chapter 3, can be used to identify possible areas. This identification may reveal the necessity of fundamental changes in the method of operation, for example, by automating previously labour-intensive production methods. One important point about cost-saving projects not to be overlooked, of which the illustration of a change in the method of operation is a good example, is that they usually involve the substitution of an avoidable variable cost with a difficult to avoid fixed cost, in order to secure forecast savings.

Finally, cost saving projects may be important to the not-for-profit organisation in which there may be no revenues associated with a project. The analysis of cost savings enables comparisons to be made with existing practice and between alternatives.

8.2.3   Expansion

Business growth can result from internal or organic expansion or by focusing upon external targets via an acquisitive strategy. Much investment activity can be related to the desire to achieve growth which many organisations (particularly smaller ones) will attempt to achieve internally. Successful internal growth will eventually permit an organisation to contemplate external expansion, particularly where its shares may be traded publicly. However, even companies with a successful track record of acquisitions will undertake internal investment resulting in business expansion to achieve growth.

8.2.4   Reactive investment

This category embraces two particular types of capital expenditure. The first type of reactive investment concerns that which is required as a defensive response to threatening changes in the commercial environment. For example, some of the changes which can be observed in major U.K. clearing bank services are the result of substantial investment caused by threats from previously dormant players in the financial services section, such as Building Societies, in recent years. The second type of reactive investment embraces that imposed upon the business because of legislative or other reasons where the benefits of the expenditure are not always readily measurable. It is perhaps, best illustrated by the following examples;

❏   As a result of new legislation, the U.K. furniture industry has been required to undertake substantial investment in fire resistant foam filling.

❏   Following the Piper Alpha disaster, North Sea Oil companies have been required to undertake safety modifications to offshore installations estimated to cost hundreds of millions of pounds.

8.2.5 Managerial responsibility for investment

In larger organisations managerial responsibility for investment is usually delegated from top management to lower levels of management. This delegation will usually exclude the raising of finance other than from short-term sources. Decisions about sources of finance with long-term implications are typically taken by top management which will try to balance proportions of debt and equity in some way as to minimise the cost of capital to the business.

The delegation of managerial responsibility for the evaluation of capital expenditure can be achieved by specifying cut-off levels, the amount of which corresponds with given levels of seniority. For example, senior divisional management may be responsible for capital expenditure up to an agreed cut-off sum, and approval would have to be obtained from top management for capital expenditure above the agreed cut-off. In addition, such senior divisional management may also be required to approve submissions for capital expenditure from its divisional management, where the capital expenditure required exceeds the level of delegated responsibility.

8.3 Appraising investment opportunities

The consideration of investments according to the needs to be addressed and clear lines of managerial responsibility will not by themselves ensure that success will result. In addition, some means of selecting from those potentially available is essential in the form of an appraisal directed at both financial and non-financial benefits. In this section we provide a background to the financial appraisal of potential investment opportunities. In common with many areas of accounting and finance, numerous terms are used to describe the financial appraisal process of which investment appraisal, project appraisal and capital budgeting are common. To avoid confusion and to reinforce the point that our concern is not with investing in securities of other organisations, we will adopt the term *project appraisal* to refer to the evaluation of capital expenditure.

You may find it easy to become lost in the detail of the financial issues associated with project appraisal, so let us take stock of the key financial requirements to be met:

❑   only those projects which meet the objectives of the business should be selected, i.e. those which provide what the business regards as a satisfactory return for the risks involved;

❑   the return to be expected from a project must exceed the financing cost that the capital expenditure will necessitate, and;

❑   the most financially desirable project must be selected from the range of opportunities available (assuming, as is normally the case, that resources are limited and that not all projects can be undertaken).

In addition to these financial requirements, it is important to stress that for many investments non-financial factors may be very important. Therefore account must also be taken of these so that both financial and non-financial considerations are given appropriate weight.

With these points in mind and before we consider individual techniques for gauging the financial benefit, let us consider the main financial variables required for a project appraisal. A definitive list is impossible, but the following items will usually occur in one form or another:

❑   The initial capital outlay including the cost of fixed assets, working capital and, if appropriate, deliberate start-up losses.

❑   The expected useful economic life of the project.

❑   An estimate of the residual value of assets remaining at the end of the project's useful economic life.

❑   The amounts and timing of all cost and revenue components associated with the project.

❑   Expected price level changes for each cost and revenue component.

❑   Taxation assumptions and any regional grants likely to affect the corporate position.

❑   The relevant cost of financing the project (cost of capital).

❑   Likely estimates of variation for each of the above variables.

Many of these financial variables will be discussed in the next section outlining the major project appraisal techniques, and the remainder are considered in the next chapter. Before considering the techniques let us review certain key points discussed in the previous chapter concerning the requirements of data for purposes of decision making. It is all to easy to focus upon the mechanics of the techniques themselves whilst losing sight of their limitations in the absence of good quality input data. It cannot be overstressed that the benefit to be derived from any technique used for appraising a project can be no better than the quality of the input data employed.

8.4   Assessing the quality of input data

The main points to consider in assessing the quality of input data are:

Future orientation

The only capital outlay, operating costs and revenues relevant to a proposed capital project are those that concern the future. Sunk, past costs are irrelevant even though there may be a temptation to treat them otherwise, as are costs to be found in a company's cost or management accounting system. This is the case whether they are past or present, and they are useful only as a guide in forecasting future cost levels.

It is not only the costs themselves that are irrelevant but also the patterns of cost behaviour. Such patterns may be appropriate to the routine accounting functions of budgeting and variance analysis, but may not be suitable for decisions, the relevant time span for which is substantially longer than that required for routine control. Assumptions which ordinarily permit different costs to be described as fixed, variable or semi-variable in their behaviour may need to be adapted when five or ten year time scales are involved, because at the time a capital project decision is being made all costs relevant to the decision are variable. It is only when the project is accepted and implemented that project associated costs become fixed.

Attributable costs and revenues

The costs and revenues relevant to a capital project are only those which can be legitimately attributed to it rather than any other source. Whilst this notion is simple and manageable in principle at the level of the individual project, difficulties can be encountered in practice when the cumulative effects of several proposed capital projects need to be anticipated.

Differential costs and revenues

Where decisions require more than one course of action to be examined, the only costs and revenues to be considered are those that will differ under the alternative courses of action. Common costs and revenues may be ignored, provided they are expected to behave identically in each of the alternatives under consideration.

Opportunity costs and benefits

These costs and benefits are usually the most difficult of all to deal with. Nevertheless, opportunity costs and benefits must be included in any project decision. For example, if a consequence of introducing a new model of a product currently sold at a profit is that sales of the existing product will be lost, then the lost contribution on the existing product is an opportunity cost of the new model which must be included in the appraisal.

Financing costs

It is often tempting but incorrect during a project appraisal to include the financing costs associated with a proposal within the estimated operating costs. As we will show in the next section, how the financing costs are compared with the financial benefits does vary according to the appraisal techniques used, but in no case are they included with the estimated operating costs.

Uncertainty and inflation

It is important that the risk and uncertainty associated with projects is incorporated within any appraisal, together with expectations about changes in costs and prices. Any failure to make appropriate allowances for risk, uncertainty and inflation can result in an appraisal of questionable value.

Qualitative issues

A serious limitation of conventional project appraisal is the omission of non-financial issues, such as improvements in product quality for corporate image, or a lower susceptibility to adverse social pressures. Whilst such benefits are often extremely difficult to assess, they should not be ignored.

8.5   Project appraisal techniques

We have now set the scene for project appraisal in our discussions of the financial variables required and important issues associated with the quality of cost and revenue inputs. The important issue for consideration now is how such data is organised for purposes of appraising a project. This we will illustrate with reference to the four major project appraisal techniques. We have deliberately omitted issues such as inflation and taxation which sit more comfortably with discussions in the next chapter.

What are the four major appraisal techniques? In common with other areas of accounting and finance some may be known by more than one name, but the most common are:

1. Payback period

2. Accounting rate of return

3. Net present value

4. Internal rate of return

The distinguishing characteristics of these four project appraisal techniques and their respective advantages and disadvantages are best illustrated with financial data. Accordingly we will use data for an imaginary organisation contemplating the following three alternative projects which are also summarised in *Table 8.1*:

Proposal 1

❑   Initial and only capital outlay of £18 million.

❑   Projected annual net cash inflows (receipts less payments) over its six year estimated economic life of £6 million per annum.

Proposal 2

❑   Initial and only capital outlay of £15 million.

❑   Projected annual net cash inflows over its estimated economic life of:

Year 1	£7 million
Year 2	£6 million
Years 3,4 & 5	£5 million

Proposal 3

- Initial and only capital outlay of £11 million.

- Projected annual net cash inflows over its three year estimated economic life of £5 million.

Table 8.1   Basic data for three projects

	Proposal 1 £'000	Proposal 2 £'000	Proposal 3 £'000
Capital Outlay	-18,000	-15,000	-11,000
Net Cash Inflows:			
Year 1	6,000	7,000	5,000
Year 2	6,000	6,000	5,000
Year 3	6,000	5,000	5,000
Year 4	6,000	5,000	
Year 5	6,000	5,000	
Year 6	6,000		

8.5.1   Payback period

The payback period is calculated with reference to cash flow data. It is expressed in terms of a number of years or years and months and summarises the time required for a project to recover its capital outlay from cash inflows. For example, for Proposal 1 which has a capital outlay of £18 million and cash inflows of £6 million for each year of its 6 year expected economic life, the payback is exactly 3 years:

$$\frac{\text{Capital outlay}}{\text{Net cash inflow}} = \frac{£18 \text{ million}}{£6 \text{ million}} = 3 \text{ years}$$

The payback period can be likened to filling a hole in the ground as illustrated in *Figure 8.1*. The outlay is the hole, £18 million in the case of Proposal 1, that is filled annually by the net cash inflows of £6 million. At the end of three years the hole is filled as illustrated in *Figure 8.1 (b)* signifying that the outlay is exactly paid back. At the end of its 6 year economic life £18 million of net cash inflows over and above the outlay will result, this being achieved from years 4, 5 and 6 inclusive as illustrated in *Figure 8.1 (c)*.

Figure 8.1   Illustration of payback period

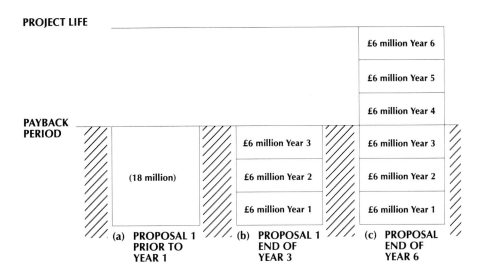

Of course Proposal 1 is straightforward because the payback period occurs exactly at the end of year 3, but this is not usually the case. For example, if you try to calculate the payback period for the other two projects you will find that it does not occur at the end of a single year. Let us see how this can be dealt with using the data for Proposal 2. The first step is to accumulate the cash flows as follows:

Table 8.2   Calculation of payback period

	£'000		
Capital Outlay	-15,000		
Net Cash Inflows:	**(i)**	**(ii)**	**(iii)**
	Annual	**Annual to payback**	**Cumulative to payback**
	£'000	**£'000**	**£'000**
Year 1	7,000	7,000	7,000
Year 2	6,000	6,000	13,000
Year 3	5,000	2,000	15,000

The figures in column (iii) show that in each of the first two years the whole of the net cash inflows are used to accumulate to £13 million. In the third year, only £2 million of the net cash flows is required to make the accumulated net cash flows equal to the capital outlay. Therefore, the payback period takes place in two and two fifth years i.e. two years, plus £2 million out of £5 million.

A similar calculation for Proposal 3 results in a payback period of 2.2 years i.e. £10 million is recovered from the first two years leaving £1 million (0.2) to be recovered from year 3. The results for all three proposals may be summarised as:

	Proposal 1	Proposal 2	Proposal 3
Payback Period (years)	3.0	2.4	2.2

The main aim in using any project appraisal technique is to find out which project should be selected from a number of competing projects. A simple ranking, in this case based on the project offering the shortest payback period, would reveal that Proposal 3 is the best project. However, some companies will evaluate the payback period in relation to the project's useful economic life. This means that Proposal 1 which pays back halfway through its estimated 6 year life may be viewed far more favourably than Proposal 3, which pays back over 70% of the way through its useful economic life. The relationship between the payback period and the useful economic life for each of the proposals may be summarised as:

	Proposal 1	Proposal 2	Proposal 3
Payback Period (years)	3.0	2.4	2.2
Useful Economic Life (years)	6.0	5.0	3.0
Payback / Economic Life	0.5	0.48	0.73

Payback period has a major advantage over other methods because it is simple to calculate, understand and implement. Against this the payback period focuses upon time taken to recover the capital outlay such that cash flows generated after the payback period may not be taken into consideration. One other major shortcoming, the substance and importance of which will become evident shortly in our discussion of the discounting principle, is that unless the cash flows are specifically adjusted, the time value of money is ignored.

8.5.2 Accounting rate of return

The accounting rate of return can be contrasted with the payback period because its calculation does draw upon data relating to the whole life of a project. You must be aware however, that it is calculated with reference to a project's profit, rather than cash flows and it is sometimes criticised because, as you have found with the definition of profit, there is no unique definition for its calculation. That said, once defined it is relatively straightforward to calculate. However, please do take note that different users may arrive at different accounting rates of return using the same input data, and what is even more confusing is that none of the resulting calculations is necessarily incorrect!

The first step in calculating the rate of return is to add the estimated annual profit flows to establish the total profit of the proposed project. If only cash flow information is available then the annual cash flows must be added together to find the total cash flows, which in our example are £36 million, £28 million, and £15 million for Proposals 1, 2 and 3, respectively. From this total the capital outlay (the total depreciation) is deducted to give the total profit. The average annual profit required for the calculation is found by dividing the total profit by the life of the proposal. This is illustrated for our three example proposals in *Table 8.3*.

Table 8.3   Calculation of accounting rate of return

		Proposal 1	Proposal 2	Proposal 3
		£'000	£'000	£'000
Total Net Cash Flow	(A)	36,000	28,000	15,000
Capital Outlay	(B)	-18,000	-15,000	-11,000
Total Profit	(C)=(A)-(B)	£18,000	£13,000	£ 3,000
Life (years)	(D)	6	5	3
Average Annual Profit	(C)/(D)	£3,000	£2,600	£1,000

The accounting rate of return is then calculated by dividing the average annual profit by the capital outlay. For proposal 1, the calculation is:

$$\text{Rate of Return (\%)} = \frac{\text{Average Annual Profit}}{\text{Capital Outlay}} \times 100$$

$$= \frac{£3 \text{ million}}{£18 \text{ million}} \times 100$$

$$= 16.7\%$$

Similar calculations for Proposal 2 and 3 produce accounting rates of return of 17.3% and 8.3%, respectively. A simple ranking from highest to lowest rate of return shows that Proposal 2 is slightly better than Proposal 1.

	Proposal 1	Proposal 2	Proposal 3
Accounting Rate of Return %	16.7	17.3	8.3
Ranking	2	1	3

It was indicated earlier that using the same input data, different accounting rates of return can be produced. How can this happen? It is conceivable that one might use some notion of average capital outlay rather than the total capital outlay adopted in our example and, indeed, some organisations do just this. As you will appreciate, anything which has the effect of reducing the capital outlay in the calculation will increase the accounting rate of return. Consider for example the effect on Proposal 1 if the average capital outlay was calculated as being £9 million. The rate of return percentage would double!

The potential ambiguity in accounting rate of return results is sometimes presented as being a shortcoming, nevertheless, the technique is used and with some success, particularly where manuals of capital expenditure procedure provide a specific definition of the items to be used in accounting rate of return calculations.

The principle of discounting

The two remaining techniques for discussion, the net present value (NPV), and the internal rate of return (IRR) are both reliant upon a principle which involves discounting, or scaling-down, future cash flows. In order to appreciate the principle involved we will compare discounting with the more familiar but related technique of compounding.

Compounding is applied to a sum of money at the present such that given a required rate of interest what it will be worth at a future period can be calculated. Discounting is the reverse, it uses cash inflows from future periods and given a required rate of interest what they will be worth at the present can be calculated. This enables a present day comparison to be made of the future cash inflows with the outlay.

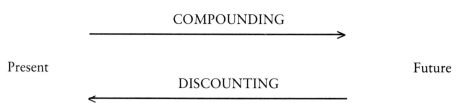

How is this discounting achieved? Cash flows can be discounted using factors which are readily available in statistical tables. The basis for their calculation is similar to the principles used in calculating compound interest. We will use the information in *Table 8.4* to show the relationship between compounding and discounting. There we make specific reference to the factors used to compound and discount cash at a 10% rate.

Table 8.4   Compound interest and discounted cash flow factors

	Compound interest factors 10%	Discounted cash flow factors (DCF) 10%
Year 0	1.000	1.000
Year 1	1.100	0.909
Year 2	1.210	0.826
Year 3	1.331	0.751
Year 4	1.464	0.683

Using the factors in *Table 8.4*, £1,000 invested today at 10% compound interest would yield £1,210 at the end of year two. i.e. £1,000 x 1.21. The reverse can be seen if we assume a forecast cash flow of £1,210 at the end of year two, discounted at 10% back to a present value would produce £1,000. i.e. £1,210 x 0.826. The principle of discounting thus operates by scaling down future cash flows to produce a present value. In this way future cash flows can be readily compared with the present value of capital outlays. You should be aware that the reduction in the value of future cash flows using the discounting process is dependent upon the rate of interest. The higher the rate of interest, the more severely will the cash flows be scaled down. The technique of adjusting cash flows might seem tedious and difficult to understand, but do bear in mind that the discount factors do not have to be calculated because tables such as that included in **Appendix A** are available. In this table the present value of £1 has been calculated for a wide range of interest rates.

Determining the relevant discount rate

In order to calculate the net present value technique (and some other discounting techniques such as, the profitability index, or the discounted payback period that we will discuss), the relevant discount factor must be known. This discount factor should be the company's *hurdle rate* as represented by its cost of capital, that is the projects' break-even point. Projects undertaken yielding a return above this hurdle rate will increase the value of the business whilst those below will decrease value. But how is this cost of capital calculated?

The components involved in the determination of a company's cost of capital have been the subject of much academic research and debate. However, there does seem to be some agreement that the appropriate rate should comprise the weighted average of the after tax cost of debt capital and the equity cost of capital. In the case of debt capital, the after tax cost is used because as you will recall from the earlier chapters, interest is deductible before tax thus providing a reduced real cost. This is unlike dividend payments which have to be met from after tax profits. How this cost of capital is arrived at is best understood with reference to the following simple example: *A company has an after tax cost of debt of 6 per cent, an estimated cost of equity of 16 per cent and future gearing comprising 20 per cent debt and 80 per cent equity.* In this simple case, the company's weighted average cost of capital is 14%, and the basis for the calculation is illustrated in *Table 8.5.*

Table 8.5   Weighted average cost of capital (WACC)

	Weight A (%)	Cost B (%)	Weighted Cost A x B % (%)
Debt	20	6	1.2
Equity	80	16	<u>12.8</u>
			14.0

This cost of capital includes the returns demanded by both debt-holders and shareholders because pre-interest cash flows are those to be discounted. Given that both debt-holders and shareholders have claims against these, the appropriate cost of capital will be one that incorporates the relative capital contribution of each group. Thus, total pre-interest cash flows which are attributable to both lenders and shareholders are discounted by a weighted cost of capital to yield a value to the business.

It is important to realise that the relative weights attached to debt and equity within the calculation should be based on the relative proportions of each targeted for the future. This is because the concern of a capital project appraisal is with the future, and not with the past. Thus, the present or previous debt to equity proportions are absolutely irrelevant, unless they apply to the future. There is also a useful analogy with the matching principle discussed in relation to accounting in Chapter 1. The objective is to compare like with like, hence the use of future orientated gearing ratio for establishing the cost of capital at which to discount future cash flows.

The determination of the relevant discount factor is important not only to project appraisal. In recognition of its importance it is discussed more fully in the next chapter.

8.5.3   Net present value (NPV)

We will now illustrate the application of the net present value (NPV) technique, whereby for a given rate of interest future cash flows are discounted using the principle discussed in the previous section. The sum total of these discounted future cash flows is compared with the capital outlay, and where it is greater than the outlay, the NPV is said to be positive and the project is acceptable on economic grounds. Conversely, if a negative NPV results (capital outlay is greater than the sum of discounted future cash flows) the project is not acceptable on economic grounds.

Using basic data for the three proposed projects illustrated earlier, and assuming a 10% cost of capital, the following NPV analysis can be carried out for Proposal 1:

Table 8.6   Calculation of net present value - Proposal 1

Year	Column 1 Discount factor 10%	Column 2 Cash flows £000	Column 3 (Column 1 x Column 2) Present value £000
1	0.909	6,000	5,454
2	0.826	6,000	4,956
3	0.751	6,000	4,506
4	0.683	6,000	4,098
5	0.621	6,000	3,726
6	0.564	6,000	3,384
Present Value of Cash Inflows			26,124
less Capital Outlay			18,000
Net Present Value			**8,124**

The annual net cash flows shown in column 2 are multiplied by the 10% discount factors in column 1 to produce the annual present value of the cash flows in column 3. These annual present values are then added together to give the total present value of the cash inflows of £26.124 million. The net present value is calculated by deducting the capital outlay from the total present value of the cash inflows (i.e. £26.124 million - £18.000 million) giving £8.124 million.

The effect of discounting the cash flows is also illustrated in *Figure 8.2*.

Figure 8.2   Comparison of cash flows - Proposal 1

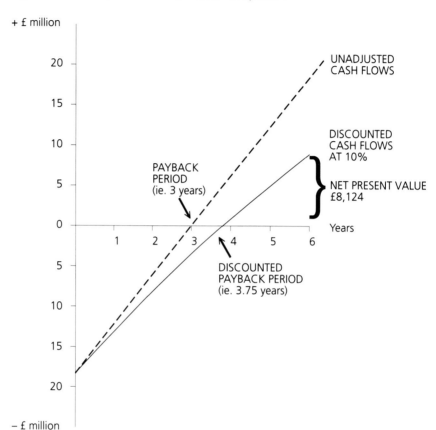

The capital outlay of £18 million is the starting point of the upper diagonal which is constructed from accumulating the annual net cash inflows of £6 million. The result is a cumulative cash inflow of £36 million at the end of year 6. When these annual cash inflows of £6 million are discounted at 10% and plotted in the diagram, the lower diagonal results. The application of the 10% discount factor can be seen to cause a scaling-down which results in a net present value of £8.124 million. Raising the discount factor would scale-down the cash flows even further, thereby resulting in a lower net present value. One other observation from the diagram is the effect upon the payback period when discounted rather than undiscounted annual net cash inflows are used. You will see from the diagram that the *discounted payback period* is 3.75 years rather than the original 3 years, when the net cash inflows are discounted at 10%. Furthermore, should the discount factor be increased resulting in a greater scaling down of cash flows, the discounted payback period becomes even longer.

We will in fact consider the discounted payback shortly once we have reviewed the net present value calculations for all three proposals.

Table 8.7   Comparison of net present values

	Proposal 1 £000	Proposal 2 £000	Proposal 3 £000
Present Value of Cash Inflows	26,124	21,594	12,430
Capital Outlay	-18,000	-15,000	-11,000
Net Present Value	**8,124**	**6,594**	**1,430**

The results show that for all three proposals the net present value is positive, and on economic grounds all would be acceptable because they:

❑   exceed the required rate of return of 10%;

❑   cover the capital outlay; and

❑   produce a sum in excess of the capital outlay which is referred to as the net present value.

Where there is a limited supply of funds the following additional calculations will provide useful information to assist in the decision. These calculations measure the discounted payback, introduced earlier, and what is known as the *profitability index*.

The profitability index is a ratio which relates the discounted net cash inflows from a project to its outlay. It is calculated by dividing the present value of the cash inflows by the capital outlay. For Proposal 1 this would be £26.124 million divided by £18 million which gives 1.45, and for Proposals 2 and 3 it is 1.44 and 1.13, respectively.

		Proposal 1 £000	Proposal 2 £000	Proposal 3 £000
Present Value of Cash Inflows	(A)	26,124	21,594	12,430
Capital Outlay	(B)	18,000	15,000	11,000
Profitability Index	(A)/(B)	1.45	1.44	1.13

The index of 1.45 for Proposal 1 means that the capital outlay is covered once plus an additional 45% and that where capital is restricted, should be preferred to the two other alternatives on economic grounds. However, before drawing any further conclusions let us consider the discounted payback.

As illustrated earlier, the discounted payback period is similar in principle to the simple payback period, the only difference being that we use the discounted annual flows, and accumulate them until their sum equals the capital outlay.

In *Figure 8.2* we illustrated the discounted payback period for Proposal 1 of 3.75 years, but how is this calculated? Using the discounted annual cash flows for Proposal 1, the discounted payback period can be calculated in a similar manner to simple payback:

Table 8.8   Calculation of discounted payback - Proposal 1

	£'000		
Capital Outlay	-18,000		
Discounted Cash Inflows:	(i)	(ii)	(iii)
	Annual	**Annual to payback**	**Cumulative to payback**
	£'000	**£'000**	**£'000**
Year 1	5,454	5,454	5,454
Year 2	4,956	4,956	10,410
Year 3	4,506	4,506	14,916
Year 4	4,098	3,084	18,000

Note. *The adjusted cash flows shown in column (i) have been extracted from Table 8.6*

The discounted cash flows to achieve the £18 million capital outlay can be monitored from column (iii). At the end of Year 3 £14.916 million will be recovered, leaving £3.084 million to be recovered in Year 4. Given that £4.098 million will be recovered from Year 4, the proportion of a year represented by £3.084 million can be readily calculated. Thus, discounted payback is achieved in three years plus £3.084 million divided by £4.098 million, which equals approximately 3.75 years.

Similar calculations for the profitability index and discounted payback can be performed for Proposals 2 and 3 to produce the following results:

Table 8.9   Comparison of net present value methods

	Proposal 1	Proposal 2	Proposal 3
Profitability Index	1.45	1.44	1.13
Discounted Payback (years)	3.75	2.98	2.62
Net Present Value (£ million)	8.124	6.594	1.430

8.5.4   Internal rate of return (IRR)

Whereas the net present value, the profitability index and the discounted payback calculations require knowledge of the company's cost of capital as necessary data input for their calculation, the internal rate of return (IRR) does not. Just what then is the IRR?

The IRR is a discounted cash flow method which seeks to find the discount rate at which the present value of cash inflows from a capital project exactly equal the capital outlay. In other words, at the IRR the net present value is zero.

The IRR can best be understood with reference to *Figure 8.3* in which you can see that the lowest line corresponds with a NPV of £0. This is achieved by scaling-down the net cash inflows by applying a discount factor corresponding with the IRR percentage. Thus the percentage which when converted to a discount factor and multiplied by the net cash inflows gives a money value equal to the capital outlay is the internal rate of return.

Figure 8.3   Graph showing internal rate of return (IRR) - Proposal 1

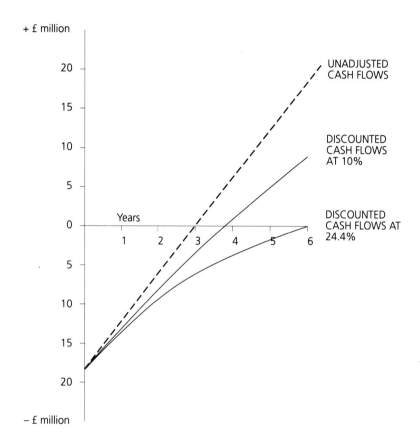

Once determined the IRR percentage should then be compared with the company's cost of capital in order to establish the economic acceptability of a project. The principle is that if the IRR exceeds the cost of capital then the project is acceptable on economic grounds. On the other hand, if the IRR from the project is lower than the cost of capital the project is not acceptable on economic grounds.

Without the aid of a computer or programmable calculator a number of manual calculations are usually required to find the IRR. The procedure involves trial and error upon the part of the user to find a discount rate corresponding with a zero net present value. The calculations necessary to find the IRR for Proposal 1 are based upon data summarised in *Table 8.10*.

Table 8.10   Trial and error calculation of internal rate of return (IRR)

Year	Cash flows £'000	DCF factor 20%	Present value £'000	DCF factor 25%	Present value £'000
1	6,000	0.833	4,998	0.800	4,800
2	6,000	0.694	4,164	0.640	3,840
3	6,000	0.579	3,474	0.512	3,072
4	6,000	0.482	2,892	0.410	2,460
5	6,000	0.402	2,412	0.328	1,968
6	6,000	0.335	2,010	0.262	1,572
Present Value of Cash Inflows			19,950		17,712
less Capital Outlay			18,000		18,000
Net Present Value			**1,950**		**-288**

The table shows that cash flows for Proposal 1, when discounted at 20%, provide a net present value of £1.950 million. To find the IRR (where the net present value is zero), in this case a higher discount is required. The result of increasing the rate to 25% shows that the net present value is negative at £-288 million. The internal rate of return must therefore fall between 20% and 25% and as illustrated below can be found approximately by linear interpolation.

$$\text{IRR} = \begin{array}{c}\text{Lower}\\ \text{discount}\\ \text{rate}\end{array} + \left(\frac{\text{NPV at lower rate}}{\begin{array}{c}\text{NPV at lower rate}\\ \text{minus NPV at}\\ \text{higher rate}\end{array}} \times \begin{array}{c}\text{Difference between}\\ \text{high and low}\\ \text{discount rates}\end{array} \right)$$

$$= \quad 20 \quad + \quad \left(\frac{1,950}{2,238} \times 5 \right)$$

$$= \quad 20 \quad + \quad 4.4$$

$$= \quad 24.4\%$$

Similar calculation carried out for Proposal 2 and 3 produce the following results shown alongside that for Proposal 1:

	Proposal 1	Proposal 2	Proposal 3
Internal Rate of Return %	24.4	27.5	17.4

The approximations of the IRR % in this case are fairly accurate. In fact, those obtained from using both a computer and a programmable calculator were 24.3%, 27.4% and 17.3% for Proposals 1, 2 and 3 respectively.

The results achieved from using manual calculations for the IRR produce satisfactory results provided that the difference between the two discount factors is not too large (e.g. greater than 5). However, it is preferable to use a computer or programmable calculator which allow the user to change any of the figures with relative ease.

You should be aware that one major problem with the IRR is that it may be impossible to provide a clear cut solution to proposals that have unconventional cash flows. In such a situation there may not be an internal rate of return, or if there is, it may not be unique.

8.5.5   Summary of key features of project appraisal techniques.

1. The payback period, the NPV and the IRR techniques are reliant upon cash flow data for their calculation, whereas the accounting rate of return is reliant upon profit data.

2. Accounting adjustments for depreciation may be required. In calculating the accounting rate of return depreciation must be deducted if you are provided with cash flow data. If you are required to calculate a measure reliant upon cash flow data (e.g. payback period, NPV, IRR) and you have profit data, then depreciation must be added back.

3. The accounting rate of return has no unique definition and is therefore far more influenced by user judgement in its calculation than the cash related techniques.

4. Only the NPV and IRR techniques directly take account of the time value of money, although a discounted payback period may also be calculated.

5. The IRR calculation can yield negative or multiple solutions because of the nature of input data used. This particular problem is unique to the technique and can make the interpretation of the results difficult.

6. The output to be interpreted from each of the techniques differs. In the

case of the payback period it is expressed in terms of time, for the NPV in monetary units, and for both the IRR and accounting rate of return it is a percentage, although what they portray differs.

Figure 8.4 Summary of project appraisal techniques if provided with cash flow data

	PAYBACK PERIOD	RATE OF RETURN	NET PRESENT VALUE	INTERNAL RATE OF RETURN
INPUT	CASH FLOW	PROFIT	CASH FLOW	CASH FLOW
ACCOUNTING ADJUSTMENTS	NO	YES	NO	NO
MORE THAN ONE DEFINITION	NO	YES	NO	NO
DISCOUNTED	SOMETIMES	NO	YES	YES
MORE THAN ONE SOLUTION	NO	NO	NO	YES
OUTPUT	YEARS AND/ OR MONTHS	%	£ PRESENT VALUE	%

8.5.6 Mutually exclusive projects (NPV or IRR?)

We have indicated that the IRR suffers from certain technical problems in comparison with the NPV. These, however, are not its only limitations and, as we will demonstrate, the technique has particular shortcomings for mutually exclusive projects, that is where one only can be selected from the available alternatives.

Whereas the decision rule for the NPV assumes that cash flows resulting during the life cycle of a project have an opportunity cost equal to the discount rate used, the decision rule for the IRR assumes that such resulting cash flows have an opportunity cost equal to the IRR which generated them. Whereas the assumption used in calculating the NPV is realistic insofar as the discount rate used is found with reference to the capital market, no such theoretical basis exists for the assumption implied by using the IRR. Second, the NPV approach provides an absolute measure that fully represents the increase in value of the company if a particular project is undertaken. The IRR, by contrast, provides a percentage figure from which the size of the benefits in terms of wealth creation cannot always be grasped. This can be readily seen with reference to the following example of two proposals:

Table 8.11   Net present value and internal rate of return

	Cash flows Proposal X £000	Cash flows Proposal Y £000
Year 0	-10,000	-16,000
1	5,000	7,500
2	5,000	7,500
3	5,000	7,500
NPV (at 10%)	£2,430	£2,645
IRR	23.4%	19.2%

For these two proposals, where only one can be selected, the IRR approach favours Proposal X, whilst in terms of increased value Proposal Y is preferable. Clearly, it is the size of the benefit rather than the percentage return, and hence the net present value, which is more important.

The problem of conflicting results between the two techniques does not always necessarily follow and, as illustrated in *Table 8.12* with reference to Proposals X and Y, will depend upon the cost of capital:

Table 8.12   Net present value at different cost of capital

Cost of Capital %	Net present value Proposal X £'000	Net present value Proposal Y £'000
15	1,420	1,130
14	1,605	1,408
13	1,805	1,708
12	2,010	2,015
11	2,220	2,330

In this case, had the cost of capital been higher than 12% Proposal X would have been shown to be preferable according to both techniques. Despite this, the NPV method does provide clear guidance and should be used where possible.

8.6 Project appraisal in practice

Many studies of project appraisal practice have been undertaken. Most studies have been orientated towards the practices of large organisations to which the following general observations apply:

1. The most frequently used technique is the payback period. This is often in conjunction with other techniques, but it may be used on its own for smaller projects.

2. When a discounted cash flow technique is used it is more likely to be the internal rate of return method rather than the net present value method.

3. Qualitative judgement is regarded as important.

4. The accounting rate of return is used despite potential ambiguities in definition.

5. The use of techniques is guided by standard procedures usually in the form of a capital budgeting manual of practice.

In addition to these five observations relating to the techniques two others are noteworthy and will be dealt with in detail in the next chapter:

❏ A formal analysis of risk is a standard pre-decision control procedure in many organisations, most often in the form of testing the sensitivity of key inputs and underlying economic assumptions.

❏ Inflation adjustments are made in appraising projects using rates applicable to specific inputs although the use of a single general rate is also practised.

One important question which emerges from the observations from the study is, why the IRR is far more popular than the theoretically preferred NPV technique. This has been attributed to a number of reasons, such as the appeal of a percentage to managers who, apparently would be far less comfortable with interpreting a NPV calculation. It should also not be ignored that from IRR calculations a ranking of projects can be obtained without the need for knowledge of the company's hurdle rate although, as indicated in the last section, this ranking may be inferior to that provided by NPV calculations. Associated with there being no need for a pre-determined cut-off rate is the political appeal of the IRR. One recognised feature of the appraisal process is the potential for playing the system by ensuring that projects which have acquired the personal commitment of management always meet or exceed the prescribed hurdle. If the hurdle is not formally communicated then perhaps this problem can be removed. Certainly our observations of practice have found some confirmation of this view in some organisations. In such cases, the IRR usually in conjunction with other techniques, is prescribed for use below corporate level. At corporate level, however, where the desired hurdle is known the NPV technique may play a more significant role.

Appendix A   PRESENT VALUE OF £1

%	6	8	10	11	12	13	14	15	16	17
Period										
1	.943	.926	.909	.901	.893	.885	.877	.870	.862	.855
2	.890	.857	.826	.812	.797	.783	.769	.756	.743	.731
3	.840	.794	.751	.731	.712	.693	.675	.658	.641	.624
4	.792	.735	.683	.659	.636	.613	.592	.572	.552	.534
5	.747	.681	.621	.593	.567	.543	.519	.497	.476	.456
6	.705	.630	.564	.535	.507	.480	.456	.432	.410	.390
7	.665	.583	.513	.482	.452	.425	.400	.376	.354	.333
8	.627	.540	.467	.434	.404	.376	.351	.327	.305	.285
9	.592	.500	.424	.391	.361	.333	.308	.284	.263	.243
10	.558	.463	.386	.352	.322	.295	.270	.247	.227	.208
11	.527	.429	.350	.317	.287	.261	.237	.215	.195	.178
12	.497	.397	.319	.286	.257	.231	.208	.187	.168	.152
13	.469	.368	.290	.258	.229	.204	.182	.163	.145	.130
14	.442	.340	.263	.232	.205	.181	.160	.141	.125	.111
15	.417	.315	.239	.209	.183	.160	.140	.123	.108	.095

%	18	19	20	21	22	23	24	26	28	30
Period										
1	.847	.840	.833	.826	.820	.813	.806	.794	.781	.769
2	.718	.706	.694	.683	.672	.661	.650	.630	.610	.592
3	.609	.593	.579	.564	.551	.537	.524	.500	.477	.455
4	.516	.499	.482	.467	.451	.437	.423	.397	.373	.350
5	.437	.419	.402	.386	.370	.355	.341	.315	.291	.269
6	.370	.352	.335	.319	.303	.289	.275	.250	.227	.207
7	.314	.296	.279	.263	.249	.235	.222	.198	.178	.159
8	.266	.249	.233	.218	.204	.191	.179	.157	.139	.123
9	.225	.209	.194	.180	.167	.155	.144	.125	.108	.094
10	.191	.176	.162	.149	.137	.126	.116	.099	.085	.073
11	.162	.148	.135	.123	.112	.103	.094	.079	.066	.056
12	.137	.124	.112	.102	.092	.083	.076	.062	.052	.043
13	.116	.104	.093	.084	.075	.068	.061	.050	.040	.033
14	.099	.088	.078	.069	.062	.055	.049	.039	.032	.025
15	.084	.074	.065	.057	.051	.045	.040	.031	.025	.020

Appendix B   ANNUITY OF £1

% Period	6	8	10	11	12	13	14	15	16	17
1	.943	.926	.909	.901	.893	.885	.877	.870	.862	.855
2	1.833	1.783	1.736	1.713	1.690	1.668	1.647	1.626	1.605	1.585
3	2.673	2.577	2.487	2.444	2.402	2.361	2.322	2.283	2.246	2.210
4	3.465	3.312	3.170	3.102	3.037	2.974	2.914	2.855	2.798	2.743
5	4.212	3.993	3.791	3.696	3.605	3.517	3.433	3.352	3.274	3.199
6	4.917	4.623	4.355	4.231	4.111	3.998	3.889	3.784	3.685	3.589
7	5.582	5.206	4.868	4.712	4.564	4.423	4.288	4.160	4.039	3.922
8	6.210	5.747	5.335	5.146	4.968	4.799	4.639	4.487	4.344	4.207
9	6.802	6.247	5.759	5.537	5.328	5.132	4.946	4.772	4.607	4.451
10	7.360	6.710	6.145	5.889	5.650	5.426	5.216	5.019	4.833	4.659
11	7.887	7.139	6.495	6.207	5.938	5.687	5.453	5.234	5.029	4.836
12	8.384	7.536	6.814	6.492	6.194	5.918	5.660	5.421	5.197	4.988
13	8.853	7.904	7.103	6.750	6.424	6.122	5.842	5.583	5.342	5.118
14	9.295	8.244	7.367	6.982	6.628	6.302	6.002	5.724	5.468	5.229
15	9.712	8.559	7.606	7.191	6.811	6.462	6.142	5.847	5.575	5.324

% Period	18	19	20	21	22	23	24	26	28	30
1	.847	.840	.833	.826	.820	.813	.806	.794	.781	.769
2	1.566	1.547	1.528	1.509	1.492	1.474	1.457	1.424	1.392	1.361
3	2.174	2.140	2.106	2.074	2.042	2.011	1.981	1.923	1.868	1.816
4	2.690	2.639	2.589	2.540	2.494	2.448	2.404	2.320	2.241	2.166
5	3.127	3.058	2.991	2.926	2.864	2.803	2.745	2.635	2.532	2.436
6	3.498	3.410	3.326	3.245	3.167	3.092	3.020	2.885	2.759	2.643
7	3.812	3.706	3.605	3.508	3.416	3.327	3.242	3.083	2.937	2.802
8	4.078	3.954	3.837	3.726	3.619	3.58	3.421	3.241	3.076	2.925
9	4.303	4.163	4.031	3.905	3.786	3.673	3.566	3.366	3.184	3.019
10	4.494	4.339	4.192	4.054	3.923	3.799	3.682	3.465	3.269	3.092
11	4.656	4.486	4.327	4.177	4.035	3.902	3.776	3.543	3.335	3.147
12	4.793	4.611	4.439	4.278	4.127	3.985	3.851	3.606	3.387	3.190
13	4.910	4.715	4.533	4.362	4.203	4.053	3.912	3.656	3.427	3.223
14	5.008	4.802	4.611	4.432	4.265	4.108	3.962	3.695	3.459	3.249
15	5.092	4.876	4.675	4.489	4.315	4.153	4.001	3.726	3.483	3.268

Appendix C

Using annuity tables

In addition to the arithmetic tables which provide a stream of discount factors (*see Appendix A*), it is also possible to obtain arithmetic tables which give cumulative discount factors over a specific period of time. These tables, which are included in *Appendix B*, are of referred to as annuity tables.

Before we go any further it might help to consider the benefit of using cumulative discount factors

Table 8.13   Discount factors at 10%

Period	Discount factors at 10%	Cumulative discount factors at 10%
1	0.909	0.909
2	0.826	1.735
3	0.751	2.486
4	0.683	3.169
5	0.621	3.790
6	0.564	4.354

From *Table 8.13* we can identify the cumulative discount factors for any period between one and five years. If we return to Proposal 1 we can calculate the present value of the cash flows in one operation:

£6 million × 4.354 = £26.124 million

A quicker method! However, we must point out that this method can only be used where the annual cash flows are equal.

A final point regarding the cumulative discount factors. Compare the figures we have just used from *Table 8.13* with the corresponding figures from *Appendix B*. The slight difference is due to rounding and for the calculation of further examples we will use the figures from *Appendix B*.

Using cumulative discount factors

In many academic environments it is possible to use cumulative discount factors to evaluate projects where the annual cash flows are equal, the benefit being a substantial saving in terms of time. (In practice it is difficult to imagine cases where the annual cash flows would be equal).

We will continue to make use of Proposal 1, (we already know the answers) and use the cumulative discount factors to calculate the following:

1. The internal rate of return given a capital outlay of £18 million, average annual savings of £6 million and a six year life.

2. The minimum average annual savings given a cost of capital (discount rate) of 24%, a capital outlay of £18 million and a six year life.

3. The maximum capital outlay given a cost of capital of 24%, average annual saving of £6 million and a six year life.

1. Calculate the internal rate of return

First, we calculate the cumulative discount factor as follows:

$$\frac{\text{Capital Outlay}}{\text{Average Annual Savings}} = \frac{£18\text{ m}}{£6\text{ m}} = 3.000$$

Second, we consult the table in *Appendix B* and check the cumulative discount factors on the line for a six year life until we obtain a value which is close to the 3.000. In this case we will see that a figure of 3.020 is the closest and this represents the cumulative discount factors at 24%. With the use of interpolation, say between 24% and 25% it is possible to arrive at rates correct to one decimal place.

2. Calculate the minimum average annual savings

In this case we are given a cost of capital and the life of the project therefore we consult *Appendix B* and extract the cumulative discount factors at 24% for a period of six years which give 3.020. To find the minimum average annual savings:

$$\frac{\text{Capital Outlay}}{\text{Cumulative Discount Factors}} = \frac{£18\text{ million}}{3.020} = £5.960\text{ m}$$

In this case, we conclude that if the capital outlay is expected to be £18 million and the company's cost of capital is 24% then the project will need to provide minimum average annual savings of £5.960 million.

3. Calculate the maximum capital outlay

In this case we follow the same procedure as in 2. above and obtain a cumulative discount factor of 3.020. The maximum capital outlay is found from:

Average annual savings $\times$ the cumulative discount factor

$$£6 \text{ million} \times 3.020 = £18.120 \text{ million}$$

Here we conclude that if the average annual savings are expected to be £6 million and the company's cost of capital is 24%, then a maximum capital outlay of £18.120 million can be spent.

Exercises

8.1 The management team of U. Dunnit Limited have four projects for consideration. In the past, they have evaluated projects against simple payback. The following information is available:

	Project A	Project B	Project C	Project D
	£'000	£ 000	£'000	£ 000
Capital Outlay	15,000	18.000	10,000	18 000
Net Cash Inflows:				
Year 1	7,000	6,000	5,000	4,000
Year 2	4,000	6,000	5,000	5,000
Year 3	3,000	6,000		6,000
Year 4	2,000	6,000		7,000
Year 5	1,000	6,000		8,000

REQUIRED

1. Evaluate the projects using each of the following methods:

   a   Simple payback

   b   Accounting rate of return

   c   Net present value and profitability index. Assuming a cost of capital of 10%.

   d   Internal rate of return (using the DCF tables given below), for the project with the best profitability index.

Period	19%	21%
1	0.840	0.826
2	0.706	0.683
3	0.593	0.564
4	0.499	0.467
5	0.419	0,386

2. Write a report to the Chairman of the management team explaining each of the evaluation methods. You are also required to make a recommendation on the method(s) which should be used by the company for future project evaluation.

8.2   A company is considering the purchase of a new machine to extend its range
       of products and have obtained the following information:

Capital Outlay   £390,000

Profit Forecast:-   £
                        Year 1   60,000
                        Year 2   45,000
                        Year 3   21,000
                        Year 4   12,000
                        Year 5   12,000

The profit before taxation figures are stated after charging £24,000 per annum
of factory overheads allocated to the project.

The scrap value of the machine at the end of the fifth year will be £60,000.

The management of the company will approve the project provided that it
will result in a minimum return of 10% per annum.

REQUIRED

1.   Advise the company management whether they should proceed with
      the project on the basis of the above figures.

2.   Suggest what other factors should be taken into consideration before
      a final decision is made.

8.3   The senior engineer of Maxifly Limited has submitted a project to install equipment to manufacture a new type of fishing rod. The following information is available:-

Capital Outlay   £480,000

Life of Project   5 years

Profit Forecast:

	£
Year 1	32,000
Year 2	48,000
Year 3	60,000
Year 4	120,000
Year 5	48,000

The scrap value of the equipment is estimated to be £80,000 and will be received at the end of year five.

The company uses the straight-line method of depreciation.

The company's cost of capital is 14 per cent.

REQUIRED

1.   Calculate the net present value and the simple payback period for the project.

2.   Although discounted cash flow is widely considered to be a superior method of investment appraisal, the simple payback method has still been shown to be the most popular method in practice. Suggest reasons why this may be the case.

8.4   A machine with a purchase price of £70,000 is estimated to eliminate manual operations costing £20,000 per year. The machine will last five years and have no residual value at the end of its life.

REQUIRED

1.   Calculate the internal rate of return.

2.   Calculate the annual saving necessary to achieve a 12% internal rate of return.

3.   Calculate the net present value and the profitability index if the company's cost of capital is 10%.

8.5 D.R. Afty Ltd., make a range of wooden doors for the building industry. The production engineer has investigated replacing three existing machines with either the latest models, or a multi-purpose model.

The following data has been collected:

Machine type	Existing machines		Proposed models	
	Original capital cost	Operating expenses per year	Capital cost	Operating expenses per year
	£	£	£	£
Cutting	20,000	15,000	27,000	9,000
Planing	30,000	25,000	35,000	17,000
Sanding	10,000	5,000	12,000	2,000
Multi-purpose model			132,000	16,000

Assume all machines to have a 10 year life.
The cost of capital within the company is 15%.
Ignore taxation

REQUIRED

Which proposal should be accepted and why?

8.6   A company is considering two mutually exclusive investment projects, A and B, each of which involves an initial cash outlay of £190,000 for A, and £300,000 for B. The estimated net cash inflows from each project are:

	A £	B £
Year 1	87,500	75,000
Year 2	87,500	150,000
Year 3	87,500	195,000
IRR	18.1%	16.2%

REQUIRED

1.   Draw a graph to show the relationship between the net present value and discount rate for the two projects, using rates of 10, 14, 18 and 22%.

2.   Use the graph to estimate the internal rate of return for each project. If the company adopts a criterion rate of 10%, which project would you recommend?

3.   Briefly summarise the relative merits of the net present value and internal rate of return as methods of investment appraisal.

8.7   A company is considering which of two mutually exclusive projects it should undertake. The finance director thinks the project with the higher NPV should be chosen whereas the managing director thinks that the one with the higher IRR should be undertaken especially as both projects have the same initial outlay and length of life. The company anticipates a cost of capital of 10% and the net after cash flows of the projects are as follows:

	Project RUF £	Project TUF £
Year 0	-160,000	-160,000
Year 1	28,000	175,000
Year 2	64,000	6,000
Year 3	72,000	6,000
Year 4	60,000	6,000
Year 5	16,000	6,000
IRR	15.6%	19.2%

REQUIRED

1. Calculate the NPV for each project.

2. Recommend, with reasons, which project if any you would undertake.

3. Explain the inconsistency in ranking of the two projects in view of the remarks of the directors.

4. Identify the cost of capital at which your recommendation in 2. would be reversed.

8.8 The most recent departmental accounts of Fringe Stores Ltd show that the household department is making a loss. Management is of the opinion that the space used by the household department could be better utilised selling furniture which has a larger mark-up.

The most recent abbreviated profit and loss account is as follows:

| | DEPARTMENTS | | | |
	Furniture £'000	Household £'000	Clothing £'000	Total £'000
Sales	1,600	200	800	2,600
less Cost of Sales	1,120	160	440	1,720
Gross Profit	480	40	360	880
Commissions	-160	-20	-80	-260
Depreciation	-48	-32	-40	-120
Other Fixed Costs	-80	-32	-60	-172
Net Profit (Loss)	£192	-£44	£180	£328

The following additional information is also available:

a. If the household department is discontinued, sales of furniture can be expanded by 25% and sales of clothing will be unaffected.

b. The fixtures and fittings at present being used in the household department could not be used in the expanded furniture department and they would have to be sold for their salvage value of £24,000. The fixtures are otherwise estimated to have a further life of eight years after which their salvage value would be nil.

c.   Since furniture is more costly than the household items held in stock, the store will have to expand its working capital investment in stock by £88,000.

d.   The added level of furniture sales would carry the same proportionate cost of sales expense as the present furniture investment and commissions would remain at 10% sales value.

e.   Expanding the furniture department would require an expenditure of £280,000 for renovation and new fixtures. The renovation and the fixtures would last for eight years before any more capital had to be spent on the department.

f.   The store uses the straight-line depreciation method.

g.   The other fixed costs of the household department includes the salaries of long-term employees, who will be made redundant at a cost of £17,600 to Fringe Stores Ltd., if the furniture department is expanded. The cost saving per year will amount to £17,600 but the remainder of the fixed costs will be chargeable to the furniture department if that department expands into the area now used by the household department.

REQUIRED

1.   Make a recommendation to management as to whether or not the household department should be discontinued and the furniture department expanded. Use both payback and a discounted cash flow approach assuming a desired rate of return of 20%.

2.   What other matters should be taken into account apart from the basic financial calculations?

AN INTRODUCTION TO FINANCIAL MANAGEMENT

LEARNING OBJECTIVES

When you have finished studying this chapter and completed the exercises you should be able to:

- ❏ Assess whether the size and composition of a company's asset structure is appropriate.

- ❏ Discuss methods to determine the size and composition of a company's future asset structure.

- ❏ Undertake sensitivity analysis on capital projects.

- ❏ Apply inflation and taxation adjustments to the cash flows of capital projects.

- ❏ Determine the volume of funds likely to be required to finance future asset structures.

- ❏ Assess the present and future capital structure.

- ❏ Describe the different methods of calculating the cost of capital.

9.1   Introduction

Financial management requires a forward looking view to be undertaken of the business as a whole. This view typically has to take account of a good deal of future uncertainty and is reliant upon the discounted cash flow principles encountered in the last chapter, in addition to many other principles and techniques encountered in earlier chapters.

In this chapter we will provide an overview rather than a detailed insight of important areas of financial management, some of which were encountered in earlier chapters. For example, we considered return on equity and associated ratios instrumental in gauging the ability of the business to generate profit for future growth. We also had a brief encounter with one other important aspect of financial management in terms of the rate of return to be used in discounting cash flows for calculating the net present value from an investment opportunity.

Good financial management is vital to the success of the business. Just as production management is concerned with handling physical resources at its disposal to increase corporate profitability and value, so financial management is concerned with improving the use of financial resources for the same objective. Financial resources represent the funds available to the business for which financial management is required to plan and control both their supply to and their use within, the business.

In this chapter we will draw together the various components of financial management by considering the following key questions:

❑   Is the size and the composition of the present asset structure appropriate?

❑   What should be the size and composition of the future asset structure?

❑   What volume of funds is likely to be required to finance the future asset structure?

❑   What should be the composition of the capital structure both now and in the future?

❑   Is there any other action that should be taken to enhance the long-term growth in market value of the equity holders' investment?

9.2 Present asset structure

Concern with the present asset structure focuses upon one key question, *"Is the volume and composition of the assets currently employed justified by the value of sales activity being achieved?"* You will recognise this question from our discussion of the sales generation ratio in Chapter 3. We saw there that the sales generation ratio is calculated from:

$$\text{Sales Generation Ratio} = \frac{\text{Sales Revenue}}{\text{Total Assets}}$$

This ratio, which shows how many £ of sales are generated per £ of total assets, can be subdivided into a number of interrelated component ratios to identify the success or otherwise of particular areas of the business such as:

❏ Stock control, to ensure that stocks and work-in-progress are no higher than is necessary to service the volume of activity achieved.

❏ Credit control, to ensure that sales effort is channelled into areas of low credit risk and that outstanding debtors (accounts receivable) are collected and banked with the minimum of delay.

❏ The control of cash and near cash funds to prevent them from lying idle, and therefore not generating any return.

❏ The existing fixed asset base. Would it be worthwhile realising the value from certain assets and subcontracting outside?

In considering the present asset structure, aspects of short-term decision analysis discussed separately earlier in Chapter 7 can be seen to be relevant. In fact, within financial management you will see a number of the principles and techniques discussed earlier being used in an integrated fashion. For example, ratio analysis covered in Chapter 3 can be used to identify the relationship between certain assets and the sales value they generate, but the benefit of the assets can only be gauged by asking the type of searching questions raised in Chapter 7 on short-term decision making.

9.3   Future asset structure

Future assets required by a business are usually the result of business plans which project business activities into the future, taking account of product/market strategies and their impact on growth and diversification. Sound financial management requires that those future assets acquired as part of the plan are indeed worthwhile to the business. We illustrated in Chapter 8 how analytical techniques can be used to appraise projects, but there is the overriding requirement that particular attention should be paid to the quality of the input data. In our opinion too much attention can be and has been given to the techniques which can only be as good as the user's judgement in selecting appropriate input data.

The most theoretically preferred appraisal technique is that requiring the calculation of a project's net present value. In calculating a project's net present value, there appear to be two discernible issues concerning cash flow estimation which form the data input:

❏   How are initial estimates to be generated as accurately as possible?

❏   How can the importance of the various components within the estimates be judged?

With regard to the first of these, forecasting methods can be used reliant upon one or more of the following; subjective managerial judgement, sensitivity analysis, consensus of expert opinion, and computer simulations. The evidence available suggests that most large companies use two or more of these and, where larger capital expenditures are involved, more quantitatively orientated methods reliant upon probability theory may well be used.

Further, and related to the second issue, the initial estimates should be broken down as far as possible. For example, in discussing the basic principles we used information about only annual cash flows from a project, which alone would be unsatisfactory for larger and therefore riskier projects. In their case, such information should be broken down into key factors and as will be illustrated later in this chapter such a break down can be powerful when using a computer spreadsheet package to investigate the importance of each factor to the end result.

Just exactly what are the factors that should be used in cash flow estimation? It is difficult to be entirely prescriptive because some factors will vary from project to project, but a useful way of considering them is within the following three groupings:

1. Financial factors

- ❏ Inflation
- ❏ Risk
- ❏ Working capital requirements
- ❏ Taxation
- ❏ Residual value

2. Marketing factors

- ❏ Sales forecast
- ❏ Product life
- ❏ Discount policy
- ❏ Promotional costs
- ❏ Selling costs
- ❏ Market test costs
- ❏ Competitive advantages and disadvantages
- ❏ Transportation costs

3. Operating factors

- ❏ Operating costs
- ❏ Material and supply costs
- ❏ Start-up costs
- ❏ Shut-down costs
- ❏ Maintenance costs
- ❏ Repair costs
- ❏ Capacity utilisation

9.3.1   Sensitivity analysis

One important management tool available for questioning both potential benefits and risks associated with a project is sensitivity analysis. In essence, the assumptions surrounding a project can be input to computer software or a programmable calculator to produce a base case net present value and internal rate of return, from which changes in assumption can easily be made to gauge the effect upon them. The mechanics of such an application we will now consider within the context of a simple example. The data to be used in our example concerns a project with the following features:

- ❏ Capital Outlay   £1,500,000
- ❏ Life   10 years
- ❏ Scrap Value   £100,000
- ❏ Sales Volume   60,000 units
- ❏ Selling Price   £30 per unit
- ❏ Labour Costs   £5 per unit
- ❏ Material Costs   £15 per unit
- ❏ Fixed Costs   £250,000 per annum
- ❏ Cost of Capital   10%

Obviously in practice the data would be far more detailed but we have deliberately made the example as simple as possible to facilitate the exposition and advantages of such an application.

This data is first input to the computer model which produces a NPV of £689,350 and an IRR of 19.7 per cent. Without the need to input any more data, each of the input variables - the scrap value, the sales volume, price, labour cost, materials cost and the fixed cost - are then varied by a specific percentage to demonstrate the effect of such a change the internal rate of return. This is illustrated in the following tables where each of the input variables have been varied adversely by 10% and the NPV and IRR recalculated.

Table 9.1   *Input variables varied adversely by 10%*

	Original estimate	Varied adversely by 10%
Capital Outlay	1,500,000	1,650,000
Life	10	9
Scrap Value	100,000	90,000
Sales Volume	60,000	54,000
Selling Price	30.00	27.00
Labour Costs	5.00	5.50
Material Costs	15.00	16.50
Fixed Costs	250,000	275,000
Cost of Capital	10%	11%

In summary, such analysis permits project proposals to be evaluated simply and the model can be easily used to identify sensitive variables without the evaluator having to input any additional data. In practice, the analysis would be extended much further than in the example, so as to explore changes in a number of variables and any interrelationships between them.

Table 9.2   *Sensitivity of input variables*

	NPV	**IRR**
Selling Price	-416,850	3.3%
Material Costs	136,840	12.0%
Sales Volume	320,650	14.6%
Capital Outlay	539,350	17.0%
Labour Costs	505,000	17.2%
Fixed Costs	535,725	17.6%
Life	558,050	18.6%
Cost of Capital	596,000	19.7%
Scrap Value	685,490	19.7%

As a result of doing nothing other than amending the original data, one really sensitive variable to the project is found to be the selling price, such that if the selling price were not £30 but £27, then the project would generate a negative NPV of £416,850 and an IRR of 3.3 per cent. In all other cases the NPV is positive and the IRR exceeds the cost of capital.

Given that the company's cost of capital is 10%, then a £3 reduction in selling price could be a potential disaster. With knowledge of this potential problem area, an investigation could be undertaken by the marketing department to establish whether difficulties in achieving a selling price of £30 are likely. If so, then despite the initially favourable NPV and IRR, the project is not acceptable on economic grounds. This, of course, assumes there to be no sales volume/selling price relationship, such that a reduction in price to £27 might well be associated with an increase in sales volume. This is one other area of investigation readily considered within the confines of such a computerised model.

9.3.2   The treatment of inflation

In calculating cash flows, if prices are expected to change because of, for example, inflation, then this must be incorporated within any appraisal. Many managers make the mistake of believing that by adopting discounted cash flow techniques, inflation has automatically been incorporated into the financial appraisal. Nothing could be further from the truth.

The principle of discounting you will recall is derived from the principle of compound interest. Even in a world with no inflation some compound interest would be present insofar as the providers of finance would wish to have some compensation for foregoing their wealth for a period of time. This being so, the principle of discounting would be equally applicable. As we will illustrate, to omit inflation can completely change the economic viability of a project. Given that inflation will not have been incorporated in a discounted cash flow technique like NPV without specific action on the part of the individual undertaking the appraisal, you are doubtless wondering what form this action should take. Let us consider this with reference to the NPV calculation for Proposal 1 from Chapter 8 :

Table 9.3   Calculation of net present value - Proposal 1

Year	Column 1 Discount factor 10%	Column 2 Cash flows £000	Column 3 (Column 1 x Column 2) Present value £000
1	0.909	6,000	5,454
2	0.826	6,000	4,956
3	0.751	6,000	4,506
4	0.683	6,000	4,098
5	0.621	6,000	3,726
6	0.564	6,000	3,384
Present Value of Cash Inflows			26,124
less Capital Outlay			18,000
Net Present Value			**8,124**

We have reproduced the NPV calculation for Proposal 1 in *Table 9.3*, where it can be seen that using a 10% discount rate, the NPV is £8.124 million. Assume now that upon investigation you discover that the cash flow forecast for the 6 years shows cash flows in real terms, for which no inflationary adjustment has been incorporated. By contrast, the 10% discount factor is a 'money' rate in which an allowance for inflation has already been included. This means that the current financial appraisal does not reflect the reality of the situation. The rule is that either inflated cash flows are discounted at a rate which incorporates an adjustment for inflation, or real cash flows are discounted at a rate which does not incorporate an adjustment for inflation.

In this example, like has not been compared with like, and a rate adjusted for inflation has been applied to pure or real cash flows. Upon examining the £6 million annual cash flow estimate for Proposal 1 it is found that these comprise £12 million of cash cost outflows and £18 million of cash revenue inflows. Because of a strongly organised labour market it is estimated that cost inflation will be 12% per annum whilst that affecting revenues will be 5%. The effect of such inflation and the impact upon the cash flows is illustrated in *Table 9.4*.

Table 9.4   Effect of inflation on net cash flows

	Revenues Inflated at 5% £'000	Costs Inflated at 12% £'000	Net Cash Flows £'000
Year 1	18,900	13,440	5,460
Year 2	19,845	15,053	4,792
Year 3	20,837	16,859	3,978
Year 4	21,879	18,882	2,997
Year 5	22,973	21,148	1,825
Year 6	24,122	23,686	436

The previously constant £6 million stream of annual cash flows is shown to be eaten away over the course of time by inflation and, in particular, the differential effects of revenue and cost inflation. The true impact of inflation upon the economic desirability of the project is summarised in *Table 9.5*, in which a revised net present value has been calculated:

Table 9.5   Effect of inflation on net present value

Year	Column 1 Discount factor 10%	Column 2 Cash flows £'000	Column 3 Present value £'000
1	0.909	5,460	4,963
2	0.826	4,792	3,958
3	0.751	3,978	2,987
4	0.683	2,997	2,047
5	0.621	1,825	1,133
6	0.564	436	246
Present Value of Cash Inflows			15,334
less Capital Outlay			18,000
Net Present Value			**-2,666**

From *Table 9.5*, where forecast information about differential rates of inflation have been built into the appraisal, you can see that Proposal 1, which was previously acceptable according to economic criteria, is now unacceptable because it will provide a negative NPV of £2.666 million.

There is one other point about inflation to bear in mind which may be of relevance to any project appraisal. This is that individual cash flow elements in the appraisal, such as the sales revenue, labour costs, materials cost and the like, may not all be subject to the same degree of inflation or price variation. In such circumstances, where there are different rates, then an adjustment should be made to each.

To summarise, inflation has to be dealt with in its own right and must never be ignored. The adjustments which have been discussed are appropriate irrespective of the techniques used in the financial appraisal. Depending upon the appraisal technique, cash flows or profit flows must be adjusted for inflation and, as illustrated, such an adjustment can have a significant impact upon the financial outcome.

9.3.3   The treatment of taxation

One other area which will impact upon a cash or profit stream to be used in project appraisal concerns taxation. Taxation is a complex subject and well beyond the scope of this book, however, the general principle to follow is similar to that discussed with regard to inflation. Just as in discounting cash flows to calculate a project's net present value inflated cash flows must be discounted using an interest rate which contains an allowance for inflation, so too must the cash flows discounted be either before or after tax, depending upon whether the required discount rate (cost of capital) is a before or after tax rate.

In reality the detail of taxation as applied to project appraisal is beyond the concern of most non-financial managers. Provided you have understood the principle of comparing 'like' cash flows with a 'like' discount rate discussed with regard to inflation, that is sufficient. It is then time to involve a taxation specialist!

An example showing how the cash flows of a capital project can be adjusted to take account of taxation is included in *Appendix A*.

9.3.4   Other factors

Before turning our attention away from the quality of data inputs that may impact upon project appraisal results, we will discuss the key question of how competitors will react which is so frequently overlooked.

The significance of competitors' reactions has been highlighted with the development of expert systems specifically for project appraisal. The point is that it is all too easy in project appraisal to consider only the detailed numerical input about sales and cost of sales, which are then checked line for line over an estimated lifetime for internal consistency, without any attempt at modelling the potential effect upon the cash flows as a result competitors' reactions. It should be recognised that scenarios for competitors' reactions can usually be generated by harnessing internal managerial knowledge and experience.

Why is the analysis of competitors' reactions so important? The successful introduction of a new product will attract competing products. Competition will tend to force prices to levels at which further investment may not be economically worthwhile. The first entrants with new products have a head start on the competition and may have some longer-term competitive advantage, for example, in terms of product protection via trade marks. Nevertheless, cash flow projections undertaken should recognise market developments and likely competitors' reactions.

We have indicated that good financial management requires more than just the appraisal of potential investments. What else is involved? In summary, sound financial management should ensure that:

❑ Individual requests are in harmony with the plan for corporate growth and development, and the risks of accepting 'no hope' capital projects should be minimised.

❑ An appropriate hierarchical structure exists for authorising capital expenditure, which should encourage all good projects, even those proposed at low levels of authority.

❑ The numbers used in appraisal calculations are complete and valid in light of the circumstances surrounding a project request.

❑ Any method used to provide a measure of the relative desirability of projects is valid.

❑ Actual expenditures are compared to planned capital outlays, and that there is an appropriate control system to prevent a waste of resources.

❑ The actual outcome of the project is compared to planned outcome by way of a post-completion audit of selected major projects so as to prevent a repetition of any mistakes encountered, and to identify good features to be encouraged for the future.

❑ A balance is maintained between those projects acquired on economic grounds and those which are a matter of necessity.

❑ A balance is maintained between high risk/high return projects and low risk/low return projects in order to prevent suffering the consequences of being at either end of the scale.

With the developments in personal computers and programmable calculators, no technical barrier should exist to the widespread use of discounting procedures for evaluating proposed capital projects. However, in spite of the extensive experience of many companies with the techniques and their relative widespread management exposure, problems still arise with the use and interpretation of project appraisal techniques. These problems arise when:

❑   Payback is required over time periods far too short for certain types of capital projects.

❑   Inappropriately high discount rates are used.

❑   New capital projects are compared with unrealistic alternatives.

❑   Capital projects selected are biased towards incremental opportunities.

❑   Evaluations ignore important capital project costs and benefits.

Payback is required over time periods far too short for certain types of capital projects

Considerable judgement is required in appraising certain types of capital project, particularly those in new untested process technologies. Many companies have been known to impose very short payback periods, such as two or three years, on all types of capital projects.

Some types of capital project, particularly those involving process technology like Flexible Manufacturing Systems (FMS) or Computer-Integrated-Manufacturing (CIM) are difficult to justify when subjected to such payback criteria in the face of more traditional alternative projects. Such projects cannot, and should not, be appraised using any criteria that do measure their benefits. Given that the benefits from such projects will arise several years in the future, when major renovation or replacement of traditional automated machines would be required, discounted cash flow analysis is far more appropriate. However, there are problems associated with quantifying the costs and benefits of such projects which makes the practical use of discounted cash flow techniques very difficult and the use of methods like the payback period far more desirable.

Inappropriately high discount rates are used

It is not uncommon to find companies using excessive discount rates for appraising capital projects. The use of an excessively high discount rate in appraising a long-lived capital project has as many drawbacks as using an arbitrarily short appraisal time. This is because discount rates compound geometrically every time period which means that cash flows received five or more years in the future will be penalised very heavily in a discounted cash flow analysis.

New capital projects are compared with unrealistic alternatives

We indicated earlier in Chapter 7 that making a decision may require a comparison to be made against an alternative involving doing nothing. Where an evaluation is made with the status quo, it is quite incorrect to assume that present cash flows can be maintained by doing nothing.

When a new technology becomes available and requires a substantial investment of funds, it will probably also be available to others. This means that a likely alternative to adopting the technology will be vulnerable market share and gross margins, with the possible consequence of declining cash flows in the future.

Capital projects selected are biased towards incremental opportunities

The project approval process for many companies specifies different levels of authorisation for different levels of management. Such a procedure can create an incentive for managers to propose a sequence of small projects that fall just below the cut-off point for higher level approval.

A consequence of this approach is that the company can become less efficient because a division never receives the full benefit from a completely re-designed and re-equipped plant that can exploit the latest technology.

Evaluations ignore important capital project costs and benefits

It is not uncommon for capital project proposals to underestimate costs quite significantly. This is particularly the case for projects that embody drastically new technological features. What are these costs? Computer software and even the training of staff may be very significant costs associated with the project which can be easily overlooked.

More importantly, whilst such costs can often be identified fairly readily, this is not so for project benefits for which major problems can arise. Whereas traditional project appraisal focuses upon future savings in materials, labour and energy, which can be readily tracked by a company's cost accounting system, innovative technologies provide benefits, some of which are more readily measured than others. Those benefits which can be estimated, albeit without enormous precision, include stock reductions, improved quality, and reduced floor space requirements. Benefits less easy to quantify include significant improvements in flexibility, faster response times to market shifts, major reductions in throughput and lead times, and opportunities to learn from and grow with technology advances.

The inadequacy of the information provided by costing systems in relation to the complex characteristics of new processes is a major source of the problem. Very simply, procedures used within companies may not be updated to respond to such complexities in the required time-frame.

Shorter product life cycles and more flexible technologies means that plant is now being installed which may last for several product life cycles, and may also be used to produce several products simultaneously. The result is that the relationship between plant life and product life has changed, with the consequence that the basis for investment must also be changed, as must the costing systems to permit an allocation of capital and running costs over a range of products.

Thus, the key problem with the conventional application of project appraisal techniques is that they are unable to quantify the technological benefits of a new investment, many of which are seen as being unquantifiable and intangible. Such intangible benefits (apparently) almost invariably appear in a different department from that where the investment is made. Furthermore, because they were not forecast or quantified, when they do appear they are recorded as an unplanned variance which is not attributed to the project.

There are no simple solutions to these problems. Current experience with such new technologies is limited such that the benefits of flexibility, reduced throughput time and lead time, organisational learning, and technology options are difficult to estimate. This does not mean however that they need necessarily be assigned a zero value when conducting a financial appraisal. As with all projects, there will be those factors difficult to quantify but which must be taken into consideration if a real view is to be formed. These are no exception.

9.4   Future requirement for funds

One important area of financial management usually assumed not to be relevant in the appraisal of capital projects is how they are to be funded. Not only is it important to ensure that there is a supply of appropriate future projects which, when taken on balance, will generate adequate return for shareholders, there is also the need to predict the future profile of cash flows to avoid unexpected cash deficits. One of the most frequent causes of bankruptcy is the inability to forecast future requirements for funds and taking on large monolithic projects.

The form that a forecast of future requirements for funds might take depends largely on the purpose for which it is needed. If concern is with a general indication of average future requirements, then a forecast funds flow statement will be sufficient. However, the problem with this is that the forecast will only illustrate the final financial position. We have reproduced the cash flow forecast from (Chapter 1 *Table 1.11*) where an equilibrium cash position was achieved at the end of the 6 month forecast but significant cash deficits were incurred at the end of some individual months, to provide and example which highlights the importance of forecasting at frequent time intervals.

Table 9.6   *Cash Flow Forecast (reproduced from Table 1.11)*

Part A

Receipts £'000	July	Aug	Sept	Oct	Nov	Dec	Total
Sales	430	600	600	800	1,300	1,600	5,330
5 year Loan	250						250
Share Capital	150						150
Sub-total A	830	600	600	800	1,300	1,600	5,730

Part B

Payments £'000 (unchanged)

	July	Aug	Sept	Oct	Nov	Dec	Total
Sub-total B	1,430	1,180	780	780	780	780	5,730

Part C

	July	Aug	Sept	Oct	Nov	Dec	
Balance A - B	-600	-580	-180	20	520	820	

Part D

Balance c/f, Cumulative Cash Position	-600	-1,180	-1,360	-1,340	-820	0	

For this reason, you will find it usual practice for cash flow forecasting as described in Chapter 1 and Chapter 6 to be used. In fact, you will find that many large organisations forecast their cash flows daily in recognition of their importance. The benefits of such a procedure in planning future cash flows are considerable and may be summarised as the following:

❑ Future requirements for funds can be planned both with respect to volume and timing. The advantages will be that time will be available to negotiate acceptable terms in advance with any prospective lender, and such a demonstration of effective management planning will assist by building confidence in the business.

❑ Future surpluses will be evident and early steps can be taken to ensure that any available are utilised adequately.

❑ The future shape of any funds required will be revealed. Such an early warning system will prevent following a course of action which is ultimately destined for disaster.

Of course, even with the best possible forecasting there will always be a chance that unexpected funds will be required not only because of poor conditions, but maybe because of good opportunities. Contingency planning is an important part of financial management and can be assisted by:

❑ Attempting to develop an awareness of the nature of the likely future contingencies and quantifying them with respect to the sensitivity of their impact upon financial resources.

❑ Developing a stock of resources that can be called upon in case of need, indicating in each case the speed by which they can be realised in cash.

❑ Formulating a strategy which can be implemented immediately to deal with emergencies that might arise.

9.5   Capital structure

We discussed capital structure briefly within the context of ratio analysis in Chapter 3. The key point about capital structure is that by raising a larger proportion of funds from debt than equity, it is quite possible to improve the return on capital employed. If debt capital can be raised and employed in the business to earn a rate which exceeds that rate being paid in fixed interest, then it must follow that a surplus will remain after payment of the interest. This surplus will clearly add to the profits available to the equity shareholder, which the following simple example demonstrates:

Example

Assume a company which presently has an all equity capital structure is to undertake an investment of £50 million which will earn incremental profit before interest and tax of £7 million. It may finance this investment either by additional equity or by a long-term loan carrying an interest of 10%. The following table demonstrates that the use of further equity dilutes the return on equity, whereas the use of debt enhances it:

		Before	After All equity	After Debt and equity
		£'m	£'m	£'m
Equity Capital	**(A)**	100.0	150.0	100.0
Debt		0.0	0.0	50.0
Profit Before Interest and Tax		20.0	27.0	27.0
less Interest Payable		0.0	0.0	5.0
Profit Before Tax		20.0	27.0	22.0
less Taxation (35%)		7.0	9.5	7.7
Profit After Tax	**(B)**	13.0	17.5	14.3
ROE %	**(B ÷ A × 100)**	**13.0%**	**11.7%**	**14.3%**

This example suggests a tremendous advantage in the use of significant amounts of debt. However, in practice, the following factors would be taken into consideration in determining the amount of debt to be used:

❑   The articles of association of a limited company normally restrict the volume of debt.

❑   The nature of the security which could be offered may detract from the acceptability of further debt.

❏   The anticipated level of future profits may provide an insufficient safety margin for future interest payments.

❏   The equity holders may not wish to accept any greater risk to dividends or share value caused by the creation of additional prior charge debt.

❏   The anticipated level of cash flow may be inadequate to service interest, debt repayment and equity dividend, thus the risk of insolvency presents itself.

Careful assessment of all of these factors enables a safe amount of debt that does not jeopardise the value of equity shareholders' investment, to be determined. The determination of the debt capacity of an organisation is an essential part of financial management, and organisations do monitor their debt position very carefully.

9.6   Dividend policy

A substantial amount of research has been undertaken about the decision to retain profit, or whether to distribute it by way of dividend. The conclusion in practice suggests that dividend policy is a vital factor in enhancing the value of shareholders' equity. However, there is still inadequate empirical evidence to confirm exactly the importance of dividends in market value, and one source of difficulty is that different shareholders have different expectations from their individual investments. Whereas some investors look for dividends, others look for capital growth. Except for very closely controlled companies, it is very difficult to establish the attitude of shareholders with any precision, nevertheless, in determining a dividend policy, the following factors do appear to be of significance:

❏   A stable dividend rather than a fluctuating one is generally regarded as a sign of strength, and should have a favourable impact upon market value.

❏   Steady growth in dividend is generally desirable, even though such growth may lag slightly behind earnings growth. Such a conservative approach is preferable to a hasty response which may subsequently require a cut in dividend.

❏   Dividend cover, although questioned by some, does provide a crude indication of the amount of retained profit which should, in principle, result in a growth in market value in the future. However, this does assume that any such retained profit will be employed successfully within the business.

In determining dividend policy, the balance between how much to distribute and how much to retain is vital and there is a crucial link between the capital investment decision discussed earlier and the financing decision.

9.7 Cost of capital

The one remaining area for consideration is the cost of capital which is a very contentious topic. This subject is supported by a substantial body of research and literature and the following discussion represents only a very brief review.

In the preceding chapter we made reference to the cost of capital for appraising potential investment opportunities. The basic guideline for investment purposes is that a return in excess of the cost of capital is required for an investment to be viable in economic terms. The problem centres upon converting this simple logic into a simple acceptable rule. There are a number of views on the subject of which we will review the two most notable. First, there is a view that the cost of capital should relate to its *marginal cost*. In this case, prospective individual investments are compared in descending order of desirability against successive alternative forms of funding. An incremental investment should be accepted if it promises a return in excess of the incremental (marginal) cost of capital necessary to finance it. The problem with this approach is that the desirability of alternatives will vary as successive types of capital are consumed. Furthermore, in times of rapidly rising interest rates, there is the danger of being locked into long-life low return projects with a consequent lack of growth in real terms from the equity investment. The second approach we encountered in the last chapter where we introduced the *weighted average cost of capital (WACC)*. You will recall that this involves listing the various sources of capital, noting their respective costs and deriving from them an arithmetic weighted average. This weighted average becomes the general index of desirability.

The weighted average cost of capital approach is generally preferred, but while there is some general agreement about the principle of having a weighted average (or blended) cost of capital, at least two areas of concern remain. These two areas of concern are, how to calculate:

❑ the weight for the future capital structure, and

❑ the cost of the debt and equity components, particularly the cost of equity.

With regard to the first of these, there is some agreement about the conceptual superiority of using market values rather than book values to establish the relative weights. Book value, which is far less volatile, can be criticised as reflecting historical costs and being inconsistent with the economic value principles associated with project appraisal. Therefore, where possible, market values should be used.

The second problem, the calculation of the individual debt and equity components, presents greater difficulties, particularly in the case of equity.

At its simplest, the cost of debt, Kd, is calculated by multiplying the interest on debt i, by (1-t), where t is the company's marginal tax rate. For example, if a company can borrow at a rate of 12%, and if it has a tax rate of 30%, its after-tax cost of debt is:

$$Kd = i(1-t)$$

$$= 12\% \times (0.7)$$

$$= 8.4\%$$

The relevant cost of the debt component is the expected cost of new debt as opposed to the costs associated with present or past long-term borrowing. Once again, and it cannot be stressed too often, the economic desirability of a capital project depends only upon future costs.

The second component of the cost of capital, the cost of equity, is more difficult to estimate. Traditionally, it was calculated using a model which attempted to measure dividend growth. This approach, still favoured by some, is based upon the proposition that the price of a company's share equals the present value of future dividends per share discounted by the company's cost of equity capital. With the assumption that future dividends per share are expected to grow at a constant rate and that this growth rate will persist forever, the present value is calculated from:

$$p = \frac{dps}{Ke-g}$$

where:

p   = current share price
dps = next year's dividend per share
g   = the perpetuity growth rate in dividends per share
Ke   = the company's cost of equity capital.

If the price of shares is determined in this manner then we can find the cost of equity capital by simply re-arranging the formula so that:

$$\text{Ke} \quad = \quad \left(\frac{\text{dps}}{\text{p}} \right) + \quad g$$

This model has a number of well documented problems that relate to:

❏ its inapplicability to companies paying no dividends or with unstable dividend patterns;

❏ the assumption of a constant, perpetual growth rate in dividends per share; and

❏ actually calculating 'g' which must be the growth rate that investors, as opposed to the company, are using to value company shares.

The deficiencies of the model stimulated further research resulting in the Capital Asset Pricing Model (known as CAPM). The CAPM views there being some implicit rate of return on equity to induce investors to buy shares and retain them within a company. Assuming investors to be rational and risk-averse, they will expect to earn a rate of return sufficient to compensate them for accepting a perceived level of risk. Thus, the cost of equity capital to a company is the minimum expected return that will induce shareholders to purchase and retain its shares, comprising a risk-free rate as reflected in current yields available in government securities, plus an additional return or equity risk premium for investing in its more risky shares. This can be expressed as:

Cost of Equity Capital = Risk Free Rate + Equity Risk Premium

Whilst government securities are not entirely risk-free and yields do fluctuate over time, they are nevertheless the best estimate available for the risk-free rate in the calculation.

The *equity risk premium* input to the calculation is the risk premium added by investors and comprises two parts. The first part is known as the *beta* coefficient, that reflects the volatility of a share price to that of the market as a whole. A share with a beta of one has a risk associated with it identical to the market. If the beta exceeds a value of one, a share is more volatile and therefore riskier than the market, while a beta of less than one is indicative of below average risk.

The second part is the market risk premium, determined from the difference between the return expected to be earned by equities in general and the risk free rate. For example, if the current rate on government securities is 8% and the return expected to be earned by equities in general is 14%, the market risk premium would be 6%. For a share with a beta of 1.5 (50% more variable than the market average) the cost of equity using the CAPM approach would be calculated as follows:

Cost of Equity Capital	=	**Risk Free Rate + Equity Risk Premium**
	=	**Risk Free Rate + (Beta $\times$ Market Risk Premium)**
	=	**8% + (1.5 x 6%)**
	=	**17%**

Whilst you are increasingly likely to encounter the CAPM approach you should be aware that it has also been criticised. Research emanating from the United States tested CAPM-based discount rates after adjusting for inflation with the actual rates for the Standard and Poor 400 (similar in principle to the Financial Times company ranking), only to find significant differences. Two reasons have been offered for these differences:

❏   The CAPM model tends to over estimate risk.

❏   It does not take into consideration the impact of personal taxes on investors.

Concerns about the inadequacy of the CAPM resulted in the search for a better model. The result of this search is the approach known as arbitrage pricing theory (or APT). This model is based upon much the same logic as the CAPM. Company *specific risk*, which is diversifiable and idiosyncratic, is not priced by the market place because it can be eliminated at virtually no cost by spreading among a large number of assets in a portfolio. This is quite unlike the *systematic risk* which cannot be diversified away in a portfolio, thereby necessitating the payment of a risk premium in order to compensate investors for bearing it. Unlike CAPM, in which the measure of systematic risk is solely the return on the market portfolio, in the APT a number of economy-wide risks are identified and used. Empirical research so far has not demonstrated APT to be sufficiently superior to the CAPM to warrant the added complexity involved. Econometric research studies continue to strive to discover those fundamental characteristics, like the industry in which a company participates, its balance sheet characteristics (e.g. gearing) and earnings performance (e.g. earnings variability), that will provide a basis for estimating a company's exposure to general market or economy-wide developments. The result of such research will hopefully be the establishment of future related betas that are not too complex to apply in practice.

Appendix A

The effect of taxation on cash flows

In this appendix it is assumed that the capital projects being appraised relate to companies which operate in a profit making environment, purchase capital assets which qualify for capital allowances and are subject to the payment of corporation tax.

There are three areas for consideration when applying tax adjustments to capital project cash flows. These are:

1. The timing of tax receipts/payments.

2. Tax payable on project savings

3. Capital allowances.

1. The timing of tax receipts/payments

When appraising capital projects, companies typically assume that:

   a. tax will be paid in the year following the one in which taxable profits (i.e. project savings/revenues) are made.

   b. tax will be reduced in the year following the one in which tax allowance are available.

2. Tax payable on project savings

It is often not appreciated that any financial benefits (i.e. savings) resulting from a capital project will typically be taxable.

3. Capital allowances

In certain circumstances the expenditure incurred on the capital outlay for a project can be deducted from the profit generated by a company in the form of a capital allowance.

These capital allowances reduce future tax payments according to the amount of allowance available, the tax rate in operation and the economic life of each project.

Capital allowances can be likened to a personal tax allowance in as much as they reduce the amount of earnings subject to assessment for tax. A company can normally reduce its taxable profits by the amount of capital allowances available.

Example

Consider the following example where there is a capital outlay of £90,000 which will result in annual savings of £30,000 for five years. Assume:

1.   A cost of capital of 10%.

2.   Capital allowances, 25% reducing balance, apply.

3.   A corporation tax rate of 35%

4.   For tax receipts and payments, a one year delay.

5.   Sufficient profits available to offset capital allowances.

Table 9.7   Calculation of after tax capital allowances

Year	A Reducing balance	B Capital allowance (at 25%)	C Tax saved using capital allowance (at 35%)
	£	£	£
1	90,000	22,500	7,875
2	67,500	16,875	5,906
3	50,625	12,656	4,430
4	37,969	9,492	3,322
5	28,477	7,119	2,492
6	21,358	21,358	7,475

The £90,000 shown in year 1 is the original capital outlay. We are allowed to apply 25% of this amount against taxable profits, hence the £22,500 in column B. However, the net tax effect is 35% of the £22,500 which equals £7,875. In year 2, the reduced balance is £67,500 (£90,000 - £22,500), and the process continues. In year 6, the reduced balance is £21,358. We assume that the project ends at year 5, therefore we take the whole of the remaining balance and offset it against our taxable profits.

The tax payable on the annual savings is simply 35% of £30,000 which equals £10,500. For purposes of project appraisal we assume that tax will be payable one year later, i.e. from year 2 through to year 6.

A fuller appraisal incorporating tax is given in *Table 9.8*

Table 9.8   Project appraisal incorporating tax

Year	A Tax saved using capital allowance £	B Savings £	C Tax on savings £	D Cash flow (A+B+C) £	E DCF 10 %	F Net present value £
1	7,875	30,000		37,875	0.909	34,428
2	5,906	30,000	-10,500	25,406	0.826	20,985
3	4,430	30,000	-10,500	23,930	0.751	17,971
4	3,322	30,000	-10,500	22,822	0.683	15,587
5	2,492	30,000	-10,500	21,992	0.621	13,657
6	7,475		-10,500	-3,025	0.564	-1,706
Present Value of Cash Inflows						100,922
less Capital Outlay						90,000
Net Present Value (NPV)						**10,922**

The tax saved by claiming capital allowances, column A, is taken from *Table 9.7*. The savings for the projects are shown in years 1 through to 5, while the tax due on the savings are shown in column C is delayed one year with the final tax due in year 6. The cash flow in column D is the sum of: columns A plus B, plus C.

The individual cash flows can then be discounted using the company's cost of capital to find their present value. Finally, these are aggregated and the capital outlay is deducted to give the net present value.

Exercises

9.1   The following data relates to a proposed capital project.

❏	Capital Outlay	£7,000,000
❏	Life	10 years
❏	Sales Volume	900,000 units
❏	Selling Price	£8.00 per unit
❏	Material Costs	£1.50 per unit
❏	Labour Costs	£3.50 per unit
❏	Fixed Costs	£1,000,000 per year
❏	Cost of Capital	14%

Ignore taxation

REQUIRED

1.   Calculate the project's NPV.

2.   Undertake a sensitivity analysis (adjust each element adversely by 10%).

3.   Comment on the results.

9.2   The following data relates to a capital project which, due to the and uncertainty of the individual elements, requires the NPV to be calculated together with a sensitivity analysis of all input variables.

❏	Capital Outlay	£500,000
❏	Life	5 years
❏	Sales Volume	50,000 units
❏	Selling Price	£25.00 per unit
❏	Material Cost	£12.00 per unit
❏	Labour Cost	£8.00 per unit
❏	Fixed Costs	£75,000 per year
❏	Cost of Capital	10%

Ignore taxation

REQUIRED

1.   Calculate the NPV for the project.

2.   Undertake a sensitivity analysis (you will find that some elements are extremely sensitive).

3.   Comment on the results.

9.3   It is your company's policy to apply inflation rates to all capital projects, these are:

❏ Revenue   +7% per annum
❏ Costs   +4% per annum
❏ Cost of Capital   +5%

The following information is available for a capital project:

❏ Capital Outlay   £200,000
❏ Revenue   £250,000 per year
❏ Costs   £180,000 per year
❏ Life   5 years
❏ Cost of Capital   12% (real)

Ignore taxation.

REQUIRED

1.   Calculate the NPV without inflation adjustments.

2.   Calculate the NPV with inflation adjustments.

3.   Comment on the results.

9.4 Using the data from question 1, apply the following inflation adjustments to the cash flows:

- Sales   +4%
- Material Costs   +3%
- Labour Costs   +8%
- Fixed Costs   +2%

Assume that the cost of capital is already adjusted.

Ignore taxation

REQUIRED

1. Calculate the NPV with inflation adjustments.

2. Comment on the results.

9.5 The following data refers to proposed capital project number 327:

- Capital Outlay   £180,000
- Life   5 years
- Residual Value   £30,000
- Annual Profit   £42,000
- Writing Down Allowance   25%
- Corporation Tax   35%
- Cost of Capital   12%

Assume straight line depreciation.

REQUIRED

Prepare a suitable financial evaluation and advise your board of directors whether or not they should acquire the machine.

9.6　The following information is given relating to a proposed capital project:

	£
❏　Capital Outlay	250,000
❏　Profit Before Tax	35,000
❏　Residual Value	40,000
❏　Cost of Capital	10% after tax
❏　Life	6 years

Working capital requirements:	£
❏　At end of year 1	10,000
❏　Released at end of the sixth year	10,000

Taxation assumptions:

- ❏　Corporation tax is at the rate of 35%.
- ❏　25% writing down allowance.
- ❏　Tax payments are made and allowances received in the year following that to which they relate.

REQUIRED

1.　Calculate the NPV for the project.

2.　Comment on the results.

9.7　What do understand by sensitivity analysis? How can it be of help in project appraisal?

9.8　'Inflation and taxation are important considerations in project appraisal, not to be confused with the basic principles underlying discounted cash flow analysis.' Do you agree?

9.9　Why is capital structure important in management decisions?

9.10　What do you understand by the cost of capital?

INTRODUCTION TO STRATEGIC FINANCIAL MANAGEMENT

LEARNING OBJECTIVES

When you have finished studying this chapter and completed the exercises you should be able to:

❏ Comment on the shortcomings of accounting based measures like earnings per share in evaluating financial strategy.

❏ Describe the relevance of discounted cash flow analysis to financial strategy.

❏ Describe the principles underpinning Shareholder Value Analysis.

❏ Identify the key drivers required as input data prior to shareholder value analysis.

❏ Calculate the cash flows and residual value and prepare a statement of shareholder value.

10.1   Introduction

The price placed by the market upon a public limited company's shares is an indicator of its perceived success. The competition for shareholders as well as customers, and hostile corporate raids that now span national barriers, requires that a company's share price performs well relative to the rest of the market and, in particular, within its own market sector.

What does a company have to do to be successful in the eyes of the market? *Peters and Waterman (1982)* in their book 'In Search of Excellence', considered this question in relation to a sample of US Corporation over a twenty-five year period. Long-term wealth creation was emphasised in the *Peters and Waterman* study as being a key contributor to excellence. Such wealth they measured using:

❑   Compound asset growth.

❑   Compound equity growth.

❑   Ratio of market value to book value.

❑   Average return on total capital.

❑   Average return on equity.

❑   Average return on sales.

To qualify for excellence a company was required by *Peters and Waterman* to have been in the top half of its industry in at least four of these six measures over a twenty year period. Those companies that qualified were then examined in more depth to find the distinguishing attributes of excellent companies.

You will recognise some of the six qualifying measures of long-term wealth from our discussions in earlier chapters. A number of them we discussed as financial measures of performance and were shown to draw heavily upon accounting principles for the measurement of profit and financial position. That they are reliant upon accounting rather than economic principles can be appreciated with reference to first three of them which require balance sheet data for their calculation, whilst the other three require profit data from the profit and loss account.

We have considered some of the limitations of accounting measures in relation to short and long-term decision making. For example, the theoretical benefits of discounted cash flows measures particularly net present value, were illustrated in Chapter 8, and compared with accounting based measures such as the rate of return. The relevance of accounting measures can also be questioned for purposes of making decisions associated with financial strategy as we will illustrate in the next section.

10.2 Shortcomings of accounting measures for financial strategy.

Why are accounting measures like profit and earnings per share inappropriate to financial strategy? The simple answer is that they have the following important shortcomings:

❑ Earnings can be calculated using alternative and equally acceptable accounting methods. A good illustration of this was provided in Chapter 2 with reference to the profit and earnings per share provided for *Cray Electronics plc* before and after an independent review of the performance of the company.

❑ Business and financial risk are excluded. A business evaluating two alternative strategies with a mean earnings growth rate of 10% might at first sight find them equally acceptable, even though the variability in their return because of financial or business risk was significantly different.

With regard to financial risk the effect of changes in the level of gearing is the important consideration. A company can improve earnings per share by using debt rather than equity financing, because of the tax shield associated with debt. Does this improvement in earnings per share necessarily improve economic value? The simple answer is no. Increases in the level of debt may increase financial risk because of the danger of insolvency. Shareholders may therefore demand higher rates of return as a consequence. The simplest way to view this is to remember that one measure of value is:

$$\text{Value} = \frac{\text{Earnings}}{\text{Required Rate of Return}}$$

Unless any added earnings are sufficiently large to offset the rise in the required rate of return, value may decline.

With accounting measures it is important to realise that:

❏ The timing of the impact of investment is ignored. Investments in working capital and fixed capital needed to sustain and make a company grow are excluded from the earnings calculations. It is therefore possible for a company to achieve high earnings even though the associated cash flow figure is much lower. For example, a company might report a net profit of £1 million but only generate £50,000 cash, the difference between the two figures being because of significant cash outflows for working capital and replacement capital expenditures, with only a small proportion being reflected in the profit reported via the depreciation charge. Thus, the net profit figure conceals the real position of a company in such a replacement programme. A relatively good net profit may not always be associated with increases in economic value which might at first sight be expected.

❏ The time value of money is ignored. Consider our earlier company evaluating two alternative strategies with a mean earnings growth rate of 10%. Both strategies might appear to be equally acceptable using an earnings criterion even though the annual cash flows associated with each may be very different. From our discussions in Chapters 8 and 9 we know that on economic grounds the preferred strategy would, other things equal, be that yielding cash flows earlier rather than later.

Our review of the shortcomings of accounting measures has focused upon earnings and earnings per share, but caution is also necessary in using the other alternatives that are available. Accounting measures, like return on capital employed (total assets) are sometimes compared to the company's cost of capital. The difference between the return on capital employed and the company's cost of capital is referred to by some authors as the 'spread'. Successful corporate performance is usually considered to correspond with a positive spread, that is where:

Return on Capital Employed is GREATER THAN Cost of Capital

For example, if the company's return on capital employed and the cost of capital have been calculated as 15% and 10%, respectively, then the spread is 5% and should, in principle, add to the value of the business. The problem with such 'spread' approaches is their reliance upon accounting numbers and, according to evidence available, the best of them leaves more than 60% of the variation in share prices unexplained. Why is this so? In effect, the return on capital employed is really adopted as a substitute for the internal rate of return, but, unfortunately, it is not an accurate or reliable estimate. Furthermore, there is no systematic pattern enabling a specific correction to be made to adjust a return on capital employed percentage to a percentage internal rate of return. With a given set of cash flows, and therefore a known internal rate of return, a book value return on capital employed calculation will either over or understate the real rate because of such factors as the:

❑   Length of project life.

❑   Capitalisation of investments in a company's books.

❑   The depreciation policy.

❑   The lag between investment outlays and their recovery in the form of cash inflows.

These problems are exacerbated when total return on capital employed is measured rather than just the increment arising from a particular strategy. This is because the measure will incorporate not only prospective investment and cash flow, but also that from earlier periods. The implications of this are that two divisions or business units with identical strategies, but with different initial values of capital employed, would face different accounting returns during the planning period in spite of identical internal rates of return!

It should also not be ignored that accounting-based measures of return typically only measure the benefits to be gained during the forecast period of the strategy and by themselves ignore key information about the value of the business after the forecast period has elapsed. In many cases, the real benefit of a strategy can only be properly evaluated with reference to the total economic return that results. This total economic return comprises not only that return provided during the forecast period of the strategy, but also the estimated value of the business at the end of the period.

Some strategies require substantial investment during the forecast period in order to grow the business and to achieve benefits beyond the forecast period. The logic of measuring the total return comprising the return associated with the plan and increases in value in the post-planning period can be likened to the increase in economic value sought by shareholders in the form of both dividends and capital gains. In fact, as we will illustrate, increases in return from a planning period may be associated with different residual values for different types of strategy, thereby making reference to a measure related to the planning period alone wholly inadequate.

However, while accounting-based numbers such as earnings per share and return on capital employed are not reliable indicators of long-term strategy and shareholder value, accounting should not be viewed as having no purpose. It may be inappropriate for evaluating financial strategy, but it is essential for assessing past performance. Performance for the most recent year cannot be properly evaluated without recognising that investments made during this and previous years may not be recouped until later years.

Accounting-based numbers do deal with this time lag and the uncertainty surrounding the amounts and timing of prospective cash flow by assigning costs systematically to a set of future time periods.

The conclusion to be drawn from this review of accounting measures is that shareholders may not to be satisfied with only excellent financial performance as conveyed by accounting numbers, particularly when it has been illustrated that such numbers can be influenced significantly within the principles of accounting and by individual company policy, for example *Cray Electronics plc*. At the end of the day the concern of shareholders is most likely to be with the total return they receive on their shareholding from dividends plus share appreciation.

In this chapter we consider financial strategy within the context of the economic orientated discounted cash flow approach discussed in Chapters 8 and 9. Before we consider the applications and implications of discounted cash flow analysis within strategy, we offer the same word of caution mentioned earlier with reference to project appraisal. It is all too easy to become immersed in the apparent precision of numbers relating to uncertain future financial data and lose sight of less tangible but equally important issues.

10.3 Discounted cash flow analysis and financial strategy

The use of discounted cash flow analysis in financial strategy has been popularised in the USA where the approach has come to be known as Shareholder Value Analysis (SVA). Shareholder value in SVA, is the NPV generated by the firm for its shareholders after all obligations have been met.

In the UK a similar approach to SVA has developed under the name of Strategic Financial Management, (SFM). For both SVA and SFM the quest for management is to maximise the cash generating potential from the business (or part of the business) as portrayed by the net present value of projected cash flows discounted at the cost of capital. By adopting this approach top management and the board of directors should be better equipped to answer the following basic questions:

❑   Will the current strategy as conveyed within corporate plan create value for its shareholders and, if so, how much?

❑   Which business units below the corporate level are creating value and which are not?

❑   How would alternative strategic plans effect shareholder value?

In principle, the approach can be applied throughout a company and be translated into a language for all levels of management and managerial functions. This means that alternative future courses of action may be compared and their desirability can be assessed by the process of discounting cash flows at the relevant cost of capital. The returns obtained from these alternatives can be converted into conventional accounting performance indicators, making the approach relevant and usable by all managerial levels. Of course, as we will demonstrate, the principles involved are not without their difficulties in terms of their application.

We will illustrate that one major advantage of adopting a discounted cash flow rather than an accounting approach is that life after the end of the current financial year is taken into consideration. In contrast to the accounting approach, where a loss in a particular activity this year may be regarded as unacceptable, that reliant upon discounted cash flow analysis takes a longer term perspective and recognises that it may well be desirable to accept such a loss in a year, if there will be a substantial profit in future years.

10.4   The principles underpinning Shareholder Value Analysis (SVA)

I n what follows we will direct our discussion of discounted cash flow analysis for financial strategy towards SVA and the measurement of shareholder value. In common with our discussion in Chapter 8 on project appraisal we require the measurement of forecast cash flows and the cost of capital in order to compute the net present value of the business according to alternative strategies. Those strategies that create positive net present values should, depending upon the quality of the assumptions made, increase shareholder value, whereas those with negative net present values are likely to reduce such value. The logic of the approach is straightforward if you have a good understanding of the material covered in Chapters 8 and 9 but, as we will identify, there are some practical difficulties.

In order to apply the net present value approach to business strategy a number of stages need to be followed:

- ❏   A projection is required of annual operating cash flows for the planning period in question for each business defined as being in the corporate portfolio. The difficulty of their estimation discussed with reference to project appraisal is equally applicable within the context of a financial strategy model.

- ❏   The cash flows, once estimated, must be discounted at the cost of capital relevant to the company during the planning period and summed to give the present value of projected cash flows.

- ❏   The final stage, and often the most difficult in practice, is the estimation the residual or terminal value of the individual businesses at the end of the planning period, discounted to its present value.

- ❏   The total present value for any particular strategy is the sum of the present values of annual operating cash flows and the residual value. As indicated earlier, there are parallels between the net present value approach and the measurement of value derived from holding a share. Just as a shareholder will usually be concerned with both dividend and capital growth potential, a company will be concerned with annual operating cash flows and the residual value.

As indicated, however, one significant problem in practice is the calculation of the residual or terminal value for the business at the end of the planning period. Whereas for capital projects terminal values are not usually a significant influence, and can usually be estimated with reference to realisable value sources, it is far more difficult for businesses which will still be going concerns at the end of the planning period.

Various approaches have been proposed for establishing residual values. Realisable values from disposal may be appealing but are not relevant if the business is to be viewed as a going concern. Two alternative traditional methods are to use the price earning (PE) multiple method and the market to book (MB) ratio method, which we have discussed in Chapter 3. Using the PE ratio method, residual value is the product of some measure of after tax earnings at the end of the forecast period and the projected PE at the end of the forecast period. A claimed advantage of this approach is that the PE is widely used and readily available from for example, the *Financial Times*. Against this must be weighed the assumption implied by its use that price is driven by earnings, and the difficulty of predicting future PE multiples.

The problem of earnings and other accounting-based measures have been discussed at length! To the concerns we have expressed about the use of earnings we need to recognise that PE ratios move over the course of time, and no reliable models exist for forecasting their future value accurately.

With the MB ratio method, the residual value is the product of the book value of equity, and the projected MB ratio at the end of the forecast period. Similar to the PE ratio, the MB is relatively easy to calculate but it has all of its shortcomings.

An alternative to both of these is to capitalise cash flow in the last planning period. This approach treats the cash flow in the last planning period as a perpetuity in the same way as a fixed income security. For example, consider a £1,000 security offering a £100 per annum. The interest rate for one year is calculated by:

$$£1,000 \div £100 = 10\%$$

Alternatively, if we know the fixed income from the security and the interest rate, the capital value of the security can be calculated by re-arranging the formula:

$$£100 \div 10\% = £1,000$$

Using such an approach the value of a fixed income security can be readily calculated in the event of a change in the interest rate. Thus, at a rate of 12.5 percent the value of the security would be:

$$£100 \div 12.5\% = £800$$

For the calculation of the residual value from a strategy, a perpetuity cash flow is taken to represent the fixed income, which is then divided by the company's cost of capital, i.e.

$$\text{Residual Value} = \frac{\text{Perpetuity Cash Flow}}{\text{Cost of Capital}}$$

The support for the perpetuity method for estimating residual value is that it is argued as corresponding broadly with the realities of business. Value creating strategies are those that yield positive net present values as a result of producing returns over the cost of capital demanded by the market. By the end of the planning period corresponding with a value creating strategy, there are likely to have been additional entrants to the market who will have identified opportunities for themselves, such that any company is not expected on average to be able to produce positive net present values.

The perpetuity cash flow assumption can of course be relaxed and modified using tailor-made computer software that is available. Commercial software is available which can be used to provide residual values involving growth rates and returns beyond the planning horizon.

10.5   Calculating shareholder value

A shareholder value calculation is reliant upon cash flow data with many of the attributes required for the type of NPV calculation discussed in Chapter 8. However, in addition to this data other inputs are required like details of fixed and working capital investment requirements. These inputs to a shareholder value calculation have collectively been labelled *value drivers*. They take their name from being key elements that drive the value of the business and to shareholders and comprise:

❑   Sales Growth

❑   Operating Margin

❑   Cash Income Taxes

❑   Working Capital Investment

❑   Fixed Capital Investment

❑   Life of Projected Strategy

❑   Cost of Capital

The first five of these value drivers are critical in determining the size of the annual cash flows generated. As we will illustrate with the aid of an example, the annual cash flow can be easily calculated using summarised data relating to each driver. This approach which has been referred to as a *scratchpad* valuation can be readily applied manually or using a computer spreadsheet or programmable calculator. For greater accuracy a more detailed valuation can be undertaken by broadening the calculation to include the elements which make up each of these five value drivers. However, such a detailed approach really warrants the use of bespoke valuation software.

Once the cash flows have been calculated, and the life of the project strategy determined, the cost of capital is required for purposes of discounting them to establish the NPV. As with the other value drivers, the cost of capital can be applied as a *scratchpad* discount factor, or if greater accuracy is required, a more detailed approach can be adopted focusing upon components like the cost of equity, cost of debt, and the tax rate.

Figure 10.1   Components of corporate value

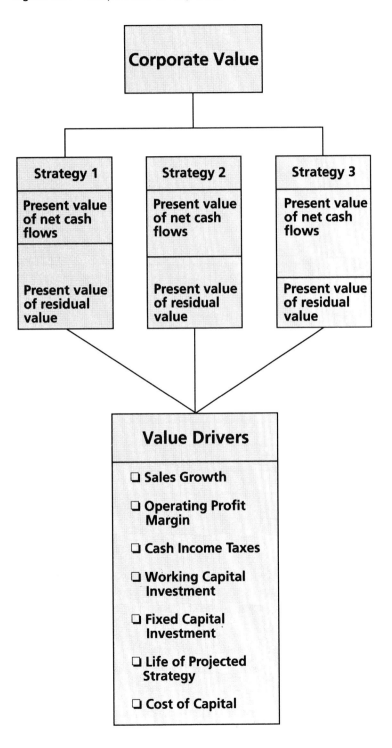

In addition to the value derived from the life of the strategy itself, the residual value at the end of the strategy must be calculated, and discounted to establish the total value resulting from the strategy. The balance between the value from the life of the strategy and the residual value will vary from strategy to strategy. Some requiring substantial fixed and working capital investment during the projected life may result in substantially higher residual values than others requiring limited investment. This is illustrated in *Figure 10.1* which portrays three strategies resulting in a different balance between the value generated during the life of the strategy and the residual value.

The value generated from this process is not however the shareholder value. Account must be taken of any market securities which add to shareholder value and also the market value of debt with reduces it. As we will demonstrate the shareholder value must be measured using the following calculation:

> Cumulative Present Value of Cash Flows
> +
> Residual Value at End of Forecast Period
> +
> Marketable Securities

=

> CORPORATE VALUE

-

> Market Value of Debt and Outside Obligations

=

> SHAREHOLDER VALUE

The easiest way to understand SVA is with reference to and example. Let us assume that the necessary cash flow and cost of capital computations are readily available together with the following forecast data:

Table 10.1   Forecast for shareholder value calculation

Number of Years in Forecast		5
Sales (base year)	(£ million)	2,000
Sales Growth	%	20.0
Operating Profit Margin	%	15.0
Incremental Fixed and Working		
Capital % of Sales	%	30.0
Cash Taxation Rate	%	50.0
Cost of Capital	%	18.0
Securities and Investments	(£ million)	30
Market Value of Debt	(£ million)	300

To start with we need to calculate the cash flow and residual value for the first year of the forecast, and the pre-forecast shareholder value as follows:

(Sales [base year] $\times$ sales growth $\times$ operating margin $\times$ taxation rate) - (Sales [base year] $\times$ sales growth $\times$ incremental fixed and working capital)

$$\textbf{Cash Flow} \quad = (2{,}000 \times 1.20 \times 0.15 \times 0.50) - (2{,}000 \times 0.20 \times 0.30)$$
$$= \qquad\qquad 180 \qquad\qquad - \qquad\qquad 120$$
$$= 60$$

$$\textbf{Residual Value} \quad = 180 \div 0.18$$
$$= 1{,}000$$

$$\textbf{Pre-Forecast}$$
$$\textbf{Shareholder Value} \quad = \frac{(2{,}000 \times 0.15 \times 0.50)}{0.18} + 30 - 300$$
$$= 833.333 + 30 - 300$$
$$= 563.333$$

Table 10.2   *Preliminary calculations for shareholder value*

Year	Discount factor 18%	Cash flow	Present value of cash flow	Cum. cash flow	Residual value	Present value of residual value
	(A)	(B) £m	(C)=(A)x(B) £m	(D) £m	(E) £m	(F)=(A)x(E) £m
1	0.847	60.000	50.820	50.820	1,000.000	847.000
2	0.718	72.000	51.696	102.516	1,200.000	861.640
3	0.609	86.400	52.618	155.134	1,440.000	876.960
4	0.516	103.680	53.499	208.632	1,728.000	891.648
5	0.437	124.416	54.370	263.002	2,073.620	906.163

The value of the five year forecast can now be obtained by adding the cumulative present value of the cash flows to the residual value at the end of the forecast period. This is shown in *Table 10.3*:

Table 10.3   *Shareholder value*

	£ m
Cumulative Present Value of Cash Flows	263.002
Present Value of Residual Value	906.163
	1,169.165
Market securities	30.000
CORPORATE VALUE	1,199.165
less Market Value of Debt	300.000
SHAREHOLDER VALUE	**899.165**

The figure of £1,199.165 million represents the corporate value. It was calculated by discounting cash flows on which both debt-holders and shareholders have claims, at a cost of capital that incorporates the returns demanded by both. From this corporate value the market value of debt of £300.000 million is deducted yielding a shareholder value of £899.165 million. What is evident from *Table 10.3* is that in this example the residual value is an important component of the total corporate value, the size of which depends upon the assumptions made for the forecast period. For example, if this company chose as an alternative to increase its market share and competitive position above that proposed in the forecast, it would doubtless have to invest more heavily in capital equipment and working capital. This course of action would decrease the annual net cash flows but would be intended to increase the growth rate and therefore future net operating cash flows. In this case, the residual value proportion would increase above that illustrated in *Table 10.3*.

Using this approach, whereby key questions are asked about important key facets of future business performance, the value of the business to the shareholders can be calculated. It can be applied to valuing parts of the business and/or measuring the benefit to be derived from the adoption of a particular strategy. For example, the value of the strategy in our example can be gauged by measuring the incremental benefit obtained. We have calculated a shareholder value in total of £899.165 million from which the value of the business at present is deducted to establish the incremental benefit. In other words £335.832 million (£899.165 million less £566.333) is created which can be compared with the relative benefit to be gained from other alternatives.

It would come as no surprise to us to discover that you found the calculation of shareholder value rather complicated and relatively difficult to follow. Yes it is in terms of calculation, hence the reliance placed upon computer software which can be used very successfully to minimise potential human error and to permit user interrogation of key assumptions with relative ease. Much of the approach is reliant upon assumptions about an uncertain future which really do have to be questioned, if not interrogated. Nevertheless, the approach does have much to commend it, because it does overcome many of the problems of accounting oriented methods with their well documented shortcomings.

Exercises

10.1 What are the shortcomings of accounting measures for evaluating business strategy?

10.2 What is shareholder value analysis? What does it have in common with net present value analysis as applied to capital project appraisal?

10.3 What is required in order to calculate shareholder value?

10.4 What is the distinction between:

- corporate value

- shareholder value

- residual value?

10.5 How can alternative strategies be compared using shareholder value analysis?

10.6 Number of Years in Forecast		5
Sales (base year)	(£ million)	400
Sales Growth	%	15.0
Operating Profit Margin	%	12.0
Incremental Fixed and Working Capital % of Sales	%	34.0
Cash Taxation Rate	%	50.0
Cost of Capital	%	10.0
Securities and Investments	(£ million)	20
Market Value of Debt	(£ million)	70

REQUIRED

1. Calculate the shareholder value created by the strategy.

2. Comment on the results.

3. Calculate the effect on the value created by the strategy if cost of capital was 20%.

Glossary of terms

Accounting period:

The period of time between two reporting dates.

Accounting policies:

These are disclosed in the annual reports published by quoted companies and represent the interpretation of accounting principles and requirements adopted by the board of directors.

Accounting practices:

The practices governing the preparation of annual reports.

Accounting principles:

These are often referred to as generally accepted accounting principles (GAAP). They are only generally accepted and do not have the force of law. You should note that sometimes they are referred to as accounting concepts and conventions.

Accounting rate of return:

A method whereby the profit generated by a capital project is expressed as a percentage of the capital outlay. There is no single correct definition for this measure, for example profit can be expressed as a percentage of half the capital outlay. The main point with this method is that the cash flows are not adjusted to take into account the time value of money.

Accounts payable:

A U.S. term for creditors.

Accounts receivable:

A U.S. term for debtors.

Acid test:

See the liquid ratio.

Acquisition:

The process by which a company acquires a controlling interest in the voting shares of another company.

Allocation:

The portion of a company's overheads which can be identified directly to a cost centre.

Amortisation:

The writing off over a period of an asset. It is often used in conjunction with intangible assets, e.g. goodwill.

Annual report:

A report usually comprising chairman's statement, report of directors, review of operations, together with financial statements and notes. It is principally for the shareholders, although it is used by many other interested parties.

Apportionment:

The process by which the main bulk of a company's overheads are spread over various cost centres for the purpose of ascertaining costs and cost control.

Audit report:

A report by an auditor in accordance with the terms of appointment. In the U.K., it usually contains "a true and fair view" statement.

Balance sheet:

A statement showing the financial position of a company in terms of its assets and liabilities as at a specified date.

Bank borrowings:

Bank overdraft and long term bank loans.

Bonus issue:

Shares issued to existing shareholders following a reorganisation of a company's share capital and reserves. The shares are issued without any monetary payment - a bonus.

Breakeven point:

It is the point at which the total revenues equal the total costs. i.e. the level of activity where a company neither makes a profit nor a loss.

Budget:

A financial plan prepared prior to a defined period of time for the purpose of meeting specific objectives.

Budgetary control:

The establishment of a budget plan and the collection and comparison of actual revenues with costs typically being controlled via variance analysis.

Budget period:

Relates to the time-span to which a budget is prepared and used. Normally one year, however it is usually sub-divided into shorter periods for control purposes.

Capital allowance:

The allowance available for tax purposes on fixed assets. Can be viewed as a standardised form of depreciation allowed by U.K. Inland Revenue.

Capital expenditure:
Expenditure on fixed assets, including commissioning. It will typically involve prior authorisation by top management.

Capital investment appraisal:
The evaluation of proposed capital projects.

Capital structure:
The size and composition of a company's sources of funds – equity and debt.

Cash budget (or cash flow forecast):
A statement of expected cash receipts, cash expenditures and period balances for the purpose of identifying cash excesses and cash shortages.

Cash flow:
Is the sum of profit before tax, interest paid, and depreciation.

Chairman's statement:
A statement by the chairman of a company, normally part of the annual report, contains reference to important events.

Consolidated (or group) balance sheet:
The balance sheet of a group of companies which is consolidated as if it were a single company.

Consolidated (or group) profit and loss account:
Similar to the consolidated balance sheet.

Contribution analysis:
A method of preparing statements, traditionally based on the separation of fixed and variable costs, that can be used to identify the most profitable areas of a business, how best to use scarce resources, whether to make or buy, and whether to accept/reject a special order.

Contribution margin:
The difference between sales revenue and variable costs. (Also the sum of fixed costs plus desired profit target)

Controllable costs:
Costs which can be influenced by the action of a person who has been given responsibility for such costs either in a budget or cost centre.

Cost centre:
A location, function or group of activities to which costs can be collected for control purposes.

Cost of capital:
The yardstick (or 'hurdle') used in the evaluation of capital projects.

Cover for creditors:
Ratio which deducts bank borrowings from liquid assets then expresses the result over creditors.

Creditors:
Amounts owing to trade suppliers and other sundry creditors, payable within one year.

Creditors, amounts falling due within one year:
Same as current liabilities.

Creditors, amounts falling due after more than one year:
Long-term loans and other liabilities.

Current assets:
Those assets in which a company trades. They include stock, debtors, short term investments, bank and cash balances.

Current liabilities:
Those liabilities which a company relies upon to finance short term activities. They include creditors, bank overdraft, proposed final dividend, and current taxation.

Current ratio:
This is the ratio of current assets divided by current liabilities. It gives an indication of a company's ability to pay its way within one year.

Current taxation:
Tax payable within one year of the balance sheet date.

Cut-off:
A term associated with Z scoring. Cut-off is a point on an arithmetic scale, using the Z scores for each company in the two groups, where the misclassifications are minimised.

Debentures:
A form of loan stock. Usually issued in multiples at a fixed rate of interest, repayable at a specified date.

Debtors:
Amounts owed to the company by its customers.

Depreciation:

An accounting adjustment to take account of the diminution in value of a fixed asset over its economic life, which affects profits but not cash flows.

Direct labour:

All labour costs which are directly associated with the conversion process of a product or service.

Direct material:

All raw material which can conveniently be assigned to a product or a service. Certain materials might be small in value and can be treated as consumable materials eg. nails, glue, fertiliser.

Discounted cash flow:

A technique used for scaling cash flows. See Time value of money, Net present value and Internal rate of return.

Discriminant analysis:

A statistical technique which in finance research studies has been used in predicting business failure to reduce a number of ratios into a single score to classify a company as belonging to a failed group or belonging to a good group.

Dividend:

The proportion of the profits of a company distributed to shareholders, usually in the form of cash.

Dividend cover:

A ratio showing the number of times the dividend of a company is covered by profit attributable to shareholders.

Dividend yield:

A ratio showing the relationship between the ordinary dividend and the market price of an ordinary share.

Earnings per share:

Profit attributable to shareholders before extraordinary items divided by the average number of ordinary shares in issue during the period. The calculation and result is shown by way of note in a company's annual report.

Equity:

The sum of issued share capital, capital reserves and revenue reserves. It is also known as shareholders' funds, or net worth.

Equity share capital:
> Normally the share capital of a company attributable to ordinary shareholders.

Exceptional items:
> Items which are derived from the ordinary activities of a company. However, due to their abnormal size and incidence are often disclosed separately.

Extraordinary items:
> These include charges such as the cost of closing a factory/shop which do not form part of normal trading. As such, they are omitted from the calculation of profit on ordinary activities and are referred to commonly as being 'below the line'.

Failed group:
> Refers to a group of companies in which individual companies will either have entered into receivership, voluntary liquidation or compulsory liquidation.

Financial ratio:
> A financial ratio is a relationship between two or more financial values which can be expressed in a number of ways, e.g. a percentage..

Financial statements:
> The most important include, the profit and loss account, the balance sheet and the cash funds statement.

Finished goods:
> A term used to describe goods available for sale/despatch as distinct from partly finished goods (work-in-progress).

Fixed assets:
> Those assets which an organisation needs in order to undertake business activity. They consist of tangible assets, like land and buildings, plant and machinery, vehicles, fixtures and fittings and intangible fixed assets, such as goodwill and brands.

Fixed charge:
> The security of a debt is 'fixed' to a specific asset or group of assets.

Fixed costs:
> A costs which tends to be unaffected by the passage of time or the level of activity (within a relevant range).

Floating charge:
Typically given as security for debt, it is a general claim against any available asset of a company.

Gearing:
The relationship between the funds provided to a company by its ordinary shareholders (including reserves) and the funds provided from other sources which usually bear fixed interest or dividend payments. High gearing refers to a significant proportion of funds being provided from sources other than shareholders' funds.

Good group:
Refers to a group of companies typically matched against a failed group of companies in assessing corporate financial health, e.g. bankruptcy prediction.

Goodwill:
The difference between the amount paid for a company as a whole and the net worth of the tangible assets and liabilities acquired.

Income statement:
A U.S. term for the profit and loss account.

Intangible assets:
Those group of assets which have no physical form, e.g. goodwill, brands.

Interest payable:
The amount payable during the year on borrowed funds.

Interim reporting:
The practice adopted in the U.K. of issuing a half yearly report to shareholders.

Internal rate of return (IRR):
The rate of return achieved when the sum of the discounted cash flows minus the capital outlay is equal to zero (net present value is zero).

Inventories:
A U.S. term for stock.

Issued share capital:
The shares issued to a company's shareholders as distinct from the amount authorised.

Key ratio:
> A term given to the profitability ratio. In the U.K. this is usually defined as profit before tax plus interest paid expressed as a percentage of total assets minus current liabilities.

Leverage:
> A U.S. term for gearing.

Liabilities:
> The financial obligations of a company, which can be to shareholders, but are more usually to other providers of debt finance, trade creditors and other creditors.

Limiting factor:
> A resource, which in the short term will limit the activities of all, or a part of a business.

Liquid assets:
> The sum of current assets minus stock.

Liquid ratio:
> This is the ratio of liquid assets divided by current liabilities. It attempts to show a company's ability to pay its way in the short term.

Loan capital:
> See long-term loans.

Long-term loans:
> The portion of interest bearing debt which is not due for repayment within one year.

Margin of safety:
> Normal expected sales less break-even sales.

Market value of equity:
> This is usually considered to correspond with market capitalisation i.e. the sum of the market value of shares times the number of shares issued.

Master budget:
> The budget which summarises a company's overall plans by way of a profit and loss account, cash flow forecast, and balance sheet.

Merchandise:
> See finished goods.

Memorandum of association:
A document which gives among other things the objects of a company.

Minority interest:
The proportion of shares in subsidiary companies which is not held by a holding company. Profit attributable to minority interests and accumulated balances are shown in the consolidated financial statements.

Net assets:
See net capital employed.

Net capital employed:
The sum of fixed assets, investments, and current assets minus current liabilities.

Net current assets:
See net working capital.

Net present value (NPV):
The sum of the cash flows discounted at the cost of capital minus the capital outlay.

Net total borrowings:
The sum of bank overdraft, plus any loans repayable within one year, plus long term loans, minus bank and cash balances.

Net working capital:
The sum of current assets minus current liabilities.

Net worth:
See equity.

No credit interval:
The ratio of liquid assets minus current liabilities divided by net operating costs.

Non-relevant costs:
Those costs that will not change as a result of making a decision. As such they can be ignored.

Ordinary shares:
Shares which attract the remaining profits after all other claims. In a liquidation, ordinary shareholders receive the remaining assets of a company after creditors and other charges have been satisfied.

Overtrading:
The process whereby a company attempts to expand at a faster rate than it can acquire and maintain resources.

Payback period:
The time taken for the cash flows of a capital project to recover the capital outlay. It is normally expressed in years and can be calculated using unadjusted and/or discounted cash flows.

Price earnings ratio:
This is the market price of an ordinary share divided by the last reported earnings per share. The PE is a multiple which shows the number of years earnings the market is willing to pay for a company's shares.

Principal budget factor:
See limiting factor.

Profit and loss account:
A statement showing the sales less the costs for the period under review. There are various "layers" of profit e.g. operating profit, profit after taxation, retained profit etc. Companies can adopt one of two formats for formal publication.

Quick assets:
See liquid assets.

Quick ratio:
See liquid ratio.

Quoted investments:
Investments in another company which has its shares quoted on a stock exchange.

Raw materials:
Unprocessed stock, which form part of the input to the production process for conversion to finished stock.

Receivables:
A U.S. term for debtors.

Reducing balance depreciation:
A method of depreciation whereby the periodic amount written off is a percentage of the reduced balance. This results in higher charges for depreciation during the earlier life of the fixed asset and correspondingly lower charges each year.

Relevant costs:
These are costs that will change as a result of making a decision.

Relevant range:
The level of activity over which sales and cost relationships do not change.

Reserves - capital:
These are reserves which are not generated through the normal trading activities of a company. They usually include one-off items such as share premium, and the revaluation of properties, and there are limits as to their distribution.

Reserves - revenue:
These are the accumulated profits generated by a company.

Retained earnings:
See reserves - revenue.

Revaluation of fixed assets:
Periodically fixed assets, normally land and buildings are revalued in the U.K. to reflect current market values. The adjustment is usually an increase in the fixed assets and a corresponding increase in the revaluation reserve.

Rights issue:
An issue of shares to which existing shareholders have a right to subscribe at a stated price, typically below the currently prevailing market price.

Residual value:
The amount expected to be obtained from the disposal of a fixed asset at the end of its useful life.

Sales:
Includes all income receivable from the principal activities of a business, net of VAT, and reported in the profit and loss account.

Script issue:
See bonus issue.

Sensitivity analysis:
This is a method used to interrogate risk and uncertainty which may often be used in capital investment appraisal, where input variables are changed to determine their effect upon a project's economic desirability.

Shareholders' funds:
Another name for owners' equity.

Share premium:
The difference between the price paid for shares and their nominal value. It arises due to the requirement to record issued share capital at its nominal value, such that the balance must be held in a share premium account. There are legal restrictions as to the uses to which a share premium may be put, e.g. it cannot be used to pay dividends.

Source and application of funds statement:
This statement shows the funds generated by the operations and funds from other sources. It also indicates how funds have been applied and whether there is a net surplus or deficiency.

Stock:
This is the name given in the U.K. to the current asset which includes raw materials, work in progress and finished goods. Stock is typically valued at lower of cost or market value.

Stock turn:
This is a ratio calculated from cost of sales or sales divided by stock. It gives an indication of the number of times stock is turned round, on average, in one year.

Straight line depreciation:
A method of depreciation whereby an equal amount is written off a fixed asset during its estimated economic life.

Sunk cost:
See non-relevant cost.

Tangible assets:
Assets having a physical identity such as land and buildings, plant and machinery, vehicles etc.

Time value of money:
A concept which is an integral part of discounted cash flow analysis used in project appraisal. It recognises that cash flows from later years cannot be compared with cash flows from earlier years without scaling them down via discounting.

Total assets:
The sum of fixed assets plus investments and current assets.

Total borrowings:
The sum of bank borrowings, long term and short term loans.

Total debt:
The sum of creditors, amounts falling due within one year plus long term loans.

Total liabilities:
See total debt

Unadjusted rate of return:
See accounting rate of return.

Variable cost:
A cost which tends to vary with the level of activity.

Working capital:
The excess of current assets (e.g. stock, debtors and cash) over creditors, amounts falling due within one year (e.g. creditors, bank overdraft etc).

Work-in-progress:
Part completed manufactured goods. Its calculation requires identification of costs and stocks associated at each stage of manufacture.

Zero based budgeting:
A term used to describe a budgeting process where the starting point for all budgets, in any budget period, is zero. This implies that all resources have to be reviewed each budget period e.g. each year.

Z scoring:
This is a technique associated with the prediction of corporate failure, where a score (Z score) is calculated from the sum of the individual ratios contained

References

Altman, E.I., *Corporate Bankruptcy in America*, Heath Lexington Books, 1971.

American Accounting Association, 'Report of the American Accounting Association's committee on international accounting operations and education 1975-1978', *The Accounting Review*, 1977.

Argenti, J., *Corporate Collapse*, McGraw-Hill, 1976.

Argyris, C., 'Human problems with budgets', *Harvard Business Review*, 1953.

European Survey of Published Financial Statements in the context of the fourth EC Directive, FEE, Brussels, 1989.

Mueller, G., *International Accounting*, Part 1, MacMillan, 1987.

Nobes, C., 'International classification of accounting systems', unpublished paper, 1980, (reported in Chen F.D.S., and G.G. Mueller, *International Accounting*, Prentice Hall, 1984.

Peters, T.J., and R.H. Waterman, *In search of excellence*, Harper and Row, 1989.

Pratt, J., and G. Behr, 'Environmental factors, transaction costs, and external reporting: a cross-national comparison', *The International Journal of Accounting Education and Research*, 1987.

Price Waterhouse International, 'Accounting principles and reporting practices - a survey in 46 countries', Price Waterhouse International, 1973, 1975.

Robertson, J., 'Company failure: measuring changes in financial health through ratio analysis', *Managemnt Accounting*, November 1983.

Taffler, R.J., 'The z-score approach to measuring company solvency', *The Accountant's Magazine*, 1983.

Index

Answers

Answer 1.1

L. DRIVER
PROFIT AND LOSS ACCOUNT
for the year ended 31st December 1990

	£	£
Sales		2,000,000
Opening Stock 1 Jan 1990	300,000	
Purchases	1,500,000	
	1,800,000	
less Closing Stock 31 Dec 1990	400,000	
Cost of Sales		1,400,000
GROSS PROFIT		600,000
Rent Received		5,000
		605,000
Wages and Salaries	100,000	
Administration Expenses	80,000	
Selling and Distribution Expenses	100,000	
Depreciation of Vehicles	55,000	
Interest Payable	20,000	
		355,000
Net Profit Before Tax		250,000

Answer 1.2

I. PING PLC
PROFIT AND LOSS ACCOUNT
for the year ended 31st March 1991

	£m	£m
Sales		450
Opening Stock 1 April 1990	100	
Purchases	300	
	400	
less Closing Stock 31 March 1991	150	
Cost of Sales		250
GROSS PROFIT		200
Interest Received		10
		210
Discounts Allowed	18	
Depreciation of Fixtures and Fittings	30	
Salaries	60	
Rent	14	
Sales Commission	18	
		140
Net Profit Before Tax		70

Answer 1.3

PLENTITURF LTD
BALANCE SHEET
as at 31st January 1991

	£	£	£
Fixed Assets			1,000,000
Current Assets			
Stock 31 Jan 1991		150,000	
Debtors		170,000	
Cash		20,000	
		340,000	
less Current Liabilities			
Creditors	160,000		
Bank Overdraft	100,000		
		260,000	
Net Current Assets			80,000
			1,080,000
			=======
Issued Share Capital			500,000
Share Premium Account			50,000
Profit and Loss Account			530,000
			1,080,000
			=======

Answer 1.4

NU-GRASS LTD.
BALANCE SHEET
as at 30th April 1991

	Cost £	Depn £	£
Fixed Assets			
Land and Buildings	2,600,000		2,600,000
Vehicles	700,000	200,000	500,000
	3,300,000	200,000	3,100,000
	=======	======	
Current Assets			
Finished Stock 30 April 1991		3,500,000	
Debtors		1,800,000	
Cash		100,000	
		5,400,000	
less Current Liabilities			
Creditors	2,500,000		
Bank Overdraft	2,000,000		
		4,500,000	
Net Current Assets			900,000
			4,000,000
			=======
Issued Share Capital			500,000
Profit and Loss Account			2,500,000
Shareholder's Fund			3,000,000
Long Term Loan			1,000,000
			4,000,000
			=======

Answer 1.5

Capital

	Jan 1 Bank 1,000

Bank

Jan 1	Capital	1,000	Jan 3	Equipment	200
Jan 5	Sales	250	Jan 10	Rent	150
Jan 19	Sales	650	Jan 23	Motor van	300
			Jan 30	Wages	200
		____	Jan 31	Balance c/d	1,050
		1,900			1,900
Jan 31	Balance b/d	1,050			

Purchases

Jan 2	G.Ashley & Co	250
Jan 8	U.Sanderson & Co	150

G.Ashley & Co

	Jan 2	Purchases	250

Equipment

Jan 3 Bank	200

Sales

Jan 5	Cash	250
Jan 19	Cash	650

U. Sanderson & Co

	Jan 8	Purchases		150

Rent

Jan 10 Cash	150		

Motor van

Jan 23 Bank	300		

Wages

Jan 30 Cash	200		

TRIAL BALANCE
as at 31st January 1991

	Dr. £	Cr. £
Capital		1,000
Bank	1,050	
Purchases	400	
G.Ashley & Co		250
Equipment	200	
Sales		900
U.Sanderson & Co		150
Rent	150	
Motor Van	300	
Wages	200	
	2,300	2,300

PROFIT AND LOSS ACCOUNT
for the month ended 31st January 1991

	£	£
Sales (250 + 650)		900
less: Purchases (250 + 150)	400	
Rent	150	
Wages	200	
	—	
		750
		—
Net Profit before Tax		150

BALANCE SHEET
as at 31st January 1991

	£	£
Fixed Assets		
Motor Van		300
Equipment		200
		—
		500
Current Assets		
Bank	1,050	
less Current Liabilities		
Creditors (250 + 150)	400	
	—	
		650
		1,150
		====
Financed as follows:		
Capital		1,000
Retained Profit *(from Profit and Loss Account)*	150	
		—
		1,150
		====

Answer 2.1

OAK Ltd
PROFIT & LOSS ACCOUNT
for the year ended 31st March 1991

	£	£
Sales		1,000,000
Opening Stock 1 April 1990	140,000	
+ Purchases	720,000	
	860,000	
- Closing Stock 31 March 1991	150,000	
Cost of Sales		710,000
Gross Profit c/d		290,000
Wages	36,500	
Rates	2,000	
Heating and Lighting	5,000	
Salaries	20,000	
Administrative Expenses	65,000	
Loan Interest	6,000	
Bad Debts	4,000	
Directors Fees	15,000	
Depreciation Vehicles	26,000	
Depreciation Furniture and Fittings	900	
		180,400
Net Profit		109,600
Dividend		54,800
Retained Profit for the year		54,800

The entries into the Profit and Loss Account follow a similar pattern to those in the Trading Account. Many of the costs / expenses can simply be recorded, however, those items which are included in the adjustments need special treatment. We will now discuss each adjustment that affects the Profit and Loss Account.

Note b. Wages outstanding £1,500.

To obtain the total wages for the period, we take the wages shown in the Trial Balance and add any wages outstanding (£35,000 + £1,500). This occurs when there are a number of working days at the end of the accounting period where wages have been earned but not paid.

Note c. Rates paid in advance £500.

To obtain the rates for the period, we take the rates shown in the Trial Balance and deduct any rates paid in advance. This occurs when a company pays rates which includes a proportion that falls into the beginning of the next year.

Note d. Depreciation of Vehicles

The provision for depreciation of vehicles is calculated using the straight line method over five years. The provision for the year is £130,000 divided by 5 which equals £26,000.

Note e. Depreciation of Furniture and Fittings

The provision for the depreciation of furniture and fittings is calculated using 5% on cost. The provision for the year is £18,000 times 5 divided by 100 which equals £900.

Note f. Provision for Bad and Doubtful Debts

The entry for bad debts in the Profit and Loss Account includes actual bad debts written off plus any adjustment between the opening provision and the closing provision. It is possible to carry out the transaction with one entry as follows:

bad debts written off (in the Trial Balance)	3,500
+ closing provision required (note f)	3,500
	7,000
- opening provision (in the Trial Balance)	3,000
	4,000

The figure of £4,000 represents; £3,500 bad debts written off plus an additional £500 which is the difference between the closing and opening provision for bad and doubtful debts.

Note g. Provide for dividend

Dividend is calculated at 50% of profit; £109,600 times 50 divided by 100 which equals £54,800.

Loan Stock: Interest at 10%

The entry in the Trial Balance for interest paid represents only six months interest. Therefore the calculation for loan stock interest for the Profit and Loss Account must include interest for the complete accounting period: £60,000 times 10 divided by 100 which equals £6,000.

OAK Ltd
BALANCE SHEET
as at 31st March 1991

	£	£	£
FIXED ASSETS	COST	DEPN	N.B.V.
Freehold Property	200,000		200,000
Vehicles	130,000	52,000	78,000
Furniture and Fittings	18,000	9,900	8,100
348,000	61,900	286,100	

CURRENT ASSETS			
Stock		150,000	
Debtors	85,000		
less Provision for Bad and Doubtful Debts	3,500	81,500	
Prepaid (Rates)		500	
Bank Balance		50,000	
	282,000		

less Creditors: amounts owing within
one year

Trade Creditors	44,000		
Accruals (Interest & Wages)	4,500		
Dividend Proposed	54,800		
	103,300		
		178,700	
			464,800

financed as follows:

Issued Share Capital		300,000
Reserves: Capital: Share Premium Account	25,000	
Revenue: Profit and Loss Account	79,800	
		104,800
		404,800
Loan Stock 10%		60,000
		464,800

A Balance Sheet is not an account, it is simply a statement which records a true and fair view of the financial position of a company. We will now discuss some of the points which often need clarification.

1. Accumulated depreciation (take Furniture and Fittings)

Accumulated depreciation shown in the closing balance sheet is calculated by taking the depreciation provision shown in the Trial Balance and adding the depreciation provision for the current year (£9,000 + £900) which equals £9,900.

2. Debtors

Debtors are taken at the value shown in the Trial Balance less the the provision for bad and doubtful debts.   In published accounts, it is normal just to show the net balance for debtors. i.e. £81,500.

3. Accruals

Accruals represent the amounts due but not paid at the end of an accounting period. They could be listed under a heading "sundry creditors".   The accruals in this example are the addition of loan interest due plus wages due: £3,000 + £1,500 which equals £4,500.

4. Dividend proposed

The dividend proposed was included in the Profit and Loss Appropriation Account and must be recorded in the Balance Sheet as a current liability.   The dividend covers the accounting period under review, but will not be paid until it is approved at the shareholder's meeting which could be a number of months into the next accounting period.

5. Reserves: Capital: Share Premium

Share premium arises when shareholders are asked to pay an amount above the nominal value of a company's shares.   The reason for this is that a company must show its issued share capital at the nominal value, therefore the difference is shown in a Share Premium account.

Answer 2.2

BEECH Ltd.
PROFIT & LOSS ACCOUNT
for the year ended 31st January 1991

	£'000	£'000
Sales		69,900
Opening Stock	18,600	
+ Purchases	48,200	
	66,800	
- Closing Stock	17,900	
Cost of Sales		48,900
Gross Profit c/d		21,000
Rent	1,058	
Marketing Expenses	1,400	
Lighting	250	
Rates	350	
General Expenses	2,600	
Selling and Commission	1,100	
Salaries	3,100	
Bad Debts	1,170	
Depreciation Plant and Equipment	2,349	
Loan Interest	350	
		13,727
Net Profit		7,273
Dividend		437
Retained Profit for the year		6,836

BEECH Ltd.
BALANCE SHEET
as at 31st January 1991

	£	£	£
FIXED ASSETS	COST	DEPN	N.B.V.
Land and Buildings	11,242		11,242
Plant and Equipment	19,124	11,518	7,606
	———	———	———
	30,366	11,518	18,848
	=====	=====	
Investment			1,486
CURRENT ASSETS			
Stock		17,900	
Debtors (16,937 - 293)	16,644		
less Provision for Bad and Doubtful Debts	1,169		
	———		
		15,475	
Cash in hand		1,042	
		34,417	
		———	
less Creditors: amounts owing within			
one year			
Creditors	12,861		
Accruals (300 + 100)	400		
Interest Due	350		
Dividend Proposed	437		
Bank Overdraft	2,479		
	———		
		16,527	
		———	
			17,890
			———
			38,224
			=====
financed as follows:			
Issued Share Capital			6,806
Reserves: Capital: Share Premium Account		4,754	
Revenue: Profit and Loss Account		22,289	
		———	
			27,043
			33,849
Long-Term Loan 8%			4,375
			———
			38,224
			=====

Answer 2.3

HORACE & DORIS MORRIS LTD.
Source and Application of Funds Statement
for the year ending 30th April 1991

	£	£
Profit Before Tax		44,300
add Depreciation		10,500
FUNDS GENERATED FROM OPERATIONS		54,800
FUNDS FROM OTHER SOURCES		
Issued Share Capital	40,000	
Share Premium Account	26,900	
Long-Term Loans	-50,000	
Sale of Asset	2,500	
		19,400
		74,200
APPLICATION OF FUNDS		
Land and Buildings	-35,000	
Vehicles	-35,800	
Taxation Paid	-18,600	
		-89,400
		-15,200
		=====
INCREASE/(DECREASE) IN WORKING CAPITAL		
Stock	-24,800	
Debtors	9,500	
Cash	-7,700	
Trade Creditors	7,800	
		-15,200
		=====

Answer 2.4

A. RETAILER PLC.
Source and Application of Funds Statement
for the year ending 30th May 1991

	£	£
Profit Before Tax		99,500
add Depreciation		36,500
FUNDS GENERATED FROM OPERATIONS		136,000
FUNDS FROM OTHER SOURCES		
Issued Share Capital	2,000	
Share Premium Account	8,300	
Long-Term Loans	-9,000	
Long-Term Investments	-900	
		400
		136,400
APPLICATION OF FUNDS		
Fixed Assets (32,300 + 36,500)	-68,800	
Taxation	-28,300	
Dividend	-11,800	
		-108,900
		27,500
		=====
INCREASE/(DECREASE) IN WORKING CAPITAL		
Stock	22,300	
Debtors	38,300	
Cash	8,400	
Trade Creditors	-43,400	
Bank Overdraft	1,900	
		27,500
		=====

Answer 3.1

R.R. Limited
BALANCE SHEET
as at 31st December 1990

	£	£	£
FIXED ASSETS			
Premises			300
Vehicles			200
			500
CURRENT ASSETS			
Stock		2,100	
Debtors		1,200	
Cash		200	
		3,500	
less CURRENT LIABILITIES			
Creditors	2,000		
Bank Overdraft	800		
		2,800	
			700
			1,200
			====
financed as follows:			
Issued Share Capital			400
Profit and Loss Account (Reserves)			800
			1,200

Profitability ratios:

$$\text{Key Ratio} = \frac{\text{PBIT}}{\text{Net Assets}} \times 100$$

$$= \frac{300}{1,200} \times 100$$

$$= 25\%$$

$$\text{Profit Margin} = \frac{\text{PBIT}}{\text{Sales}} \times 100$$

$$= \frac{300}{3,500} \times 100$$

$$= 8.6\%$$

$$\text{Sales Generation} = \frac{\text{Sales}}{\text{Net Assets}}$$

$$= \frac{3,500}{1,200}$$

$$= 2.92$$

Liquidity and working capital ratios

$$\text{Current Ratio} = \frac{\text{Current Assets}}{\text{Current Liabilities}}$$

$$= \frac{3,500}{2,800}$$

$$= 1.25$$

$$\text{Liquid Ratio} = \frac{(\text{Current Assets - Stock})}{\text{Current Liabilities}}$$

$$= \frac{(3,500 - 2,100)}{2,800}$$

$$= 0.50$$

2.

	RR Ltd	Industry
Profit / Net Assets	25.0 %	32.0 %
Profit / Sales	8.6 %	4.0 %
Sales / Net Assets	2.92 to 1	8.00 to 1
Current Ratio	1.25 to 1	1.60 to 1
Liquid Ratio (or acid test)	0.50 to 1	0.60 to 1

3.

Profitability ratios: (using total assets)

$$\text{Key Ratio} = \frac{\text{PBIT}}{\text{Total Assets}} \times 100$$

$$= \frac{300}{4{,}000} \times 100$$

$$= 7.5\%$$

$$\text{Profit Margin} = \frac{\text{PBIT}}{\text{Sales}} \times 100$$

$$= \frac{300}{3{,}500} \times 100$$

$$= 8.6\%$$

$$\text{Sales Generation} = \frac{\text{Sales}}{\text{Total Assets}}$$

$$= \frac{3{,}500}{4{,}000}$$

$$= 0.88$$

Answer 3.2

Preparatory work:

Current Assets	=	1.75 x £125,000	=	£218,750
Liquid Assets	=	1.05 x £125,000	=	£131,250
Stock	=	£218,750 - £131,250	=	£87,500
Net Current Assets	=	£218,750 - £125,000	=	£93,750
Net Profit	=	£93,750 x 20%	=	£18,750
Gross Profit	=	£18,750 + £33,250	=	£52,000
Cost of Sales	=	£52,000 ÷ 20 x 80	=	£208,000
Sales	=	£208,000 + £52,000	=	£260,000
Debtors	=	£260,000 ÷ 52 x 12	=	£60,000
Fixed Assets	=	£258,750 - £218,750	=	£50,000

H.O. Ratio Limited
Profit and Loss Account
for the year ended 31st October 1990

	£
Sales	260,000
Cost of Sales	-208,000
Gross Profit	52,000
Expenses	-33,250
Net Profit	18,750

H.O. Ratio Limited
Balance Sheet
as at 31st October 1990

	£	£
Fixed Assets		50,000
Current Assets		
Stock	87,500	
Debtors	60,000	
Cash	71,250	
	218,750	
less Current Liabilities	125,000	
Net Current Assets		93,750
Net Assets		143,750
financed as follows:		
Issued Share Capital		125,000
Profit and Loss Account		18,750
		143,750

Answer 3.3

	1986	1987	1988	1989	1990
	£000s	£000s	£000s	£000s	£000s
PBIT	12,000	15,000	19,500	28,600	35,000
Net Assets	37,000	83,000	93,000	109,000	125,000
Total Assets	102,000	147,000	160,000	179,000	225,000
PBIT / Net Assets %	32.43	18.07	20.97	26.24	28.00
PBIT / Sales %	13.33	12.71	15.73	20.43	20.59
Sales / Net Assets (times)	2.43	1.42	1.33	1.28	1.3
PBIT / Total Assets %	11.76	10.20	12.19	15.98	15.56
PBIT / Sales %	13.33	12.71	15.73	20.43	20.59
Sales / Total Assets (times)	.88	.80	.78	.78	.76

Answer 3.4

	1986	1987	1988	1989	1990
	£000s	£000s	£000s	£000s	£000s
Current Assets	76,000	77,000	80,000	83,000	90,000
Current Liabilities	65,000	64,000	67,000	70,000	100,000
Stock	50,000	50,000	51,000	52,000	58,000
Debtors	24,000	25,000	26,000	28,000	24,000
Sales	90,000	118,000	124,000	140,000	170,000
Current Ratio (times)	1.17	1.20	1.19	1.19	0.90
Liquid Ratio (times)	0.40	0.42	0.43	0.44	0.32
Sales/Stock (times)	1.80	2.36	2..43	2.69	2.93
Sales/Debtors (times)	3.75	4.72	4.77	5.00	7.08

Answer 3.5

	1986	1987	1988	1989	1990
	£000s	£000s	£000s	£000s	£000s
Total Debt	84,000	90,000	93,000	99,000	133,000
Total Assets	102,000	147,000	160,000	179,000	225,000
Equity	18,000	57,000	67,000	80,000	92,000
Debt (interest bearing)	30,000	38,000	38,000	41,000	65,000
Total Debt/Total Assets %	82.4	61.2	58.1	55.3	59.1
Debt/Equity %	166.7	66.7	56.7	51.3	70.7
Total Assets/Equity	5.67	2.58	2.39	2.24	2.45
Equity/Total Assets %	17.6	38.8	41.9	44.7	40.9

Answer 3-6

	1989	1990
	£000s	£000s
Sales	140,000	170,000
Fixed Assets	96,000	135,000
Current Assets	83,000	90,000
Total Assets	179,000	225,000
Total Asset utilisation (times)	0.78	0.76
Fixed Asset utilisation (times)	1.46	1.26
Current Asset utilisation (times)	1.69	1.89

Answer 3.7

1. **GOODPILE CARPETS Ltd**
   BALANCE SHEET
   as at 27th April 1991

	£000s	£000s	£000s
Fixed Assets			
Leasehold Property			2,755
Plant and Equipment			11,126
Motor Vehicles			20,278
			34,159
Current Assets			
Stock		98,662	
Trade Debtors		92,757	
Prepayments		4,449	
Cash		1,121	
		196,989	
less Current Liabilities			
Trade Creditors	75,926		
Bank Overdraft	27,805		
Accrued Expenses	16,108		
		119,839	
Net Current Assets			77,150
Net Assets			111,309
			=====

financed as follows:

Issued Share Capital			14,500
Share Premium			14,500
Profit and Loss Account			14,159
			43,159
Long Term Loans			68,150
			111,309
			=====

2.   a. Liquidity

Current Ratio   = $\dfrac{\text{Current Assets}}{\text{Current Liabilities}}$

= $\dfrac{196{,}989}{119{,}839}$

=   1.64 to 1

Liquid Ratio   = $\dfrac{(\text{Current Assets - Stock})}{\text{Current Liabilities}}$

= $\dfrac{(196{,}989 - 98{,}662)}{119{,}839}$

=   0.82 to 1

2.   b. Gearing:

= $\dfrac{\text{Total Assets}}{\text{Equity}}$

= $\dfrac{231{,}148}{43{,}159}$

=   5.36 to 1

2.   c.   Sales Generation:

$$\text{Total Asset} = \frac{\text{Sales}}{\text{Total Assets}}$$

$$= \frac{522,000}{231,148}$$

$$= 2.26 \text{ to } 1$$

$$\text{Fixed Asset} = \frac{\text{Sales}}{\text{Fixed Assets}}$$

$$= \frac{522,000}{34,159}$$

$$= 15.28 \text{ to } 1$$

$$\text{Current Asset} = \frac{\text{Sales}}{\text{Current Assets}}$$

$$= \frac{522,000}{196,989}$$

$$= 2.65 \text{ to } 1$$

Answer 4.1

Altman's 1968 model

			1986	1987	1988	1989	1990
X_1 =	NWC / T.ASSETS x 1.2		0.34	0.38	0.30	0.21	0.24
X_2 =	RET.EARN / T.ASSETS x 1.4		0.46	0.49	0.48	0.42	0.31
X_3 =	PBIT / T.ASSETS x 3.3		0.60	0.61	0.43	0.46	0.25
X_4 =	MVOE [†] / T.DEBT x 0.6		1.41	1.45	1.35	1.16	0.43
X_5 =	SALES / T.ASSETS x 1.0		1.10	1.11	1.14	1.24	1.17
TOTAL SCORE			3.91	4.04	3.70	3.49	2.40

[†] MVOE = Issued Share Capital / Nominal Value of Share x Market Value of Share

Robertson's 1983 model

			1986	1987	1988	1989	1990
R_1 =	SA–T.ASS / SALES x 0.3		0.03	0.03	0.04	0.06	0.04
R_2 =	PBT / T.ASSETS x 3.0		0.46	0.45	0.28	0.31	0.14
R_3 =	CA–T.DEBT / CL x 0.6		0.09	0.15	-0.04	-0.35	-0.79
R_4 =	EQ–TB [‡] / T.DEBT x 0.3		0.12	0.12	0.08	0.00	-0.12
R_5 =	LA–BANK / CREDITORS x 0.3		0.42	0.58	0.41	0.34	0.30
TOTAL SCORE			1.12	1.33	0.77	0.36	-0.43

[‡] Total Borrowings (TB) = Short–term loans + Bank Overdraft + Long–term loans

Please refer to textbook for full descriptions of the ratios

Answer 4.2

1. **B. Clumsy Limited**
    Profit and Loss Account
    for the year ended 30th October 1990

	£000s
Sales	27,200
Cost of Sales *(balancing figure)*	-24,850
Interest Payable	-2,500
Profit/Loss Before Tax	-150

B. Clumsy Limited
Balance Sheet
as at 31st October 1990

	£000s	£000s	£000s
Fixed assets			
Land and Buildings			3,000
Plant and Machinery			15,000
Vehicles			2,500
			20,500
Current Assets			
Stock		1,500	
Debtors		3,000	
Cash		20	
		4,520	
less Current Liabilities			
Creditors	4,000		
Bank Overdraft	1,000		
		5,000	
Net Current Liabilities			-480
Net Assets			20,020
financed as follows:			
Issued Share Capital			500
Share Premium			20
Profit and Loss Account			-500
			20
Long Term Loans			20,000
			20,020

2.   Altman's 1968 model

$$\frac{\text{Net Working Capital}}{\text{Total Assets}} \quad \times \quad 1.2$$

$$\frac{\text{Retained Earnings}}{\text{Total Assets}} \quad \times \quad 1.4$$

$$\frac{\text{Profit Before Interest and Tax}}{\text{Total Assets}} \quad \times \quad 3.3$$

$$\frac{\text{Market Value of Equity}}{\text{Total Debt}} \quad \times \quad 0.6$$

$$\frac{\text{Sales}}{\text{Total Assets}} \quad \times \quad 1.0$$

NWC / TA x 1.2   =   -480 / 25,020 x 1.2   =   -0.02

RE / TA x 1.4   =   -500 / 25,020 x 1.4   =   -0.03

PBIT / TA x 3.3   =   2,350 / 25,020 x 3.3   =   0.31

MVOE / TD x 0.6   =   500 / 25,000 x 0.6   =   0.01

Sales / TA x 1.0   =   27,200 / 25,020 x 1.0   =   1.09
                                                          ___
                                                          1.36

To find the market value of equity we have assumed that the market value of an equity share is equal to its nominal value.

Answer 6.1

E. TEE Ltd
CASH BUDGET
for the quarter ending 31st March 1992

	Jan £	Feb £	Mar £
Part A			
Receipts:			
Sales	216,000	144,000	132,000
Cash Sales	36,000	33,000	30,000
Fixtures and Fittings			1,500
Sub Total A	252,000	177,000	163,500
Part B			
Payments:			
Creditors	87,750	58,500	117,000
Overhead Expense	28,500	26,500	31,500
Wages	60,000	51,000	52,000
Computer		37,500	
Sub Total B	176,250	173,500	200,500
Part C			
Balance (A-B)	75,750	3,500	-37,000
Part D			
Balance b/f	30,000	105,750	109,250
Balance c/f	105,750	109,250	72,250

Answer 6.2

DREAM Ltd
CASH BUDGET
for the six months ending 30th June 1992

£	Jan £	Feb £	Mar £	Apr £	May £	Jun
Part A						
Receipts:						
Sales	0	20,000	40,000	40,000	50,000	60,000
Sub Total A	0	20,000	40,000	40,000	50,000	60,000
Part B						
Payments:						
Raw Materials	0	12,000	12,000	12,000	18,000	18,000
Wages	8,000	8,000	8,000	12,000	12,000	12,000
Rent	10,000			10,000		
Heat and Light			5,000			5,000
Other Expenses	10,000	10,000	10,000	10,000	10,000	10,000
Capital Equipment	5,000	5,000	5,000	5,000	5,000	5,000
Sub Total B	33,000	35,000	40,000	49,000	45,000	50,000
Part C						
Balance (A-B)	-33,000	-15,000	0	-9,000	5,000	10,000
Part D						
Balance b/f	25,000	-8,000	-23,000	-23,000	-32,000	-27,000
Balance c/f	-8,000	-23,000	-23,000	-32,000	-27,000	-17,000

2.

DREAM Ltd
BUDGETED PROFIT & LOSS ACCOUNT
for the six months ended 30th June 1992

	£	£
Sales		300,000
Raw Materials	90,000	
Wages and Salaries	60,000	
Rent	20,000	
Heat and Light	10,000	
Other Expenses	60,000	
Depreciation (50,000 x 25% ÷ 2)	6,250	
		246,250
Net Profit		53,750

DREAM Ltd
BUDGETED BALANCE SHEET
as at   30th June 1992

	£	£	£
Fixed Assets:	Cost	Depn.	N.B.V.
Plant and Machinery	50,000	6,250	43,750
Current Assets:			
Debtors		90,000	
Cash		0	
		90,000	
less Current Liabilities:			
Creditors	38,000		
Bank Overdraft	17,000		
		55,000	
			35,000
			78,750
financed as follows:			
Issued Share Capital			25,000
Profit and Loss Account			53,750
			78,750

Answer 6.3

ALASTAIR DRYANT
CASH BUDGET
for the four months ending 30th April 1992

	Jan £	Feb £	Mar £	Apr £
Part A Receipts:				
Sales		4,500	6,000	9,000
Cash Sales	4,500	6,000	9,000	10,000
Sub Total A	4,500	10,500	15,000	19,000
Part B Payments:				
Raw Materials	0	0	8,400	7,200
Wages and Expenses	2,700	3,600	5,400	6,000
Fixed Expenses	1,800	1,800	1,800	1,800
Managers Salary	2,000	2,000	2,000	2,000
Machinery	0	12,000	12,000	12,000
Sub Total B	6,500	19,400	29,600	29,000
Part C				
Balance (A-B)	-2,000	-8,900	-14,600	-10,000
Part D				
Balance b/f	25,000	23,000	14,100	-500
Balance c/f	23,000	14,100	-500	-10,500

Calculation of purchases and creditors:

	Jan £	Feb £	Mar £	Apr £
Sales	9,000	12,000	18,000	20,000
Materials: 40%	3,600	4,800	7,200	8,000
Purchases				
January	3,600			
February	4,800			
March		7,200		
April			8,000	
May				8,000

Calculation of expenses:
Fixed expenses of £2,200 less £400 per month depreciation.

Answer 6.4

P.C Ltd
CASH BUDGET
for the six months to 31st December 1991

	Jul £	Aug £	Sep £	Oct £	Nov £	Dec £
Part A Receipts:						
Sales	70,000	40,000	40,000	50,000	70,000	80,000
Sub Total A	70,000	40,000	40,000	50,000	70,000	80,000
Part B Payments:						
Creditors	40,000	25,000	15,000	39,000	46,000	60,000
Wages	5,000	7,000	8,000	10,000	6,000	4,000
Capital Equipment		40,000				
Fixed Costs	5,000	5,000	5,000	5,000	5,000	5,000
Dividend	10,000					
Sub Total B	60,000	77,000	28,000	54,000	57,000	69,000
Part C						
Balance (A-B)	10,000	-37,000	12,000	-4,000	13,000	11,000
Part D						
Balance b/f	0	10,000	-27,000	-15,000	-19,000	-6,000
Balance c/f	10,000	-27,000	-15,000	-19,000	-6,000	5,000

Calculation to determine purchases:

	Jul £000	Aug £000	Sep £000	Oct £000	Nov £000	Dec £000
Sales	50	70	80	100	60	40
- Gross profit	15	21	24	30	18	12
= Cost of sales	35	49	56	70	42	28
+ Closing stock	200	190	180	170	170	160
	235	239	236	240	212	188
- Opening stock	220	200	190	180	170	170
= Purchases	15	39	46	60	42	18

Answer 6.5

THRUST LIMITED
CASH BUDGET
for the quarter ending 30th September 1991

	Jul £	Aug £	Sep £
Part A Receipts:			
Sales	260,650	241,250	194,000
Loan Stock		30,000	
Sub Total A	260,650	271,250	194,000
Part B Payments:			
Purchases	60,000	55,000	80,000
Wages	46,250	32,500	33,750
Research and Development	9,000	12,500	13,500
Administration Costs	25,000	30,000	25,000
Production Costs	25,000	20,000	18,000
Taxation		110,000	
Dividend	50,000		
Capital Expenditure			40,000
Commissions	5,800	4,900	3,600
Sub Total B	221,050	264,900	213,850
Part C			
Balance (A-B)	39,600	6,350	-19,850
Part D			
Balance b/f	30,000	69,600	75,950
Balance c/f	69,600	75,950	56,100

Calculation of Sales:

	May	Jun	Jul	Aug	Sep
Sales (£)	240,000	290,000	245,000	180,000	170,000
20%			49,000	36,000	34,000
1 month 50%			145,000	122,500	90,000
2 months 30%			72,000	87,000	73,500
			266,000	245,500	197,500
less cash discount 5%			-2,450	-1,800	-1,700
cash discount 2%			-2,900	-2,450	-1,800
			260,650	241,250	194,000

Calculation of Labour:

	Jun £	Jul £	Aug £	Sep £
Labour	65,000	40,000	30,000	35,000
3/4		30,000	22,500	26,250
1/4		16,250	10,000	7,500
		46,250	32,500	33,750

Answer 6.6

FINDINGS Ltd
CASH BUDGET
for the quarter ending 30th April 1991

	Jan £	Feb £	Mar £	Apr £
Part A Receipts:				
Sales	10,800	71,700	120,560	105,880
Sub Total A	10,800	71,700	120,560	105,880
Part B Payments:				
Purchases	-	62,000	50,000	40,000
Labour	34,000	34,000	26,000	36,000
Capital Expenditure	180,000		20,000	
Production Expenses	8,500	5,500	4,500	5,500
Administration Expenses	9,200	7,200	7,200	7,200
Selling and Distribution	7,500	8,500	7,000	9,500
Sub Total B	239,200	117,200	114,700	98,200
Part C				
Balance (A-B)	-228,400	-45,500	5,860	7,680
Part D				
Balance b/f	-	-228,400	-273,900	-268,040
Balance c/f	-228,400	-273,900	-268,040	-260,360

Calculation of sales

	Jan £	Feb £	Mar £	Apr £
Sales	120,000	130,000	84,000	132,000
10%	12,000	13,000	8,400	13,200
1 month 50%	-	60,000	65,000	42,000
2 months 40%	-	-	48,000	52,000
	12,000	73,000	121,400	107,200
less cash discount 10%	-1,200	-1,300	-840	-1,320
	10,800	71,700	120,560	105,880

Calculation of production costs

	Jan £	Feb £	Mar £	Apr £
Production Costs	7,000	8,000	7,000	8,000
deduct Depreciation	-1,500	-1,500	-1,500	-1,500
deduct Monthly Charge	-1,000	-1,000	-1,000	-1,000
add Cash Payment	4,000			
	8,500	5,500	4,500	5,500

Answer 6.11

PVY Plc

The following budgets will be shown:

1. Sales Budget
2. Production Budget
3. Materials Usage Budget
4. Material Purchases Budget
5. Direct Labour Budget
6. Factory Overhead Budget
7. Product Cost: Production Budget
8. Ending Stock Budget
9. Cost of Goods Sold Budget
10. Selling and Administration Budget
11. Cash Budget
12. Budgeted Profit and Loss Account
13. Budgeted Balance Sheet

1. SALES BUDGET

	Units	Selling price £	Total sales £
Product A	25,000	45	1,125,000
Product B	70,000	35	2,450,000
			3,575,000

2. PRODUCTION BUDGET

	Units of product A	B
Desired Ending Stock	2,500	6,000
+ Expected Sales	25,000	70,000
	27,500	76,000
- Stock at Beginning	3,000	2,000
UNITS TO BE PRODUCED	24,500	74,000

3. MATERIAL USAGE BUDGET

Material	ProductA 24,500 units Qty	Total	ProductB 74,000 units Qty	Total	Total usage Kilos	Price £	Material usage £
101	2	49,000	4	296,000	345,000	3.00	1,035,000
102	1	24,500	2	148,000	172,500	1.00	172,500
							1,207,500

4. MATERIAL PURCHASES BUDGET

	Material 101	Material 102	Total £
Desired Ending Stock	90,000	15,000	
+ Production Usage	345,000	172,500	
	435,000	187,500	
- Stock at Beginning	70,000	10,000	
MATERIALS TO PURCHASE	365,000	177,500	
Purchase Price	3.00	1.00	
PURCHASE COST	1,095,000	177,500	1,272,500

5. DIRECT LABOUR BUDGET

	Units	Hours per unit	Total hours	Labour rate £	Total Cost £
Product A	24,500	3	73,500	6.00	441,000
Product B	74,000	2	148,000	6.00	888,000
			221,500		1,329,000

6. FACTORY OVERHEAD BUDGET

	£	£
Consumable Materials	80,000	
Indirect Labour	100,000	
Wages and Salaries	100,000	
Electricity	40,000	
Maintenance	40,000	
Total Variable Overhead		360,000
Depreciation	50,000	
Rates	20,000	
Insurance	5,000	
Supervision	70,000	
Stores and Handling	10,000	
Miscellaneous	5,000	
Total Fixed Overhead		160,000
		520,000

$$\text{Overhead Absorption Rate} = \frac{£520,000}{221,500} = £2.35$$

7. PRODUCT COST - PRODUCTION

	Unit Cost	Product A Units	Product A Cost	Product B Units	Product B Cost
	£		£		£
Material 101	3.00	2	6.00	4	12.00
Material 102	1.00	1	1.00	2	2.00
Direct Labour	6.00	3	18.00	2	12.00
Factory Overhead	2.35	3	7.05	2	4.70
			32.05		30.70

8. ENDING STOCK BUDGET

	Units	Unit Cost		Total
		£	£	£
Material 101	90,000	3.00	270,000	
Material 102	15,000	1.00	15,000	
				285,000
Product A	2,500	32.05	80,125	
Product B	6,000	30.70	184,200	
				264,325

9. COST OF GOODS SOLD BUDGET

	£	£
Opening Stock Finished goods		145,000
Direct Materials	1,207,500	
Direct Labour	1,329,000	
Factory Overheads	520,000	
		3,056,500
		3,201,500
less Closing Stock Finished Goods		264,325
		2,937,175

10. SELLING AND ADMINISTRATION BUDGET

	£	£
Sales Commissions	80,000	
Advertising	20,000	
Sales Salaries	50,000	
Distribution	10,000	
Administration Expenses	50,000	
Personnel	5,000	
Administration Salaries	80,000	
Management Services	15,000	
		310,000

11. CASH BUDGET

	Qtr 1 £	Qtr 2 £	Qtr 3 £	Qtr 4 £	Annual £
Part A Receipts:					
Sales	700,000	750,000	750,000	950,000	3,150,000
Sub Total A	700,000	750,000	750,000	950,000	3,150,000
Part B Payments:					
Materials	250,000	300,000	350,000	300,000	1,200,000
Other Costs	40,000	60,000	65,000	45,000	210,000
Wages and Salaries	360,000	400,000	400,000	480,000	1,640,000
Current Taxation	20,000	0	0	0	20,000
New Plant	0	0	90,000	0	90,000
Sub Total B	670,000	760,000	905,000	825,000	3,160,000
Part C:					
Balance (A - B)	30,000	-10,000	-155,000	125,000	-10,000
Part D:					
Opening Balance	30,000	60,000	50,000	-105,000	30,000
Closing Balance	60,000	50,000	-105,000	20,000	20,000

12. BUDGETED PROFIT AND LOSS ACCOUNT

	Schedule	£
Sales	1	3,575,000
Cost of Goods Sold	9	-2,937,175
Gross Profit		637,825
Selling and Administration	10	-310,000
Net Profit before Tax		327,825
Taxation	given	-100,000
Net Profit after Tax		227,825

13. BUDGET BALANCE SHEET

		£	£	£
FIXED ASSETS				
Land and Buildings				130,000
Plant and Machinery	(1,000,000 + 90,000)		1,090,000	
less Depreciation	(200,000 + 50,000)		250,000	
				840,000
				970,000
CURRENT ASSETS				
Stock Finished Goods	(Schedule 8)		264,325	
Stock Raw Materials	(Schedule 8)		285,000	
Debtors	(90,000 + 3,575,000 - 3,150,000)		515,000	
Cash	(Schedule 11)		20,000	
			1,084,325	
CURRENT LIABILITIES				
Creditors	(See Note (1))	621,500		
Taxation		100,000		
		721,500		
			362,825	
			1,332,825	
financed as follows				
Share Capital				200,000
Profit and Loss Account	(905,000 + 227,825)			1,132,825
				1,332,825

Note 1

Creditors	Opening balance £	Cost for year £	less Paid £	Closing balance £
Material Purchases		1,272,500	1,200,000	
Director Labour		1,329,000	1,640,000	
Factory Overhead (less depn.)		470,000		
Selling and Administration		310,000		
Other Overhead Costs			210,000	
	290,000	3,381,500	3,050,000	621,500

Answer 7.1

Workings	Total £	Per unit £	2(b) £	2(c) £
Sales	210,00	30.00	30.00	31.20
Variable Costs	140,000	20.00	21.00	20.00
Contribution	70,000	10.00	9.00	11.20
Fixed Costs	40,000			
Profit	30,000			

1. Break even point $= \dfrac{\text{Fixed Costs}}{\text{Contribution Per Unit}}$

   $= \dfrac{£40,000}{£10.00}$

   $=$ 4,000 units

2. a. $= \dfrac{£44,000}{£10.00}$

   $=$ 4,400 units

   b. $= \dfrac{£40,000}{£9.00}$

   $=$ 4,445 units   *(rounded up to fully recover fixed costs)*

   c. $= \dfrac{£40,000}{£11.20}$

   $=$ 3,572 units   *(rounded up to fully recover fixed costs)*

   d. No change in break even

Answer 7.2

Workings	Total £	Per unit £	(b) £	(c) £
Sales	750,000	25.00	25.00	23.00
Variable Costs	450,000	15.00	16.00	15.00
Contribution	300,000	10.00	9.00	8.00
Fixed Costs	200,000			
Profit	100,000			

1. Break even point (units) = $\dfrac{\text{Fixed Costs}}{\text{Contribution Per Unit}}$

   = $\dfrac{£200,000}{£10.00}$

   = 20,000 units

   Break even point (£ sterling) = 20,000 x £25.00

   = £500,000

2. Break even point (units) = $\dfrac{£200,000}{£9.00}$

   = 22,223 units *(rounded up to fully recover fixed costs)*

3. Break even point (£ sterling) = $\dfrac{£235,000}{£10.00}$ x 25.00

   = £587,500

4. Minimum selling price $= \dfrac{\text{(Fixed Costs + Pofit}}{\text{Volume}} + \text{VCpU}$

$= \dfrac{(£200,000 + £70,000)}{30,000} + £15.00$

$= \dfrac{£270,000}{30,000} + £15.00$

$= £9.00 + £15.00$

$= £24.00$

5. Volume $= \dfrac{\text{(Fixed Costs + Profit)}}{\text{Contribution Per Unit}}$

$= \dfrac{(£200,000 + £100,000)}{£8.00}$

$= \dfrac{£300,000}{£8.00}$

$= 37,500 \text{ units}$

6. Additional units $= \dfrac{£40,000}{£10.00}$

$= 4,000 \text{ units}$

Answer 7.3

Workings	£	Total £	Per unit £	(b) £	(d) £
Sales		6,000,000	300.00	280.00	280.00
Materials	2,200,000				
Labour	640,000				
Variable Production Costs	160,000				
Total Variable Costs		3,000,000	150.00	150.00	156.00
Contribution		3,000,000	150.00	130.00	124.00
Fixed Production Costs	1,440,000				
Selling and Administration	1,960,000				
Total Fixed Costs		3,400,000			
Profit		-400,000			

1. Break even point (units) $= \dfrac{\text{Fixed Costs}}{\text{Contribution Per Unit}}$

   $= \dfrac{£3,400,000}{£150.00}$

   $= 22,667$ units

2. Break even point (units) $= \dfrac{£3,400,000}{£130.00}$

   $= 26,154$ units

3. Contribution (30,000 x £130.00)   3,900,000
   Fixed Costs   3,400,000
   Profit   500,000

4. Contribution (60,000 x £124.00)   7,440,000
   Fixed costs (2 x £3,400,000 x 1.10)   7,480,000
   Profit / loss   -40,000

   Break even point (units) $= \dfrac{£7,480,000}{£124.00}$

   $= 60,323$ units

Answer 7.4

Workings	£	Total £	Per unit £	%	£
Sales (1,000,000 units)		4,000,000	4.00	100	
Purchases	1,500,000				
Packing	500,000				
Selling Overheads	200,000				
Total Variable Costs		2,200,000	2.20	55	
Contribution		1,800,000	1.80	45	2,600,000
Administration	500,000				
Marketing and Selling	300,000				
Total Fixed Costs		800,000		20	1,100,000
Profit		1,000,000		25	1,500,000

1. Break even point (units) $= \dfrac{\text{Fixed Costs}}{\text{Contribution Per Unit}}$

$$= \frac{£800,000}{£1.80}$$

$$= 444,445 \text{ units}$$

2a. Minimum Selling Price $= \dfrac{(\text{Fixed Costs} + \text{Profit})}{\text{Volume}} + VCperUnit$

$$= \frac{(£1,100,000 + £1,500,000)}{1,000,000} + £2.20$$

$$= \frac{£2,600,000}{1,000,000} + £2.20$$

$$= £2.60 + £2.20$$

$$= £4.80$$

2b. Volume $\quad=\quad \dfrac{\text{(Fixed Costs + Profit)}}{\text{Contribution Per Unit}}$

$\quad=\quad \dfrac{(£1,100,000 \;+\; £1,500,000)}{£1.80}$

$\quad=\quad \dfrac{£2,600,000}{£1.80}$

$\quad=\quad 1,444,445 \text{ units}$

3a. Minimum Selling Price $\quad=\quad \dfrac{\dfrac{\text{(Total Costs)}}{((1 - \text{TPdec}))}}{\text{Volume}}$ *TPdec = Target Profit as a decimal*

$\quad=\quad \dfrac{\dfrac{(£2,200,000 \;+\; £800,000)}{(1 - 0.20)}}{1,000,000}$

$\quad=\quad \dfrac{£3,750,000}{1,000,000}$

$\quad=\quad £3.75$

3b. Volume $\quad=\quad \dfrac{\text{Fixed Costs}}{\text{FCdec} \;\times\; \text{Selling Price}}$ *FCdec = Fixed Cost% as a decimal i.e. 0.25*

$\quad=\quad \dfrac{£800,000}{0.25 \;\times\; £4.00}$ *If Sellingprice remains at £4.00, Contribution equals 45%, Fixed Costs 25%, Profit Margin 20%.*

$\quad=\quad 800,000 \text{ units}$

Answer 7.5

1.

		Standard £	Super £	Deluxe £	Total £
Selling Price	(A)	300.00	375.00	550.00	
Direct Material		90.00	120.00	160.00	
Direct Labour		45.00	45.00	90.00	
Variable Overhead		20.00	30.00	50.00	
Variable Costs	(B)	155.00	195.00	300.00	
Contribution Per Unit (A - B)		145.00	180.00	250.00	
Sales Volume (units)		4,000	3,000	1,000	
Contribution Margin		580,000	540,000	250,000	1,370,000
Fixed Costs					1,000,000
Profit					370,000

2.   Choice - Reduce Selling Price of Delux by £75.00

Contribution Per Unit	£250.00 - £75.00	=	£175.00
Volume Change	1,000 x 1.50	=	1,500 units
Contribution Margin	1,500 x £175.00	=	£262,500
Profit Increase	£262,500 - £250,000	=	£12,500

Choice - Drop Delux, increase production of Super (i.e. highest contribution)

	Standard	Super	Total
Extra Volume Super [1]		2,000	
Contribution Per Unit		£180.00	
	£	£	£
Extra Contribution		360,000	360,000
Contribution Margin	580,000	540,000	1,120,000
			1,480,000
Fixed Costs [2]			1,000,000
Profit			480,000

Profit Increase   £480,000 - £370,000   =   £110,000

[1]   £90.00 x 1,000 units / £45.00 = 2,000 units
[2]   Assumes no immediate change in the level of fixed costs

Answer 7.6

1. Statement showing Bristol and Reading Depots making losses

		Swindon	Bristol	Reading	Total
Sales Volume		67,000	22,000	10,000	99,000
	£	£	£	£	£
Sales Revenue	22.00	1,474,000	484,000	220,000	2,178,000
Direct Material	6.50	435,500	143,000	65,000	643,500
Direct Labour	3.40	227,800	74,800	34,000	336,600
Variable Overhead	5.10	341,700	112,200	51,000	504,900
Selling and distribution:					
Variable		117,920	48,400	26,400	192,720
Fixed		70,000	60,000	60,000	190,000
Factory Fixed Costs		169,192	55,556	25,252	250,000
Total Costs		1,362,112	493,956	261,652	2,117,720
Profit / Loss		111,888	-9,956	-41,652	60,280

2a. Statement showing effect of closure of Bristol and Reading Depots

		Swindon	Total
Sales Volume		67,000	67,000
	£	£	£
Sales Revenue	22.00	1,474,000	1,474,000
Direct Material	6.50	435,500	435,500
Direct Labour	3.40	227,800	227,800
Variable Overhead	5.10	341,700	341,700
Selling and Distribution:			
Variable		117,920	117,920
Fixed		70,000	70,000
Contribution to Factory Fixed		281,080	281,080
Factory Fixed Costs			250,000
Profit / Loss			31,080

2b.   Statement showing effect of closure of the Reading depot

		Swindon	Bristol	Total
Sales Volume		67,000	22,000	89,000
	£	£	£	£
Sales Revenue	22.00	1,474,000	484,000	1,958,000
Direct Material	6.50	435,500	143,000	578,500
Direct Labour	3.40	227,800	74,800	302,600
Variable Overhead	5.10	341,700	112,200	453,900
Selling and Distribution:				
Variable		117,920	48,400	166,320
Fixed		70,000	60,000	130,000
Contribution to Factory Fixed		281,080	45,600	326,680
Factory Fixed Costs				250,000
Profit / Loss				76,680

Answer 7.7

1. Best use of scarce resources - ranking

	A	B	C	D	E	F	G
Contribution £	1,000	600	300	500	2,000	800	1,400
Machine Hours	40	20	20	60	80	20	120
Contribution £ per Machine Hour	25.00	30.00	15.00	8.33	25.00	40.00	11.67
Ranking	3=	2	5	7	3=	1	6

2. Product income statement (for a single week)

	F	B	A	E	Total
Machine Hours	20	20	40	80	160
	£	£	£	£	£
Sales	2,000	2,000	7,000	6,000	17,000
Materials	600	800	4,000	3,000	8,400
Labour	600	600	2,000	1,000	4,200
Variable Costs	1,200	1,400	6,000	4,000	12,600
Contribution	800	600	1,000	2,000	4,400
Fixed Costs (£115,440 ÷ 52)					2,220
Profit					2,180

Answer 7.8

Best use of scarce resources - determine labour hours

	A	B	C	D	E	F
Units	400	1,000	300	800	500	300
Labour Cost per Unit	40.00	90.00	90.00	50.00	70.00	90.00
Labour Cost	16,000	90,000	27,000	40,000	35,000	27,000
Labour Hours [1]	2,000	11,250	3,375	5,000	4,375	3,375

[1] labour cost divided by £8.00 per hour

Best use of scarce resources - ranking

	A	B	C	D	E	F
Units	400	1,000	300	800	500	300
Contribution Per Unit	140.00	295.00	265.00	185.00	195.00	275.00
Contribution	56,000	295,000	79,500	148,000	97,500	82,500
Labour Hours	2,000	11,250	3,375	5,000	4,375	3,375
Contribution per Labour Hour	28.00	26.22	23.56	29.60	22.29	24.44
Ranking	2	3	5	1	6	4

Product income statement

	D	A	B	F	C	Total
Labour Hours	5,000	2,000	11,250	3,375	3,375	25,000
	£	£	£	£	£	£
Sales	384,000	168,000	570,000	171,000	153,000	
Materials	164,000	76,000	160,000	45,000	39,000	
Labour	40,000	16,000	90,000	27,000	27,000	
Variable Overhead	32,000	20,000	25,000	16,500	7,500	
Total Variable Costs	236,000	112,000	275,000	88,500	73,500	
Contribution	148,000	56,000	295,000	82,500	79,500	661,000
Fixed Overheads [2]						300,000
Profit						361,000

[2] Fixed Overheads = Labour Rate x Hours x 1.50
                     = £8.00 x 25,000 x 1.5
                     = £300,000

Answer 7.9

WITHOUT RESTRICTION

	A	B	C	D	Total
Amill (Kgs) [1]	2,700	5,184	3,240	11,520	
Selling Price (£)	3.24	4.92	4.62	6.00	
Variable Costs (£)	1.80	2.76	2.28	4.20	
Contribution Per Unit (£)	1.44	2.16	2.34	1.80	
Volume	18,000	21,600	18,000	28,800	
	£	£	£	£	£
Contribution	25,920	46,656	42,120	51,840	166,536
Fixed Costs					30,000
Profit					136,536

[1]   Calculation to find the amount of Amill used for Product A

$$\frac{£0.90}{£6.00} \quad x \quad 18,000 \quad = \quad 2,700 \text{ kgs}$$

CONTRIBUTION PER UNIT OF LIMITING FACTOR

	A	B	C	D
Contribution £	25,920	46,656	42,120	51,840
AMILL (kgs)	2,700	5,184	3,240	11,520
Contribution Per Unit of Limiting Factor	9.60	9.00	13.00	4.50
Ranking	2	3	1	4

(Continued)

WITH RESTRICTION

	C	A	B	D	Total
Contribution Per Unit (£)	2.34	1.44	2.16	1.80	
Volume (2)	18,000	18,000	21,600	2,190	
	£	£	£	£	£
Contribution £	42,120	25,920	46,656	3,942	118,638
Fixed Costs					30,000
Profit					88,638

(2)   Calculation to determine the balance of Amill to produce/sell Product D.

Product	C	3,240
	A	2,700
	B	5,184
		11,124
Product	D	876
		12,000

$$\text{Units of Product D} = \frac{876}{11,520} \times 28,800 = 2,190$$

Answer 7.10

MARS PACKERS LTD.

1. Variable costs of making cartons:

	£ p.a.
Direct materials	84,000
Direct labour	18,000
Electricity (power costs)	4,500
Repairs to plant	3,000
	109,500

Cost of buying in cartons:

360,000 cartons at £325 per 1,000	117,000
additional storage costs	9,000
	126,000

The variable costs of making the cartons is less than the cost of buying in the cartons, therefore Mars Packers Ltd should continue to produce their own cartons.

Answer 7.11

WHINES LTD.

1. Relevant costs which would be eliminated if electric motors were bought-in.

Direct Materials	16,000
Direct Labour	24,000
Variable Production Overhead	16,000
Fixed Production Overhead	12,000
	£68,000

Cost of buying in cartons:

32,000 motors at £2.50 per unit	80,000
less Rent Received	8,000
	£72,000

The relevant costs of manufacture are less than the cost of buying the electric motors from Wedge Ltd, therefore the company should continue to produce their own motors.

Answer 7.12

DYMOND LTD.

1.

$$\text{Production capacity} = \frac{300{,}000}{0.60} = 500{,}000 \text{ units}$$

Therefore, increase in capacity/sales = 200,000 units

	Total p.a. £	Per unit £
Sales		5.60
Variable Costs		4.80
Contribution	160,000	0.80
Additional Fixed Costs	0	
Increase in Profit	160,000	

2. Re-evaluate the offer: additional fixed costs of £80,000

	Total p.a. £	Per unit £
Sales		5.60
Variable Costs		4.80
Contribution	160,000	0.80
Additional Fixed Costs	80,000	
Increase in Profit	80,000	

Answer 8.1

Payback period - Project A = 3 years 6 months

	£'000		
Capital Outlay	-15,000		
Cash Inflows:	Annual	Annual to payback	Cumulative to payback
	£'000	£'000	£'000
Year 1	7,000	7,000	7,000
Year 2	4,000	4,000	11,000
Year 3	3,000	3,000	14,000
Year 4	2,000	1,000	15,000

Payback period - Project B = 3 years

	£'000		
Capital Outlay	-18,000		
Cash Inflows:	Annual	Annual to payback	Cumulative to payback
	£'000	£'000	£'000
Year 1	6,000	6,000	6,000
Year 2	6,000	6,000	12,000
Year 3	6,000	6,000	18,000

Payback period - Project C = 2 years

	£'000		
Capital Outlay	-10,000		
Cash Inflows:	Annual	Annual to payback	Cumulative to payback
	£'000	£'000	£'000
Year 1	5,000	5,000	5,000
Year 2	5,000	5,000	10,000

Payback period - Project D = 3 years 5 months

	£'000		
Capital Outlay	-18,000		
Cash Inflows:	Annual	Annual to payback	Cumulative to payback
	£'000	£'000	£'000
Year 1	4,000	4,000	4,000
Year 2	5,000	5,000	9,000
Year 3	(1) 6,000	6,000	15,000
Year 4	7,000	3,000	18,000

Accounting rate of return

	A £000	B £000	C £000	D £000
Net Cash Inflows	17,000	30,000	10,000	30,000
less Capital Outlay	15,000	18,000	10,000	18,000
Profit over the Life of each Project	2,000	12,000	0	12,000
Life (years)	5	5	2	5
Average Annual Profit	400	2,400	0	2,400

Accounting rate of return: calculations

$$\text{Project A} = \frac{400}{15,000} \times 100$$

$$= 2.7\%$$

$$\text{Project B} = \frac{2,400}{18,000} \times 100$$

$$= 13.3\%$$

$$\text{Project C} = \frac{0}{10,000} \times 100$$

$$= 0\%$$

$$\text{Project D} = \frac{2,400}{18,000} \times 100$$

$$= 13.3\%$$

Net present value - Project A

Year	Cash flows £000	DCF factor 10 %	Present value £000
1	7,000	0.909	6,363
2	4,000	0.826	3,304
3	3,000	0.751	2,253
4	2,000	0.683	1,366
5	1,000	0.621	621
Present Value of Cash Inflows			13,907
less Capital Outlay			15,000
Net Present Value			-1,093

Net present value - Project B

Year	Cash flows £000	DCF factor 10 %	Present value £000
1	6,000	0.909	5,454
2	6,000	0.826	4,956
3	6,000	0.751	4,506
4	6,000	0.683	4,098
5	6,000	0.621	3,726
Present Value of Cash Inflows			22,740
less Capital Outlay			18,000
Net Present Value			4,740

Net present value - Project C

Year	Cash flows £000	DCF factor 10 %	Present value £000
1	5,000	0.909	4,545
2	5,000	0.826	4,130
Present Value of Cash Inflows			8,675
less Capital Outlay			10,000
Net Present Value			-1,325

Net present value - Project D

Year	Cash flows £000	DCF factor 10 %	Present value £000
1	4,000	0.909	3,636
2	5,000	0.826	4,130
3	6,000	0.751	4,506
4	7,000	0.683	4,781
5	8,000	0.621	4,968

Present Value of Cash Inflows	22,021
less Capital Outlay	18,000
Net Present Value	4,021

Internal rate of return - Project B

Year	Cash Flows £000	DCF Factor 19%	Present Value £000	DCF Factor 21%	Present Value £000
1	6,000	0.840	5,040	0.826	4,956
2	6,000	0.706	4,236	0.683	4,098
3	6,000	0.593	3,558	0.564	3,384
4	6,000	0.499	2,994	0.467	2,802
5	6,000	0.419	2,514	0.386	2,316

Present Value of Cash Inflows	18,342	17,556
less Capital Outlay	18,000	18,000
Net Present Value	+342	-444

$$\text{Internal Rate of Return} = 19 + \left(\frac{342}{(342 + 444)} \times 2 \right)$$

$$= 19 + 0.87$$

$$= 19.87\%$$

Answer 8.2

Convert profit to cash flows:

Year	Profit		Overhead		Depn (1)		Cash flow
	£		£		£		£
1	60,000	+	24,000	+	66,000	=	150,000
2	45,000	+	24,000	+	66,000	=	135,000
3	21,000	+	24,000	+	66,000	=	111,000
4	12,000	+	24,000	+	66,000	=	102,000
5	12,000	+	24,000	+	66,000	=	102,000

$$^{(1)}\ \text{Depreciation} = \frac{(\text{Capital Outlay - Residual Value})}{\text{Life}}$$

Year	Cash flows (2) £	DCF factor 10 %	Present value £
1	150,000	0.909	136,350
2	135,000	0.826	111,510
3	111,000	0.751	83,361
4	102,000	0.683	69,666
5	162,000	0.621	100,602

Present Value of Cash Inflows	501,489
less Capital Outlay	390,000
Net Present Value	111,489

(2)   The residual value of £60,000 will be added to the cash flow for year 5 to give £162,000.

Answer 8.3

Convert profit to cash flows:

Year	Profit		Depn [1]		Cash flow
	£		£		£
1	32,000	+	80,000	=	112,000
2	48,000	+	80,000	=	128,000
3	60,000	+	80,000	=	140,000
4	120,000	+	80,000	=	200,000
5	48,000	+	80,000	=	128,000

$$[1]\ \text{Depreciation} = \frac{(\text{Capital Outlay} - \text{Residual Value})}{\text{Life}}$$

Net Present Value:

Year	Cash flows [2] £	DCF factor 14 %	Present value £
1	112,000	0.877	98,224
2	128,000	0.769	98,432
3	140,000	0.675	94,500
4	200,000	0.592	118,400
5	208,000	0.519	97,572

Present Value of Cash Inflows	507,128
less Capital Outlay	480,000
Net Present Value	27,128

[2] The residual value of £80,000 will be added to the cash flow for year 5 to give £208,000.

Payback period:

	£		
Capital Outlay	-480,000		
Cash Inflows:	Annual	Annual to payback	Cumulative to payback
	£	£	£
Year 1	112,000	112,000	112,000
Year 2	128,000	128,000	240,000
Year 3	140,000	140,000	380,000
Year 4	200,000	100,000	480,000

Payback period = 3.5 years

Answer 8.4

1. To find IRR

$$= \frac{\text{Capital Outlay}}{\text{Average Annual Savings}}$$

$$= \frac{£70,000}{£20,000}$$

$$= 3.500$$

Consult annuity table for five year life.

13%	14%	Difference
3.517	3.433	0.084

$$\text{IRR} = 13 + \frac{(3.517 - 3.500)}{0.084} \times 2$$

$$= 13 + 0.2$$

$$= 13.2\% \text{ approx}$$

2. Savings

$$= \frac{\text{Capital Outlay}}{\text{Cumulative Discount Factor}}$$

$$= \frac{£70,000}{3.605}$$

$$= £19,417$$

3. Present Value of Cash Inflows £20,000 x 3.791 = 75,820
    less Capital Outlay   70,000
    Net Present Value   5,820

Profitability Index

$$= \frac{\text{Present Value of Cash Inflows}}{\text{Capital Outlay}}$$

$$= \frac{£75,820}{£70,000}$$

$$= 1.08$$

Answer 8.5

The original cost of the existing machines is in the past and must be ignored. The proceeds (if any) from selling the existing machines is common to both options so can be ignored.

REPLACE EXISTING MACHINES:

	Outlay £	Annual Savings £
Cutting machine	27,000	6,000
Planing machine	35,000	8,000
Sanding machine	12,000	3,000
	74,000	17,000

Present Value of Cash Inflows £17,000 x 5.019 =	85,323
less Capital Outlay	74,000
Net Present Value	11,323

REPLACE EXISTING MACHINES WITH A MULTI-PURPOSE MACHINE

Annual Savings   £45,000 - £16,000   =   £29,000

	£
Present Value of Cash Inflows £29,000 x 5.019 =	145,551
less Capital Outlay	132,000
Net Present Value	13,551

INCREMENTAL CASH FLOWS

	Multi-purpose	Proposed machines	Incremental cash flows
Capital Outlay £	132,000	74,000	58,000
Annual Savings £	29,000	17,000	12,000
Annuity Factor	4.552	4.353	4.833
I.R.R.	17.6%	18.9%	16.0%

To find incremental IRR

$$= \frac{\text{Capital Outlay}}{\text{Average Annual Saving}}$$

$$= \frac{£58,000}{£12,000}$$

$$= 4.833$$

Which proposal should be accepted?

IF cost of capital is less than 16% then choose the multi-purpose machine.

IF cost of capital is more than 18.9% then choose neither option

Answer 8.6

CALCULATE NPV's FOR PROJECT A USING ANNUITY TABLES

At 10% discount rate:

		£
Present Value of Cash Inflows £87,500 x 2.487	=	217,613
less Capital Outlay		190,000
Net Present Value		27,613

At 14% discount rate:

		£
Present Value of Cash Inflows £87,500 x 2.322	=	203,175
less Capital Outlay		190,000
Net Present Value		13,175

At 18% discount rate:

		£
Present Value of Cash Inflows £87,500 x 2.174	=	190,225
less Capital Outlay		190,000
Net Present Value		225

At 22% discount rate:

		£
Present Value of Cash Inflows £87,500 x 2.042	=	178,675
less Capital Outlay		190,000
Net Present Value		-11,325

CALCULATE NPV'S FOR PROJECT B

Year	Cash flows £	DCF factor 10 %	Present value £
1	75,000	0.909	68,175
2	150,000	0.826	123,900
3	195,000	0.751	146,445
Present Value of Cash Inflows			338,520
less Capital Outlay			300,000
Net Present Value			38,520

Year	Cash flows £	DCF factor 14 %	Present value £
1	75,000	0.877	65,775
2	150,000	0.769	115,350
3	195,000	0.675	131,625
Present Value of Cash Inflows			312,750
less Capital Outlay			300,000
Net Present Value			12,750

Year	Cash flows £	DCF factor 18 %	Present value £
1	75,000	0.847	63,525
2	150,000	0.718	107,700
3	195,000	0.609	118,755
Present Value of Cash Inflows			289,980
less Capital Outlay			300,000
Net Present Value			-10,020

Year	Cash flows £	DCF factor 22 %	Present value £
1	75,000	0.820	61,500
2	150,000	0.672	100,800
3	195,000	0.551	107,445
Present Value of Cash Inflows			269,745
less Capital Outlay			300,000
Net Present Value			-30,255

SUMMARY OF NPV'S AND INCREMENTAL NPV

Discount rate	Project B £	Project A £	Incremental NPV (B - A) £
10%	38,520	27,613	10,907
14%	12,750	13,175	-425
18%	-10,020	225	-10,245
22%	-30,255	-11,325	-18,930

Project A

Incremental

Project B

Answer 8.7

1.

Year	Cash flows £	DCF factor 10 %	Present value £
1	28,000	0.909	25,452
2	64,000	0.826	52,864
3	72,000	0.751	54,072
4	60,000	0.683	40,980
5	16,000	0.621	9,936

Present Value of Cash Inflows	183,304
less Capital Outlay	160,000
Net Present Value	23,304

Year	Cash flows £	DCF factor 10%	Present value £
1	175,000	0.909	159,075
2	6,000	0.826	4,956
3	6,000	0.751	4,506
4	6,000	0.683	4,098
5	6,000	0.621	3,726

Present Value of Cash Inflows	176,361
less Capital Outlay	160,000
Net Present Value	16,361

2.

Year	Project RUF £	Project TUF £	Incremental cash flows (RUF - TUF) £
1	28,000	175,000	-147,000
2	64,000	6,000	58,000
3	72,000	6,000	66,000
4	60,000	6,000	54,000
5	16,000	6,000	10,000

Year	Incremental cash flows £	Discount rate 10%	Present value £	Discount rate 15%	Present value £
1	-147,000	0.909	-133,623	0.870	-127,890
2	58,000	0.826	47,908	0.756	43,848
3	66,000	0.751	49,566	0.658	43,428
4	54,000	0.683	36,882	0.572	30,888
5	10,000	0.621	6,210	0.497	4,970
			6,943		-4,756

$$\text{IRR} = 10 + \frac{6,943}{(6,943 + 4,756)} \times 5$$

$$= 10 + 2.967$$

$$= 13\% \quad \text{approx}$$

Answer 8.8

Determine changes in cash flows:

	Furniture £	Household £	Difference £
Sales	400,000	200,000	200,000
Cost of Sales	-280,000	-160,000	-120,000
Commissions	- 40,000	- 20,000	- 20,000
Fixed Costs [1]	- 14,400	- 32,000	17,600
	60,000	- 12,000	77,600

(1) *Fixed Costs = 32,000 - 17,600 (redundancy payments)*

Determine capital inflow/outlay:

	£
Salvage: Fixtures and Fittings	24,000
Renovation of Furniture Department	-280,000
Redundancy Payments	- 17,600
	273,600
Increase in Working Capital (*end year 1*)	88,000
	361,600

CALCULATE SIMPLE PAYBACK

$$= \frac{£273,600}{£72,000}$$

$$= 3.8 \text{ years}$$

CALCULATE NET PRESENT VALUE

Year	Working capital £	Savings £	Cash flows £	Discount rate 20%	Present value £
1	-88,000	77,600	-10,400	0.833	-8,663
2		77,600	77,600	0.694	53,854
3		77,600	77,600	0.579	44,930
4		77,600	77,600	0.482	37,403
5		77,600	77,600	0.402	31,195
6		77,600	77,600	0.335	25,996
7		77,600	77,600	0.279	21,650
8	88,000	77,600	165,600	0.233	38,585

Present Value of Cash Inflows 244,950
less Capital Outlay 273,600

-28,650

CLOSING THE HOUSEHOLD DEPARTMENT

	£
Present Value of Cash Savings (£12,000 x 3.837)	46,044
Other cash flows:	
Salvage of Fixtures and Fittings	24,000
Redundancy Costs	-17,600
Net Present Value	52,444

Question the need to renovate the furniture department.

What will happen to the space vacated by the household dept?

Answer 9.1

Method:

1. Determine the cash flow and calculate the net present value before making any adjustments to the input variables.

2. Adjust each of the input variables adversely by 10%.

3. Determine the alternative cash flows and calculate revised net present values.

4. Rank each of the input variables according to the sensitivity of the net present values.

1. Determine the annual net cash flow

(Sales Volume x Contribution Per Unit)   -   Specific Fixed Costs

= (900,000 x £3.00) - £1,000,000

= £1,700,000

Calculate the project's NPV:

(Annual Net Cash Flow x Annuity Factor)   -   Capital Outlay

= (£1,700,000 x 5.216) - £7,000,000

= £1,867,200

2. Adjust the input variables adversely by 10%

Input variables adversely affected by 10%

	Original Estimate	Varied Adversely by 10%
Capital Outlay	£7,000,000	£7,700,000
Life	10	9.091 (say 9)
Sales Volume	900,000	818,182
Selling Price	£8.00	£7.27
Material Cost	£1.50	£1.65
Labour Cost	£3.50	£3.85
Specific Fixed	£1,000,000	£1,100,000

3. Determine alternative cash flows and calculate revised NPV's

	A Sales volume	B Contri- bution p.unit	C Fixed costs	D Cash flow (A*B)-C
	Units	£	£	£
Capital Outlay	900,000	3.00	1,000,000	1,700,000
Life (years)	900,000	3.00	1,000,000	1,700,000
Sales Volume (units)	818,182	3.00	1,000,000	1,454,546
Selling Price	900,000	2.27	1,000,000	1,043,000
Material Cost	900,000	2.85	1,000,000	1,565,000
Labour Cost	900,000	2.65	1,000,000	1,385,000
Specific Fixed Costs	900,000	3.00	1,100,000	1,600,000

Calculate NPV's using annuity tables

	A Cash flow	B Annuity factor	C Present value of cash flow	D Capital outlay	E Net Present value
	£		£	£	£
Capital Outlay	1,700,000	5.216	8,867,200	7,700,000	1,167,200
Life	1,700,000	4.946	8,408,200	7,000,000	1,408,200
Sales Volume	1,454,546	5.216	7,586,912	7,000,000	586,912
Selling Price	1,043,000	5.216	5,440,288	7,000,000	-1,559,712
Material Cost	1,565,000	5.216	8,163,040	7,000,000	1,163,040
Labour Cost	1,385,000	5.216	7,224,160	7,000,000	224,160
Specific Fixed Cost	1,600,000	5.216	8,345,600	7,000,000	1,345,600

4.   Rank input variables according to sensitivity of NPV's

          Sensitivity of input variables

	NPV £
Selling Price	-1,559,712
Labour Cost	224,160
Sales Volume	586,912
Material Cost	1,163,040
Capital Outlay	1,167,200
Specific Fixed Costs	1,345,600
Life	1,408,200

Answer 9.2

1.   Determine the annual net cash flow:

(Sales Volume x Contribution Per Unit) - Specific Fixed Costs

-    (50,000 x £5.00) - £75,000

=   £175,000

Calculate the project's NPV:

(Annual Net Cash Flow x Annuity Factor) - Capital Outlay

=   (£175,000 x 3.791) - £500,000

=   £163,425

2.   Adjust the input variables adversely by 5%

Input variables adversely affected by 5%

	Original estimate	Varied adversely by 5%
Capital Outlay	£500,000	£525,000
Life (years)	5	4.76 (say 5)
Sales Volume (units)	50,000	47,619
Selling Price	£25.00	£23.81
Material Cost	£12.00	£12.60
Labour Cost	£8.00	£8.40
Specific Fixed	£75,000	£78,750

25

3. Determine alternative cash flows and calculate revised NPV's

	A Sales volume	B Contri- bution p.unit	C Fixed cost	D Cash flow (A*B)-C
	Units	£	£	£
Capital Outlay	50,000	5.00	75,000	175,000
Life	50,000	5.00	75,000	175,000
Sales Volume	47,619	5.00	75,000	163,095
Selling Price	50,000	3.81	75,000	115,500
Material Cost	50,000	4.40	75,000	145,000
Labour Cost	50,000	4.60	75,000	155,000
Specific Fixed Costs	50,000	5.00	78,750	171,250

Calculate NPV's using annuity tables

	A Cash flow	B Annuity factor	C Present value of cash flow	D Capital outlay	E Net Present value
	£		£	£	£
Capital Outlay	175,000	3.791	663,425	525,000	138,425
Life	175,000	3.791	663,425	500,000	163,425
Sales Volume	163,095	3.791	618,293	500,000	118,293
Selling Price	115,500	3.791	437,861	500,000	-62,139
Material Cost	145,000	3.791	549,695	500,000	49,695
Labour Cost	155,000	3.791	587,605	500,000	87,605
Specific Fixed Costs	171,250	3.791	649,209	500,000	149,209

4. Rank input variables according to sensitivity of NPV's

Sensitivity of input variables

	NPV £
Selling Price	-62,139
Material Cost	49,695
Labour Cost	87,605
Sales Volume	118,293
Capital Outlay	138,425
Specific Fixed Costs	149,209
Life	163,425

Answer 9.3

1. No adjustments for inflation

   Net present value with no inflation

   | (£250,000 | - | £180,000) | * | 3.605 | = | £252,350 |
   less Capital Outlay £200,000

   Net Present Value £252,350 - £200,000 = £52,350

   (£250,000 - £180,000) * 3.605 = £252,350
   less Capital Outlay   £200,000

   Net Present Value   £52,350

2. Adjusting revenues and costs for inflation

Year	Revenues 1.07 £	Costs 1.04 £	Net cash flows £
0	250,000	180,000	
1	267,500	187,200	80,300
2	286,225	194,688	91,537
3	306,261	202,476	103,785
4	327,699	210,575	117,124
5	350,638	218,998	131,640

   Adjusting the cost of capital:
   1.12   x   1.05   =   1.176   therefore   17.6%

   Net present value - with differential inflation

Year	Savings £	DFC 17.6%	Present value £
1	80,300	0.850	68,255
2	91,537	0.723	66,181
3	103,785	0.615	63,828
4	117,124	0.523	61,256
5	131,640	0.445	58,580
Present Value of Cash Inflows			318,100
Capital Outlay			200,000
Net Present Value (NPV)			118,100

Answer 9.4

Adjusting revenues and costs for inflation:

Year	Sales 1.04 £000	Material costs 1.03 £000	Labour costs 1.08 £000	Specific fixed costs 1.02 £000	Net cash flows £000
0	7,200	1,350	3,150	1,000	
1	7,488	1,391	3,402	1,020	1,675
2	7,788	1,432	3,674	1,040	1,642
3	8,099	1,475	3,968	1,061	1,595
4	8,423	1,519	4,286	1,082	1,536
5	8,760	1,565	4,628	1,104	1,463
6	9,110	1,612	4,999	1,126	1,373
7	9,475	1,660	5,399	1,149	1,267
8	9,854	1,710	5,830	1,172	1,142
9	10,248	1,761	6,297	1,195	995
10	10,658	1,814	6,801	1,219	824

Net present value - with differential inflation

Year	Savings £000	DCF 14.0%	Present value £000
1	1,675	0.877	1,469
2	1,642	0.769	1,263
3	1,595	0.675	1,077
4	1,536	0.592	909
5	1,463	0.519	759
6	1,373	0.456	626
7	1,267	0.400	507
8	1,142	0.351	401
9	995	0.308	306
10	824	0.270	222

Present Value of Cash Inflows	7,539
Capital Outlay	7,000
Net Present Value (NPV)	539

Answer 9.5

Calculation of after tax capital allowance

Year	A Reducing balance £	B Capital allowance (at 25%) £	C Tax saved using capital allowance (at 35%) £
1	180,000	45,000	15,750
2	135,000	33,750	11,813
3	101,250	25,313	8,860
4	75,937	18,984	6,644
5	56,953	14,238	4,983
6	42,715	12,715 [1]	4,450

[1]   *In the final year the capital allowance if any balance remaining, £42,715 less the expected receipts on disposal £30,000.*

Project appraisal incorporating tax

Year	C Tax saved using cap allowance £	D Operating cash inflow [2] £	E Tax on cash inflow £	F Residual value £	G Cash flow £	H DCF 12 %	I Present value £
1	15,750	72,000			87,750	0.893	78,361
2	11,813	72,000	-25,200		58,613	0.797	46,715
3	8,860	72,000	-25,200		55,660	0.712	39,630
4	6,644	72,000	-25,200		53,444	0.636	33,990
5	4,983	72,000	-25,200	30,000	81,783	0.567	46,371
6	4,450		-25,200		-20,750	0.507	-10,520

Present Value of Cash Inflows	234,547
Capital Outlay	180,000
Net Present Value (NPV)	54,547

[2]   *Annual depreciation (£180,000 - £30,000) ÷ 5 years = £30,000*
Annual operating cash flow = £42,000 + £30,000 = £72,000

Answer 9.6

Calculation of after tax capital allowances

Year	A Reducing balance £	B Capital Allowance (at 25%) £	C Tax saved using capital allowance (at 35%) £
1	250,000	62,500	21,875
2	187,500	46,875	16,406
3	140,625	35,156	12,305
4	105,469	26,367	9,228
5	79,102	19,776	6,922
6	59,326	14,832	5,191
7	44,494	4,494 [1]	1,573

[1]   *In the final year the capital allowances is any balance remaining £44,494 less the expected receipts on disposal £40,000.*

Project appraisal incorporating tax

Year	C Tax saved using cap allowance £	D Operating cash inflow £	E Tax on cash inflow £	F Working capital & residual value £	G Cash flow £	H DCF 12 %	I Present value £
1	21,875	70,000		-10,000	81,875	0.909	74,424
2	16,406	70,000	-24,500		61,906	0.826	51,134
3	12,305	70,000	-24,500		57,805	0.751	43,412
4	9,228	70,000	-24,500		54,728	0.683	37,379
5	6,922	70,000	-24,500		52,422	0.621	32,554
6	5,191	70,000	-24,500	50,000	100,691	0.564	56,790
7	1,573		-24,500		-22,927	0.513	-11,762

[2]

Present Value of Cash Inflows	283,931
Capital Outlay	250,000
Net Present Value (NPV)	33,931

[2]   *Annual depreciation (£250,000 - £40,000) ÷ 6 years = £35,000*
Annual operating cash flow = £35,000 + £35,000 = £70,000

Answer 10.6

Calculation of cash flow and residual value for the first year of the forecast, and the pre-forecast shareholder value as follows:

(Sales [base year] x Sales Growth x Operating Margin x Taxation Rate) - (Sales [base year] x Sales Growth x Incremental Fixed and Working Capital)

Cash Flow   =   (400 x 1.15 x 0.12 x 0.50) - (400 x 0.15 x 0.34)

       =   27.6   -   20.4

       =   £7.2m

Residual Value   =   27.6 ÷ 0.10

       =   £276m

Pre-Forecast Shareholder Value   = $\dfrac{(400 \times 0.12 \times 0.50)}{0.10}$ + 20 - 70

       =   240 + 20 - 70

       =   £190m

Preliminary calculations for shareholder value:

Year	Discount rate 10%	Cash flow	Present value of cash flow	Cumulative present value of cash flow	Residual value	Present value of residual value
		£m	£m	£m	£m	£m
	(A)	(B)	(C)=(A)x(B)	(D)	(E)	(F)=(A)x(E)
1	0.909	7.200	6.545	6.545	276.000	250.884
2	0.826	8.280	6.839	13.384	317.400	262.172
3	0.751	9.522	7.151	20.535	365.010	274.123
4	0.683	10.950	7.479	28.014	419.762	286.697
5	0.621	12.593	7.820	35.834	482.726	299.773

The value of the five year forecast can now be obtained by adding the cumulative present value of the cash flows to the residual value at the end of the forecast period. This is shown in the following table:

Value created by the forecast:

	£m
Cumulative Present Value of Cash Flows	35.834
Increase in Residual Value (299.773 - 190.000)	109.773
Marketable Securities	20.000
CORPORATE VALUE	165.607
less Market Value of Debt	70.000
SHAREHOLDER VALUE CREATED BY FORECAST	95.607

Residual Value   = $27.6 \div 0.20$

                     =   £138m

Preforecast
Shareholder Value $= \dfrac{(400 \times 0.12 \times 0.50)}{0.20} + 20 - 70$

                     = $120 + 20 - 70$

                     =   70

Preliminary calculations for shareholder value:

Year	Discount rate 10% £m (A)	Cash flow £m (B)	Present value of cash flow £m (C)=(A)x(B)	Cumulative present value of cash flow £m (D)	Residual value £m (E)	Present value of residual value £m (F)=(A)x(E)
1	0.833	7.200	5.998	5.998	138.000	114.954
2	0.694	8.280	5.746	11.744	158.700	110.138
3	0.579	9.522	5.513	17.257	182.505	105.670
4	0.482	10.950	5.278	22.535	209.881	101.163
5	0.402	12.593	5.062	27.597	241.363	97.028

The value of the five year forecast can now be obtained by adding the cumulative present value of the cash flows to the residual value at the end of the forecast period. This is shown in the following table:

Value created by the forecast:

	£m
Cumulative Present Value of Cash Flows	27.597
Increase in residual Value (97.028 - 70.000)	27.028
Marketable Securities	20.000
CORPORATE VALUE	74.625
less Market Value of Debt	70.000
SHAREHOLDER VALUE CREATED BY FORECAST	4.625